Post-Communist Transition

Emerging Pluralism in Hungary

Edited by
András Bozóki
András Körösényi
and
George Schöpflin

Pinter Publishers, London
St. Martin's Press, New York

© Editors and contributors, 1992

First published in Great Britain in 1992 by
Pinter Publishers Limited
25 Floral Street, London WC2E 9DS

First published in the United States of America in 1992 by
St. Martin's Press, Inc.
175 Fifth Avenue, New York, N.Y. 10010

British Library Cataloguing in Publication Data
A CIP catalogue record for this book is available from the
British Library

ISBN 1 85567 014 3 (Pinter)
ISBN 0–312–08092–1 (St. Martin's)

Library of Congress Cataloging-in-Publication Data
Post-communist transition / edited by András Bozóki, András Körösényi,
  and George Schöpflin.
    p. cm.
  Includes index.
  ISBN 0–312–08092–1 (U.S.)
  1. Hungary – Politics and government – 1989–   2. Post-communism –
Hungary. 3. Pluralism (Social sciences) – Hungary.   I. Bozóki,
András.   II. Körösényi, András.   III. Schöpflin, George.
JN2067.P67 1992   92–6508
943.905′ 3–dc20   CIP

Typeset by Mayhew Typesetting, Rhayader, Powys
Printed and bound in Great Britain by Biddles Ltd., Guildford and King's Lynn

Post-Communist Transition

Contents

vi   *Contents*

List of contributors

András Bozóki is Associate Professor of Sociology at Eötvös University of Budapest.

László Bruszt is a sociologist and research fellow at the Sociological Research Institute, Budapest.

Tamás Kolosi is a sociologist and director of the Social Science Information Centre, Budapest.

András Körösényi is Associate Professor of Political Science at Eötvös University of Budapest.

László Lengyel is an economist and political essayist. He is Director of the Financial Research Institute Co. Ltd., Budapest.

George Schöpflin is Professor of Political Science at the London School of Economics.

Iván Szelényi is Professor of Sociology at the University of California at Los Angeles (UCLA).

Szonja Szelényi is Assistant Professor of Sociology at Stanford University.

László Urbán is an economist at Eötvös University of Budapest.

Bruce Western is a sociologist at the University of California at Los Angeles (UCLA).

Preface

George Schöpflin

The idea of compiling a book on Hungarian political science emerged, as many a book has in the past, from regular contact among the three editors. On my repeated visits to Hungary in 1989 and after, I discussed this with András Bozóki and András Körösényi and they took the initiative to launch this collection. But the book is more than just the outcome of a series of conversations. It constitutes a serious contribution to the understanding of a former communist country at the moment when it cast off the Soviet-type system and began to journey towards democracy. As such it offers a comprehensive picture of the beginnings of post-Communism. But it is more than a mere profile of a smallish country in Central Europe; it is also an attempt to give a Western readership access to the way in which Hungarian social scientists see their political processes and thereby to contribute to the mainstream of political science. Over the last two decades and more, a large number of scholarly contributions have been published in Hungary, in Hungarian, which means that access to them is limited. This volume is intended to breach the salami and paprika curtain.

Why Hungary? There are several reasons why studies of Hungary can provide insights of a particularly fruitful and cogent kind to the social sciences. Unlike several other East European states, the last years of Communism were relatively relaxed – relative for a communist state, that is – so much so that the Kádár years are widely referred to as a 'soft' dictatorship. The crucial benefit to be derived from this by the social sciences was that party control was looser and the limits of what could be studied and published were expanded outwards all the time, even if certain constraints and conventions remained relevant. By the 1980s, it was also possible for Hungarian scholars to spend time in the West and to absorb the ideas circulating there at first hand.

In many ways, Hungary became a laboratory for the social sciences, essentially from the 1960s, when, in the heyday of the Kádárist 'liberalization' in the run-up to the New Economic Mechanism, the party relaxed the prohibition on the study of society. This permitted a generation of scholars to embark on the reception of Western sociology, mostly American and British, but with French and German inputs as well. At the same time, there was a re-examination of the earlier, pre-communist traditions of studying society and the two currents merged to produce a vigorous discourse that offered countless insights into the way in which communist modernization had transformed the country and society. In addition to sociology, for a long time the most sensitive field of study, as it directly challenged many of the legitimating myths of Marxism-Leninism, contributions came from economics, law, history and other approaches. The exception was political science itself. Any scrutiny of the nature of political power, the way in which it was exerted, generated or legitimated was too sensitive and attracted interventions by the party censor. Thus social stratification could be studied, but the possible political implications of the differentials among the different strata could not.

It was only very gradually, even tangentially, that these issues could be smuggled into the public sphere. Iván Szelényi has written elsewhere of ideas that were 'camouflaged into conformity' as a way of avoiding censorship.[1] Certainly, by the mid-1980s, there was a readiness to investigate questions of politics as well and the last two or three years of the Kádár régime saw the crumbling of numerous taboos and the period under Károly Grósz (1988–89) was clearly the beginning of the end for the Soviet-type system. In May 1988, the Political Science Department of the Eötvös Loránd University in Budapest organized the first conference of Hungarian political scientists from Hungary and abroad under the auspices of Professor Mihály Bihari in Eger. It proved to be an extremely interesting meeting, where many ideas were exchanged and debated. Coincidentally, it was held during the week when the Conference of the Hungarian Socialist Workers' Party, that removed Kádár, was held in Budapest. In this sense, these years constituted a vital preparation for the studies which are included in this volume.

Another important influence on the development of political research in Hungary was *samizdat*. The writings of the democratic opposition appeared in two regularly published journals and in several *ad hoc* publications.[2] These had wide circulation and were very significant in structuring ideas about political participation, the nature of authority, the functioning of communist institutions and the shortcomings of official legitimation. Mention must also be made here of the role of the writings of István Bibó, by common consent the greatest thinker on politics in Hungary in the 20th century. Much of Bibó's work was published first in the West and then, with some omissions, in Hungary itself.[3] The rediscovery of Bibó, who had died in 1979, by younger scholars, who encountered his ideas in the various post-war journals and the Western emigré publications, proved to be a major factor in the methodologies of political analysis and through the emphasis that he placed on the context of political conflict.

With the end of Communism, a great deal (though, needless to say, not everything) changed. Above all, the political constraints on research and publication disappeared, political science entered the universities as a recognized and popular field of study and, given the Hungarian tradition of placing high value on intellectual enquiry, there was a great deal of curiosity about the state of the state and nation and what the social sciences had to say about them. The new political system attracted considerable attention. It instantly raised questions of the transfer of power, of party formation, the nature of representation and the relationship between the new parties and their electorates, the characteristics of the new élites, the impact of the electoral system, the launching of new institutions, the character of the dominant ideologies, the role of intellectuals, the relationship between state and society and countless others. All of these issues are in some way, directly or indirectly, mirrored in this volume.

From mid-1989 to around the autumn of 1990 in Hungary was an extraordinarily exciting period for anyone with any interest in the development of politics and the nature of political processes. Some of this excitement has found expression in some of the studies included in this volume, although the editors have avoided including any material that was of short-term interest only.

The intellectual coherence of this volume is provided by the nature of subject matter – political change in one country, over a limited time-span – and by the intellectual commitment to the contributors, whose approach is broadly critical of Communism and committed to the values of democracy and the methodologies of the social sciences.

Notes

1. See his 'Socialist opposition in Eastern Europe: dilemmas and prospects', in (editor) Rudolf Tökés, *Opposition in Eastern Europe*, (London: Macmillan, 1979).
2. Some of the writings of János Kis, a leading figure in the democratic opposition and subsequently chairman of the Alliance of Free Democrats, were published as *Politics in Hungary: For a Democratic Alternative*, Social Science Monographs series, (Boulder, CO: 1989).
3. István Bibó, *Összegyüjtött munkát*, 4 vols (Bern: Európai Protestáns Magyar Szabadegyetem, 1981–1984) and István Bibó, *Válogatott tanulmányok 1935–1979*, 4 vols (Budapest: Magvetö, 1986–1990). A selection of Bibó's work appeared in English under the title, *Democracy, Revolution, Self-Determination*, edited by Károly Nagy, in the Social Science Monographs series, (Boulder, CO: 1991).

List of abbreviations

Abbreviations are given in English and are followed by the Hungarian version in brackets.

AFD (SZDSZ)   Alliance of Free Democrats
BZSFS (BZSBT)   Bajcsy-Zsilinszky Friendship Society
CDPP (KDNP)   Christian Democratic People's Party
DYA (DEMISZ)   Democratic Youth Alliance
FMS (MFT)   Ferenc Münnich Society
FYD (FIDESZ)   Federation of Young Democrats
HDF (MDF)   Hungarian Democratic Forum
HOP (MOP)   Hungarian October Party
HPI (MFP)   Hungarian Party for Independence
HPP (MNP)   Hungarian People's Party
HSDP (MSZDP)   Hungarian Social Democratic Party
HSP (MSZP)   Hungarian Socialist Party
HSWP (MSZMP)   Hungarian Socialist Workers' Party
(I)SHP (FKGP)   Independent Smallholders' Party
NFI (SZKH)   Network of Free Initiatives
NMF (UMF)   New March Front
PPF (HNF)   Patriotic People's Front

Acknowledgements

Pinter Publishers would like to acknowledge the generous assistance of the Central and East European Publishing Project, who provided a grant towards translation costs of this volume.

1 The decay of communist rule in Hungary*

András Körösényi

The collapse of the communist regime in Hungary in 1989 occurred fast, but not without prehistory. The first signs of the crisis had already appeared in 1985; however, the years 1985–87 were the golden age of communist reformism (1st Period). Then, very soon after, the opposition entered the stage (2nd Period). The next two periods of the transition can be characterized by a two-sided process: a rapid decay of the Communist Party and a slow, gradual rise of the opposition (3rd–4th Period). There were no two strong, determined and self-confident characters in this political drama, as with Solidarity and the Communist Party in Poland, but rather several hesitant second fiddlers. The Communists resigned under rather weak pressure, because even they themselves had lost their belief in the legitimacy of their rule, as well as their self-interest in maintaining it (5th Period). The regime had collapsed before the opposition could take power. The five-month power vacuum (6th Period) lasted until the first post-communist parliamentary elections in March 1990.

1st Period The first signs of dissatisfaction: the golden age of political reformism (June 1985–September 1987)

The first signs of dissatisfaction appeared in 1985. The regime could not solve the economic crisis which had lasted more than five years. The moderate but continuous rise in living standards had stopped at the end of the seventies. The first half of the eighties saw the failure of necessary economic reforms. The new economic policy of 'speeding up', announced by János Kádár at the 1985 Congress of the ruling Communist Party, called the Hungarian Socialist Workers' Party (HSWP), led to the mismanagement of the economy and to a deepening debt crisis.

The political signs of growing dissatisfaction appeared on two levels.

* First published in *Slovo*, a journal of contemporary Soviet and East European affairs. Vol. 4, no. 1, June 1991, pp. 47–57.

On the elite level it was expressed by the disappointment of professional groups, like the 'reform economists', who had given economic advice to the government. Realizing that their commitment to economic reforms had not yielded anything, they turned towards the public for support.[1] They also took part in the Monor-meeting, where various dissident groups of Hungarian intellectuals held a three-day political meeting.[2]

Signs of growing dissatisfaction and a legitimacy crisis appeared at the mass level as well. Independent candidates were nominated at the 1985 parliamentary election, and about 40–45 of them were finally elected[3] after a bitter and unequal fight against the local Communist Party apparatus, which kept control over the whole election process. Their voices could be heard in Parliament in the following years. The flourishing of quasi-political clubs and societies in civil society also characterized this period.

The years 1986–87 brought growing pressure for political reforms from below. All the political reform concepts, worked out either by dissident intellectuals or by communist reformers, pointed towards some *power sharing* between the Communist Party and the people. The aim of the reformers was to create a constitutional regime, where the ruling party could keep a significant part of its power but its prerogatives would be legally limited. On the other hand, the rights of citizens, as well as the way they can practise them, would be constitutionally defined. This concept aimed at a switch from a one-party dictatorship towards constitutional power sharing and a semi-parliamentary regime.[4]

Behind this liberal and open-minded reformism two kinds of political thinking existed. The first one was a *reform Communist* attitude, which tried to make *socialism* and *democracy* compatible. It had not lost its belief in the possibility of democratic socialism and its ideological way of thinking. The second one was the attitude of *opposition*, which did not believe in any kind of socialism. For them the political reforms towards a constitutional but non-democratic, semi-parliamentary regime simply meant a political compromise. Their long-term task remained to create a parliamentary democracy. The opposition as a political force, however, had not appeared yet. The political scene was dominated by the 'reformer' and the 'hard-liner' wing of the ruling HSWP.

The hard-liners of the HSWP tried to defend their monopoly of power and keep the one-party system. They were also for reforms and for constitutional government in their rhetoric. Reforms, however, meant for them a peculiar thing: the strengthening of their power by legalizing it. Since under the Communists the Hungarian constitution was much more liberal than the regime itself, on a legal level there were no limitations on the rights of assembly and association. Therefore, the aim of the legal reform drafts of 1988 was to fill these gaps in the legal system, regulating the rights of assembly and the rights of association by the law, in such a way that the state administration could keep control over these rights. These reactionary reforms were, however, rejected by society in the second half of 1988. The government had to withdraw them.

The main aims of the hard-liners were in 1988 to keep the reforms within the framework of the one-party system. Being unsuccessful, in 1989 they turned their attention to preserving the privileges of the ruling HSWP, such as the *nomenklatura* system, the presence of party cells at workplaces, the Workers Militia, and the property of the party. The most well-known politicians of the hard-line Communists were Károly Grósz, János Berecz, until his fall János Kádár, and a representative of the extreme left Róbert Ribánszki, who appeared on the political scene in the autumn of 1988. These politicians, however, did not represent a united group of conservatives, but rather politicians who were competing for power. Their strongholds were the county and local party apparatuses which were interwoven with the parallel state and business administration. More or less formalized factions of the hard-liners had been established since the autumn of 1988, such as the Ferenc Münnich Society (1988), the Marxist-Leninist Unity-Platform (Ribánszky, 1989), and the Union for Renewal of the HSWP (Berecz, 1989).

On the other side of the party was the *reform wing* of the HSWP. It was also a loose alliance of party politicians and technocrats of the government, primarily of the economic administration. The market-oriented liberal economic experts and bureaucrats of the civil service supported the Grósz-government in 1987–88 as well as the following Németh-government. Grósz tried to present himself as a committed reformer, at least in the sphere of the economy. He was regarded as the father of some 'reform dictatorship' as a 'red Pinochet', who was ready to combine tough economic liberalism with a new political dictatorship. Therefore, diverging from the Grósz-line, the main features of the 'genuine' reform wing were in the realm of politics. The leading figure of the reformers was Imre Pozsgay from the beginning of the eighties. He incorporated more and more national and democratic slogans into his rhetoric and gained prestige among the reform-oriented intellectuals, and also among professionals both within and outside the party. As general secretary of the Patriotic Peoples Front (PPF), which had been a satellite organization of the party since the fifties, Pozsgay transformed it into an 'umbrella' organization of the reviving civil society, comprising memorial and patriotic clubs, associations and the people's college movement, and made room for the reform initiatives of professional groups as well. The stamp of the PPF was a great help to the 'reform economists' in publishing *Turn and Reform* in 1987, which opened the series of political reform packages.

Diverging from the old Kádárist leadership, Pozsgay appealed for a national debate on the future of 'reform'. ('Reform' was still a key word in Hungarian political discussion in 1987.) The most detailed expression of Pozsgay's political philosophy, the concept of 'democratic socialism', was worked out by Mihály Bihari, a well-known political scientist, in the summer of 1987. It was entitled '*Reform and Democracy*' and was spread like a *samizdat* in the following months.[5] Beside 'democratic socialism', Pozsgay's political message was also *national*. He had supporters among the national-populist intellectuals and he was present, at Lakitelek, at the foundation of the Hungarian Democratic Forum (HDF). The 'third way socialist' ideology of the populist movement was compatible at several points with the ideas of 'democratic socialism'. Zoltán Biró, the first president of the HDF, had a close personal and political connection with Pozsgay.[6] Reformist factions within or around the Communist Party were the New March Front (Nyers, 1988), the Reform circles (spontaneous movement of the rank and file, 1989) and the Movement for Democratic Hungary (Pozsgay, 1989).

2nd Period The opposition enters the stage: the succession crisis of the Kádár regime (September 1987–May 1988)

The years 1988–89 marked the re-emergence of political pluralism in Hungary. The starting point was at Lakitelek, in September 1987. There, at the meeting of populist writers and intellectuals, was founded the first big opposition movement, called Hungarian Democratic Forum (Forum). The Forum tried to keep an intermediate position very consciously between the regime and the Democratic Opposition,[7] and enjoyed some support from the reform wing of the Communist Party. In spite of some personal overlapping with the reform Communists, the HDF was definitely an independent movement from the very beginning. It had its own ideology, 'populism', and began its own independent political activity. The winter of 1987–88 was the beginning of public mass meetings, organized by the Forum, where more and more citizens took part and criticized the policy of the communist regime.[8] Issues like the oppression of the Hungarian minority in Rumania, press censorship, the constitutional prerogatives of the Communist Party, the lack of free elections and parliamentary government, etc. were raised and the achievements of the four-decade-long communist regime were discredited.

The political consequences of the deepening economic crisis appeared within the Communist Party as well. Kádár's reputation was declining among his comrades and he was criticized at local party meetings all over the country. The succession crisis became evident and visible, but the big competition for power among the three main potential successors, Grósz, Berecz and Pozsgay, had not been decided up until the extraordinary party conference in May 1988.[9]

3rd Period Kádár's fall: the Grósz-era (May 1988–January 1989)

The May party conference did not take place according to a scenario written in advance. Besides the succession crisis, it reflected the revolt of the rank and file of the Communist Party. The 'putsch' against Kádár would not have been as successful without the anger of the dissatisfied delegates elected by the local party committees. The old Kádárist leadership was swept away. Eight old Kádárists, even János Kádár himself, were ousted from the Politburo. Kádár became the President of the party without authority. The winner of the game was Grósz, who became General

Table 1.1 Political cleavages along the regime-opposition dimension

Regime (HSWP)		Opposition	
Hard-liners	*Reformers*	*Moderates*	*Radicals*
F. Münnich Society	Nyers Pozsgay Gy. Horn M. Németh	Hungarian Democratic Forum	Alliance of Free Democrats
Marxist-Leninist Unity Platform	New March Front	Smallholder Party	Young Democrats
		Socialdemocrats	
J. Berecz R. Ribánszki K. Grósz F. Puja	Movement for Democratic Hungary	People's Party	
	Reform-circles	Christian Democratic Party	
after October 1989: HSWP	Hungarian Socialist Party		

Secretary and could keep the Premiership as well.[10]

During the months of the Grósz era nothing was decided. In the period between June 1988 and January 1989 the future was still doubtful. The political demonstrations of the radical Democratic Opposition, on 16 June, 23 October and 7 November, were banned or dispersed by the police, while the anti-Ceaucescu demonstration organized by the moderate opposition Forum on 27 June was permitted. While the former demonstration was held by a few hundred people, more than 100,000 people participated in the latter.

The summer of 1988 marked the beginning of the freedom of the press. In July, for the first time, an action of the opposition was reported on the front pages of the papers with no condemnation. The censorship was first lightened then lifted by the end of the year. The press became more and more liberal and informative. This was the first year for decades when it became worth buying and reading a daily paper in Hungary.

Within the HSWP, the fight between the hard-liners and the reform communists continued. The hard-liner Grósz, in spite of his victory in May, could not stabilize his power. Due to his contradictory speeches he could not keep even the support of the party apparatus. By the end of 1988 he was considered a fallen politician. He had to resign from the Premiership and his attempt to turn the whole process back and to keep it within the framework of a one-party system was unsuccessful. In his last great hard-liner speech for party activists, referring to the opposition, he spoke about an 'impending white terror'.[11] His words caused huge nationwide indignation, so Grósz had to moderate his statement later. Even such hard-liners as János Berecz, the former party secretary of ideological affairs, tried to escape from the sinking ship. He moved from Grósz towards Pozsgay, but it was too late.

However, nothing could stop the foundation of new political parties and the reorganization of old ones. From a loose movement, by September the Hungarian Democratic Forum had become a political organization with more than 10,000 members. The Federation of Young Democrats, which survived accusations of 'anti-state and anti-socialist conspiracy' in the spring, held its first National Congress in October. The groups of the former Democratic Opposition established the Alliance of Free Democrats in November. The historical parties of the last multi-party period of 1945–48, like the Smallholders and the Social Democrats, had come to life again by the end of the year. All these parties demanded free elections, and a new constitution which would abolish the prerogatives of the Communist Party, guarantee the freedom of the press and the rights of assembly, and create a parliamentary government.

During the Grósz era, the Government and the HSWP attempted through legal reforms to keep the processes within the one-party regime. The communist rhetoric used the term 'socialist pluralism', which meant the liberalization of the system without political democracy. According to this concept, the Communist Party would remain the 'mediator' between the different interest groups and organizations, and define the 'social' interest. Even the most radical reform Communist party leaders, like Pozsgay, never spoke about free multiparty parliamentarism at this time. They spoke about 'democratic socialism' within a one-party system or with the competition of those political parties which *accept* socialism. So the idea of a *limited* multiparty system was still very popular among communist reformers in this period.

The people and the opposition, however, refused this version of reforms. Bills on the right of assembly, on the right of association and on the new election law, which reflected this concept, were deliberately refused even by the officially organized 'social discussion' and by the liberal press, so the government had to withdraw them. The pressure for constitutional reforms intensified. The Federation of Young Democrats pressed unpopular MPs, even the Speaker of the House, to resign. The popular demand to stop the construction of a dam on the Danube was also a heavy burden on the government; this was the most sensitive issue, and the only one which produced a popular movement and mass demonstrations against the government. The regime was on the defensive and in decay. The opposition, however, was still not strong enough to take over the direction of events. The process came to a deadlock for a while.

4th Period The advance of Pozsgay: the opposition is ready for the battle (January 1989–16th June 1989)

What pushed events forward was Pozsgay's action at the end of January

1989. Pozsgay recognized that there would be no consensus without the revaluation of the events of 1956. While Károly Grósz enjoyed the mountains of the Alps in Switzerland, Pozsgay declared in a radio interview that what happened in Hungary in 1956 was not a counter-revolution, as the official communist historiography considered the events, but a 'national uprising'. The effect was dramatic. Grósz called together an extraordinary session of the Central Committee of the HSWP in two weeks' time. During those two weeks hundreds of social and political organizations expressed their agreement with Pozsgay, or at least their appreciation of his statement. Backed by public opinion and the press, Pozsgay and the reformers won the battle. The Central Committee session of February accepted not only the revaluation of the events of 1956, but the multiparty system as well.[12]

The new short-run programme of the Communist Party, issued on 7 March, committed itself to a reform Communist and social democratic orientation. But all for nothing; it could not restore the people's confidence in the party. While one face of the party smiled at the people, the other face showed its teeth. The Communist Party was like a dragon with different heads, each speaking a different language. While Pozsgay began to speak about multiparty democracy, Grósz and Fejti still refused to consider the opposition as legitimate. In fact, the ruling party refused to begin negotiations with the Round-Table of the Opposition Parties for months.

The concept of the opposition was to begin negotiations with the ruling party on questions of transformation, such as the new election law, the review of criminal law, the dissolution of the Workers Militia (the private army of the Communist Party) and the amendments to the Constitution. They did not want to leave these crucial questions of legislation to the government and the parliament, which were not regarded as legitimate by the opposition, and where more than two-thirds of the MPs were Communist Party members.

The resistance of the HSWP did not last long. The coming national and political anniversaries did not help them. On 15 March, the anniversary of the War of Independence and the Revolution of 1848, more than 100,000 people took part in a demonstration of the opposition in Budapest and tens of thousands in the countryside. The demonstrators accused the communist regime of having ruined the country during their four-decade rule.

The reformers and the technocrats of the HSWP, however, were seeking consensus and legitimacy. Beside Pozsgay, there were others like Miklós Németh, who succeeded the unpopular Grósz in the position of Prime Minister,[13] Gyula Horn, the Minister of Foreign Affairs, and Mátyás Szürös, the new Speaker of the Parliament.[14] They were successful in creating personal prestige, but the fate of the Communist Party as a whole was sealed.

8 *András Körösényi*

5th Period The Communists pushed on to the defensive (16th June 1989–October 1989)

The crucial event that caused the psychological breakdown of the communist regime was the Imre Nagy question: the re-burial and rehabilitation of the Prime Minister of the 1956 revolution. The coming anniversary of his execution kept the regime under intense pressure for months. As an uprising against a communist dictatorship, 1956 was a leading topic in the mass media. The Communists and János Kádár himself were blamed for the executions and for the suppression of the revolution. The HSWP were not even allowed to take part in the re-burial ceremony, which turned into a huge demonstration against the system. The HSWP never recovered from this humiliation, and *psychologically* collapsed at this time.

In addition to this, the next stroke came very soon, with the by-elections of the summer. Since a couple of communist MPs were 'called back' or pressed to resign by the pressure of the opposition, by-elections were held in four single-member constituencies at the end of July. The communist candidates were defeated in three out of the four constituencies. Two-thirds of the electorate voted for the candidates of the opposition parties.

The wind of the Imre Nagy affair and the coming visit of George Bush, the American President, made the HSWP begin negotiations with the Round-Table of the Opposition. The negotiations, due to the divergent viewpoints, were unsuccessful for several months.[15] The moderates of both sides, however, urged the others towards a compromise. As a result of these efforts, the Great Pact was worked out and signed by both sides on 18 September. However, the compromise caused a serious rift within the opposition. The radicals, like the Young Democrats and the Free Democrats, refused to sign it.

Until the autumn of 1989, it looked as though the Forum and the reform wing of the Communist Party would dominate the new political scene.[16] The following six months, however, were marked by two big political landslides. The first was the collapse of the reform Communists.

The 'reform circles', the local bases of the communist reform wing, forced the HSWP leadership to call an extraordinary party congress by the beginning of October. It was expected to be the final battle between the hard-liners and the reformers. The revolt of the rank and file helped the reformers to push the conservatives back and to change the party's image from Communist to social democratic. Yet, the result of the congress was not clear for weeks. They aimed to reorganize the party under a new name: it was to be called the Hungarian Socialist Party (HSP). However, the continuity of the membership was not automatic, and in the meantime the parliament, under pressure of public opinion, banned party activity at workplaces. The practical consequence of these two coincidental events was equal to the dissolution of the party. The Communist Party became completely disorganized, and most of its 700,000 former members did not join either the new reform-oriented HSP or the old hard-liner HSWP.

They were happy to be out of the party without taking any personal risk. The heart of the communist rule, the old *nomenklatura* system, suddenly collapsed. The new Hungarian Socialist Party had less than 20,000 members at the beginning of November 1989, and not more than 50,000 by March 1990. (The old HSWP, which was able to recruit 100,000 members[17] from the older comrades, lost all its power. The HSWP did not have any influence beyond its own members.)

6th Period The power vacuum: from the collapse of the Communist Party to free elections (October 1989–March 1990)

In the meantime the radical opposition, which did not sign the pact with the Communists, began a campaign for a referendum on those four questions which were not settled by the pact, namely: 1. the dissolution of the Workers Militia; 2. the banishment of party activity from workplaces; 3. the HSWP should account for its property (i.e. most of it comes from the state budget and not from membership fees); and 4. the most controversial question of contemporary Hungarian politics, the timing and the procedure of the presidential election.

Regarding the first three questions, the only difference between the radical and the soft opposition was whether to accept a temporary compromise or not. The real cause of the split, however, was the fourth question. The parties of the moderate opposition, such as the Hungarian Democratic Forum, the People's Party, the Christian Democrats and the Smallholders, accepted the reform Communist concept of the transition, which focused on a directly elected president with significant constitutional power. The reform Communists and the moderate opposition thought that a legitimate constitutional power, a president, could make the transition smooth and safe and could guarantee political stability for the months before the first free parliamentary elections. All of them regarded Pozsgay as the right person to do this job. The radical opposition, however, refused this concept. They regarded it as giving the Communists a chance to preserve their power behind the facade of a presidential system. They preferred a solution in which parliamentary elections would be held first, and then the new, freely elected parliament would elect a president.[18]

In addition, the Free Democrats accused the Hungarian Democratic Forum of betraying the opposition and of making a secret pact with Pozsgay. Their campaign for a referendum on the four crucial questions of the transition was quite successful. Their petition was signed by 200,000 people, so the parliament had to call a referendum on these debated areas. The November referendum ended with a marginal victory for the radicals.[19] The presidential elections were postponed.

The victory of the communist reformers at the October party conference and the offensive of the radical opposition with their referendum campaign ruined the communist rule. The old power structure collapsed without changing the members of the government, and the parliament. A real power vacuum came into being, since no political power stood behind the government and the legislature. The government was like a provisional one, consisting of technocrats without authority. The parliament passed laws under mass pressure. The opposition was out of the parliament and heavily divided. The new, reformed Hungarian Socialist Party lost its members and could not win the confidence of society. Contemporary opinion polls predicted for the first time the victory of the opposition at the coming parliamentary elections, which were scheduled for March 1990.

The second big political landslide was the advance of the most important radical opposition party, the Free Democrats. Whereas before their campaign for the referendum they were hardly known by the electorate, by February 1990 they had caught up with the Forum in terms of popularity. Since the referendum the political scene and the agenda have been determined less by the fight between the opposition and the (ex-) communist parties, and much more by the debate between the two major opposition parties, the Forum and Free Democrats.[20]

The Hungarian Democratic Forum was the strongest party of a potential 'national centre' coalition and on the political scene as a whole.[21] The political character of the HDF had significantly changed since its foundation. It had lost its original populist character and had become a 'catch-all' party. After J. Antall followed Z. Biró in the office of Chairman of the HDF in October, the party aimed to play the same role as the West-German CDU or the Austrian Volkspartei had played in post-war politics. Stressing the Christian and national values and the historical and constitutional legacy of Hungary, the Forum relied on the votes of the middle-class and provincial Hungary.

The Free Democrats on the other side of the new political scene, became popular among intellectuals, professionals and the urban population. Having its roots in the human rights movement and in the radical 'Democratic Opposition' of the seventies, the Free Democrats did not make any compromise with reformer Communist successors of the former communist state party. Making no distinction between reformers and hard-liners, the Free Democrats discredited both Pozsgay and the Forum and won the November referendum. This unexpected victory brought the Free Democrats up to second place in the political competition.

The results of the March/April 1990 parliamentary elections showed that the majority of Hungarians voted for moderate centre–right parties (the Forum, the Christian Democrats and the Smallholders), about a third of them voted for the radical left-liberals (Free Democrats, Young Democrats and Social Democrats), and about a sixth of them voted for the stability-oriented former communist parties (HSP, HSWP). Four and a half decades of Hungarian history ended.

Notes

1. A group of 'reform economists' wrote and published an analysis and reform project on the Hungarian economy, entitled '*Turn and Reform*'. (László Antal et al., 'Fordulat és reform' *Medvetánc* 1987/2 *Melléklet*).
2. László Lengyel's article gives an insight into the changing attitude and behaviour pattern of the 'reform economists' in this period. ('Adalékok a fordulat és reform történetéhez' *Medvetánc* 1987/2 *Melléklet*).
3. On the 1985 parliamentary elections the most comprehensive study is written by *István Kukorelli*, *Igy választottunk* (Budapest, 1988); on the 1985–90 parliament see B. *Rácz*: 'The parliamentary infrastructure and political reforms in Hungary' *Soviet Studies* Vol. XLI, no. 1, Jan. 1989.
4. Elemér Hankiss's book gives a comprehensive analysis of these reform concepts: *Kelet-Europai Alternativák* (KJK, Budapest, 1989). English Version: *East-European Alternatives*, Oxford University Press, 1990.
5. Finally it was published. Mihály Bihari, 'Reform és demokrácia' *Medvetánc* 1987/2 *Melléklet*.
6. M. Bihari, Z. Biró, Z. Király and L. Lengyel, *Kizárt a párt* (Budapest 1988); Z. Biró, *Elsö beszélgetésem Pozgay Imrével* (Püski, 1989); Z. Biró, *Második beszélgetésem Pozgay Imrével* (Püski, 1990).
7. The Democratic Opposition was a group of dissident intellectuals and human rights activists. It came into being in 1977, when they expressed their solidarity with the activity of the Czechoslovak Charter 77 and began to publish *samizdat*. They were an opposition *in principle*. Though they had never engaged in political (organizational) activity beyond the *samizdat* publishing until 1988, they were regarded as and accused of being 'opposition' by the regime. The Democratic Opposition began its political activity on an organizational level, founding its umbrella organization, the Network of Free Initiatives, on 1 May 1988. It existed until the foundation of the Alliance of Free Democrats on 12 November 1988.
8. These meetings were held in the Jurta Szinház, the only theatre in Budapest that was not state owned.
9. About the power struggle within the HSWP, see: G. Schöpflin, R. Tökés and I. Völgyes, 'Leadership change and crisis in Hungary' *Problems of communism*, 1988/5.
10. op. cit.
11. The speech was given for Budapest party activists in the Budapest Sportcsarnok on 29 November 1988 (*HVG* 1990, márciusi különszám, p. 43).
12. About Pozsgay's role and the phases of the crisis of the regime see Béla Faragó's brilliant article: 'Mi történt Magyarországon? Történelem jelenidöben' *Századvég* 1989/1–2.
13. Grósz resigned on 24 November 1988.
14. The former Speaker of the House, István Stadinger, resigned under the pressure of the opposition and public opinion on 8 March 1989.
15. A series of articles were written about the history of the round-table negotiations by A. Bozóki in the *Beszélö* (1990 március).
16. Public opinion polls in June also confirmed this view. The HSWP still had about a third of the potential votes, i.e. the highest number of potential votes among the political parties. (MKI survey, *Magyarország Politikai Évkönyve 1990*, p. 463. Edited by S. Kurtán, P. Sándor and L. Vass.)
17. Groups of hard-liners, declaring that they were still Communists, did not give up. They appealed to the party cells and party committees of the old party

not to dissolve themselves but to keep their basic organizations and begin to restore the old Communist Party (HSWP) from below. It was successful, as far as the high figure of party membership is concerned. They didn't accept the resolutions of the October party congress and considered the reformers as traitors of the workers' movement. Their own party congress was held in December 1989.

18. In fact, the 'danger' of a presidential system was rather low, since the constitutional rights of the president were limited. Besides the preference of the radical opposition for a parliamentary system, their real aim was to prevent Pozsgay from becoming president. They regarded Pozsgay as the political leader of a potential (reformer) Communist-HDF coalition, which might have pushed the radicals to the margin of the political scene.

19. While 95 per cent of the voters agreed with the radicals on the first three questions, only 50.1 per cent voted for the postponement of the presidential election.

20. Both the Hungarian Democratic Forum and the Alliance of Free Democrats were originally formed by intellectuals, therefore their cleavage reflects a traditional split of the Hungarian intelligentsia between the *populist* (népi) and *urbanist* (urbánus) wing. This split had its origin in the inter-war period, but appeared again in the 1980s and marked the re-emerging political pluralism.

21. András Körösényi, 'Coalitions in the making in Hungarian politics' p. 30–31. In: *East European Reporter*, Vol. 4, no. 1 (Winter 1989/90).

2 Post-communist transition: political tendencies in Hungary*

András Bozóki

Any definition of the economic and political transitions occurring in Hungary today must begin with an analysis of the earlier structures that are now being dissolved. For a long time the system had no longer been Stalinist, that is, based on a totalitarian ideology which systematically used terror in the exercise of autocratic control over the everyday personal and professional lives of the people. After the 1956 uprising the system could not continue without change. People's memory of the event might be pushed out of their consciousness by the government's retaliation, but the Rákosi dictatorship could not continue as if nothing had happened;[1] the basic economic and political system remained the same, but the political style changed. The party leaders held on to their political monopoly, but stopped trying to persuade the people, reasoning that if the conditions of their lives improved, they would not be interested in politics. When the private sector became free, the decline of Stalinism was possible, Kádár adopted Khrushchev's policy, and remained loyal even after Khrushchevism was abandoned in the Soviet Union. Although it was impossible to prevent the damaging impacts of neo-Stalinism associated with Brezhnev, Kádárism was able to keep its post-Stalinist nature, supporting a higher standard of living and increased consumption while doing its best to isolate the social conflicts; thus, it was a *paternal dictatorship*. But these goals were unrealizable and the country became poor, burdened by international debts, while the Kádár regime lost its credibility.

Now the conditions were established for a transition from a post-Stalinist to a post-communist system.[2] The weak spot of the post-Stalinist economic structure had been its sluggish productivity, and it

* This article was written in September 1989 and updated in February 1990 by the editors of *EEPS* (East European Politics and Societies) with the permission of the author in order to include some factual changes that had taken place over the previous five months. Vol. 4, no. 2, pp. 211–30.

became clear that it was not only wasteful, as economists already knew, but unable to reach levels achieved earlier. This system could function only when it was *closed*, which was why Stalin tried to pursue a policy of economic autarchy, forcing his allies to keep their commercial relations behind the Iron Curtain. But as the dynamics of the world economy speeded up, this policy could only preserve the underdevelopment of the region. The failure of post-Stalinism proved the insufficiency of a 'reform of economic structure'. It was not only the Stalinist model of socialism that could not work, but also the 'softer' Lenin-Bukharin model. Socialism as a system was not able to fulfil its historical promise and became the dead end of modernization; the promise of catching up became the fact of falling behind. Earlier efforts to revive this system had been isolated and unique to Eastern Europe. Its complete crisis was revealed when the Soviet system lost the Cold War to the Americans in the eighties.[3] It was questionable whether the Communists could maintain the experiment called socialism in disregard of the societies subjected to it, and against their will. This has lately stimulated more than just theoretical arguments. Fewer and fewer people accept the idea, once popular, of socialism as a transition to Communism. It has become clear that one cannot suppose this from a projected image of the future of history, fitting real events into an imaginary evolution leading from capitalism to Communism and forgetting whatever does not fit the theory, or forcing it into some Procrustean bed of social theory.

While an orthodox minority thinks this way, the anti-Stalinist proponents of the socialist models insist that one cannot talk about socialism *yet*, because what we have been seeing is actually a transition period before 'real' socialism.[4] In their opinion, socialism can only be democratic, economically and politically, but this assertion can be put in doubt by historical and theoretical arguments: nowadays the majority of the opposition groups reject this ideal explanation of socialism.

Up to now, socialism has existed only in a state of war, and in a centralized structure. 'Real socialism' has always been a state-socialism. Where, as in the Paris Commune, the Kronstadt Uprising, or the Spanish Civil War, it was not supported by a party-state, it failed within weeks or months. Those revolutionary experiments failed too, whose goal was the revival of 'real socialism'. Since these experiments were crushed by interventions, many people remained hopeful about the possibility of a viable non-statist socialism. Historical examples seem to deny this possibility, but their validity is only partial, since they are all in the past, and the fact that the system has failed everywhere does not prove in theory that it cannot succeed in the future.

It is difficult to picture an economic democracy without a political democracy. It has not worked anywhere. The example of Yugoslavia proves that in a one-party system economic democracy cannot exist – workers' self-management failed within the limits of a party-state.[5]

However, it is difficult to picture a political democracy that does not accept private property and a market economy – it could not exist today. But economic democracy would not be decisive even if the administrative distribution of goods was replaced by the market and political democracy was established at the same time. The private sector is mainly interested in profit. This feature of capitalism can be modified by the economic intervention of the state and by the trade unions' defence of workers' interests, but it cannot be basically changed. The plants, factories and enterprises are not democratic forums. Self-government could not become a system. In the East, it has failed because of the lack of democracy; in the West, it remains on the periphery of the private sector.

If an economic democracy cannot exist in the broad sense of the term, neither can 'ideal' socialism. 'Ideal' socialism is not based upon the formal procedures of democracy but upon its substantive notion, which derives from an idealized image of man, anthropology's ideal-type, the 'cooperating man'. This concept presumes that men are sometimes ready to give up personal success for the sake of abstract social ideas. In some extreme situations they may do so, but not usually during times of social peace. Socialism, as a system, can only exist as state-socialism. (This is not to say that socialism cannot be effective as an ideology or a movement against social inequalities.)

There are differences among various political groups or parties in Hungary today concerning the aim of the transition. The representatives of the ruling party want to change certain key elements of the socialist model but they do not want to change the system itself. The populist parties are looking at the possibility of an organic 'third way'. The liberal parties declare, following the above-mentioned arguments, that it would be an illusion to aim for a socialism that does not yet exist, since unreal socialism is really impossible. Societies are either based on redistribution or on the market: there is no 'third way' between socialism and capitalism.

The current transition tends towards the growth of capitalism in Hungary. Yet we do not know how long this will take because there is no really strong national bourgeoisie of any significance in Hungary. Nor do we know what the capitalist structure will be like when it emerges: will it resemble the model of nineteenth-century free competition, the Latin American model of 'comprador bourgeoisie', or the West European welfare model? It seems certain that the path Hungary must follow from its present state to the much favoured welfare state can be covered only slowly, step by step.

From the ideals of the welfare state, Eastern Europe got only the state, which has monopolized politics and the economy. Here is the real problem for the transition: the radical reorganization of both politics and the economy.

It is well known that in the modernized 'model countries', the market did not have to be restored, since it had not been demolished. Authoritarian right-wing dictatorships are *political* dictatorships. They are often more cruel than those of the left, but when they fail, society can more quickly resume its normal functioning. The question of transition there is limited to the political field, with the elaboration of democratic rules and their acceptance. This process of liberalization took place in

Spain after Franco and in Greece after the military dictatorship, and the same tendency has begun in South Korea, Chile and some other countries in recent years. But this model of transition has little relevance for Eastern Europe.[6]

Political tendencies and actors

Since the autumn of 1987, the previously hidden ideological fragmentation of Hungarian society has become apparent.[7] Today in Hungary there are not only different ways of thinking and different value systems, but there are also different, competing political orientations, parties, organizations and movements. Hungary differed from Poland, where before the recent changes a cohesive opposition confronted a fairly cohesive power; in Hungary, an increasingly pluralistic opposition faced a factional power. Many observers believe that Hungary's lack of rigid social stratification offers the possibility of a smooth transition. To some of them, the pluralism that already precedes the power shift is a promising circumstance, while to others it is dangerous. The optimism of the first comes from the reasoning that there are already the social conditions for a pluralistic democracy, there being relatively few at the extremes of power and powerlessness, so that a large majority is in a position to enter negotiations. The darker view is that the ruling party may take advantage of the opposition's divisiveness and succeed in being overrepresented in the new parliament. The ruling party itself, however, may be too divided to exploit this situation.

During the last year, critical questions and topics surfaced and pushed apart the different groups. Although ideology does not completely determine political structures, in Hungary today there is a strong correlation between political and ideological divisions. In Western societies with well-established and de-ideologized democratic systems, catch-all parties entered the limelight. In Hungary, the formation of parties and ideological diversification are still underway. The new groups are searching for their own identity, and therefore for an ideology to motivate and justify their actions. But the organized opposition appeared as the result of a longer process. After 1956 the opposition first demanded the renewal of Marxism, and as an intra-party opposition it influenced the intellectual circles. Its representatives were later expelled from the Communist Party – and a few, indeed, from the country.

In the late seventies there appeared a new, intellectual opposition group to champion human rights, and this changed in time from a kind of political subculture to a counterculture. This group broke with Marxism and the idea of the system's internal reform, gave up the language of the party bureaucracy, and created an independent press and a new, oppositional style of behaviour.

 The late eighties saw a revival of the traditional political parties[8] and of ideologies that had been silenced for the previous four decades. Politics got the impact of renewed global value systems – Christianity, populism, socialism, liberalism – and every political tendency reflected some mixture of them.

I shall discuss here the seven important political tendencies that, in my opinion, we can observe in Hungary today, ranging from the left to the right. (See Table 2.1.) I use these terms in their ordinary sense: the left supports government interventions in social life and has faith in the possibility of progress; the right believes in organic change and respect for tradition and authority. Where the left in democracies wants the same or even more government intervention, the right calls for less. For the left, society is based on natural law; for the right, on history and religion. In anti-democratic systems, the extreme left may strive for ideologically justified totalitarian rule, while the rule of the extreme right may result in racial, ethnic or national discrimination.

It is a sign of democratic progress in Hungarian politics that the extreme right, a significant force in the thirties and early forties, has almost completely disappeared, while the extreme left of the post-war era is gradually losing its earlier importance, although it still exists.

1. For the time being, the extreme left is represented by the *conservative Bolshevik* forces. Their model is Leninist-Stalinist, i.e. a centralized, planned economy, a one-party system in which the autonomy of bourgeois society is replaced by central control and mobilization. Their political structure follows the logic of war and the belief that without a vanguard elite to maintain social order and progress, society would fall into chaos. Bolshevik conservatism places the need for order and discipline above all else, and regards conflict as a social anomaly and not a natural phenomenon. It believes in maintaining the existing economic and political system, along with its alliances (COMECON, the Warsaw Pact) and its isolation from Western markets. Here we may mention the Ferenc Münnich Society (MFT) with its 10–12,000 members, and the approximate 100,000 members of that faction of the former Communist Party, which after the October 1989 conference retained its old name of the Hungarian Socialist Workers' Party (MSZMP).

Socially these groups are based on the privileged stratum of the Stalinist or post-Stalinist system. The power and clout of the Hungarian Socialist Workers' Party has decreased since the party congress of May 1988. At the October 1989 conference they decided to join a pragmatic and reformist tendency because of their old age and ideological convictions. They believe that they need above all to be strong in order to resist the powers of 'uprising, revision, and restoration'. The largest proportion of their disciples is probably from among the older party bureaucrats, the police and the paramilitary troops. At the November 1989 referendum they supported the maintenance of the Workers Militia (*Munkásörség*, with 60,000 members), which was dismantled by the Hungarian parliament. The Workers Militia, actually a private army of the Hungarian Socialist Workers' Party, was organized at the beginning of 1957 to threaten society after the crushed revolution.

2. In October 1989 a new party, the Hungarian Socialist Party (MSZP) was formed by the non-conservative members of the Hungarian Socialist

Workers' Party (MSZMP). It actually embraced two political tendencies –
the pragmatic technocrats and the reform Communists, or democratic
socialists. The *pragmatic technocrats* are a distinct political group whose
members are not bound by the above-mentioned ideological convictions.
They can be described by their neutral system of values, conformism and
readiness to make adjustments. They are most interested in stability and
the maintenance of their power, to which ends they are willing to make
small reforms. For the same reasons they had earlier defended the one-
party system, but gave this up later under political pressure.

Before the October 1989 conference this group considered party unity
and the Leninist principle of democratic centralism important, seeing less
danger in the pluralism of society than in the MSZMP, which directly
threatened them. They wanted very much to stay at the centre of the
party, but at the conference they joined the centre group led by Rezsö
Nyers and voted for the new Hungarian Socialist Party. Their group,
more than others, contains those who are trying to exchange their
political power for economic power so that they can survive a possible
change in regime. Members of a small circle may keep their positions in
or near the elite by virtue of their skill and connections, and here we see
most bureaucrats, the cadre-elite of the party and those who work for the
state administration. They have an aversion to both the former dictatorship and the spontaneously organized reform movement. They would be
willing to accept a reformist dictatorship, but they are not in a position
to make it acceptable to the broader society. To save their power, they
would support both reform and a partial restoration of dictatorship.

3. The next grouping is that of the *reform Communists* and *democratic
socialists*, the other component of the Hungarian Socialist Party (MSZP).
Their basic principle is socialist democracy. They think that democracy
and socialism can co-exist and thus the system can be reformed; therefore
they press for radical reforms – while it is not too late. According to
them, state socialism is not the only possible expression of the socialist
system. They demand social control of institutions, and the sooner the
better. Instead of 'real socialism', they design a non-statist, 'ideal'
socialism, looking back to the young Marx and non-Marxist socialist
traditions. To them, democracy is not just form but substance; they do
not want a democracy limited to the politics of consent, but rather
democracy realized in workers' councils, cooperatives and local self-
government, for the development of mankind. Their economic experts
project the distribution of state property as a transfer of those estates to
equities available to everybody, or as a fair distribution among the
workers. From this point of view, their ideology stands closer to the
value-system of the traditional left than does that of the politically more
'leftist' but ideologically disengaged, pragmatic party elite.

This group of course accepts the multiparty system, but they see it as
merely creating competing elites, not guaranteeing the real participation of
society in decision-making. They firmly reject both a rigid Stalinist
dictatorship and a competitive capitalist system. They accept the idea of
a mixed economy, but question what they regard as an overemphasis on

economic rationality. They are ready to limit efficiency for the sake of solidarity.

The *reform circles* were the hard core from which MSZP emerged. They were spontaneously organized and are growing horizontally, with at least 100,000 sympathetic party members. Today, MSZP may have some 30–40,000 members. Most cells of the Hungarian Democratic Youth Alliance (DEMISZ) also belong to this group. This organization is the successor of the Hungarian Communist Youth Alliance (KISZ), which was dissolved in the spring of 1989. It is difficult to estimate the number of DEMISZ supporters: it inherited a large organization, but its members are only 'registered', not card-carrying. The Patriotic People's Front (HNF) follows a similar line. The HNF has a national network but no members; this is why it entered the electoral campaign for the March 1990 elections as a quasi-electoral party.

The most important question for Hungary's political life may be the future of the ruling party. In the decades of Kádárism, the MSZMP operated as a state party, collecting under its wing representatives of the middle class who wished to have a successful career; old-fashioned Communists; former Social Democrats; and loyal populists. There were more than 700,000 MSZMP members. With the split of the party into MSZMP and MSZP following the October 1989 conference, MSZMP claims to have retained a relatively large membership, while MSZP has not been very successful in its membership recruitment. Still, the results of the referendum of November 1989 and opinion polls conducted since show that MSZP may do better in the elections. MSZMP would do well if it could get 5 per cent of the popular vote; MSZP still seems to have a hold on some 10 to 15 per cent of the electorate.[9]

4. The fourth grouping is that of the *Social Democrats*, who are living in a state of schizophrenia. Their basic value is a welfare state, and their ideal those Western countries that have such a state. They believe that a multiparty system, mixed economy and strong compensatory social policy are needed to reach this goal. In spite of similarities and overlaps, they differ from the reformist Communists in certain respects. On the one hand, they do not adhere to the social system of socialism; in fact many would welcome a capitalist-type economy and a bourgeois democracy. On the other hand, they are thinking of a representative democracy with trade unions instead of direct socialization. Like the other opposition parties, they want to prohibit political organizations in the workplace, rejecting the system used by the MSZMP for decades.

The present identity crisis of Social Democrats is caused by the two contradictory images they hold of their own party: the traditional and the Western-type image. Traditionally, the Hungarian Social Democratic Party (MSZDP) is a Marxist class-party, the authentic representative of the workers. It has to resume the activity it was forced to abandon when the two parties merged in 1948. This is emphasized by the so-called 'historic platform' of the Social Democrats. Its members had participated in their party's struggle in the forties, when they were young.[10] They were ousted from power in the late forties or early fifties. They do not trust the former MSZMP members who are joining the party now.

But the party's division is not just due to the generation gap and political apprehensions. Representatives of the other view want the party to follow the way of the western Social Democrats, that is, to become a democratic populist party. They think that the Social Democratic movement has to be bourgeois and democratic, and should represent the idea of social equality and justice within a capitalist society – without any Marxist principles. This is the concept of the so-called 'renewal platform'.

The ideology of the Social Democrats influences not only the organizations that declare themselves social-democratic (MSZDP and the Social Democratic Youth Movement), but also the MSZP and DEMISZ and even the Alliance of Free Democrats (SZDSZ) and the Federation of Young Democrats (FIDESZ). The electoral base of this circle is in the urban middle class and the workers.

It is difficult to guess the real strength of the MSZDP because the published data are contradictory. It probably has more than 10,000 members. If some reform wing left the MSZMP, it could give a serious boost to the Social Democratic party, but it might also be a strong rival as an independent party. Still, if the economic situation deteriorates, and inflation and unemployment increase, it is likely that the Social Democrats will become a strong political power. No consistent liberal programme can be popular now, and the orthodox Communists can only gain the confidence of a minor group. The Social Democrats are therefore the only other serious political representatives of those who dislike the world of populist thought.

5. The next group of the political spectrum is the *radical and liberal democrats*. Their central concern is human rights. They advocate a mixed market economy, a multiparty system based on representative democracy, and the acceptance of basic human rights. This centrist-type includes the Social Democratic sympathizers who stand somewhat to the left, but also the Anglo-Saxon kind of conservative free thinkers who stand to the right of centre. The common element in the different platforms is their rejection of the idea of a 'third way' between capitalism and 'real socialism'. The path of progress they recommend is to try to catch up with Europe and accept the Western value system in Hungarian economic and political institutions.

They equally underline unlimited liberty of ventures and the defence of social minorities (Gypsies, ethnic groups, religious groups, the poor), and they fight against anti-Semitism. The most famous representatives of this tendency are the SZDSZ and the FIDESZ. But elements of economic liberalism can be observed also in the Party of Independent Smallholders (FKGP).

The SZDSZ grew from the subculture of democratic opposition which became stronger in the early seventies. Later it was enlarged with 'fifty-sixers', liberal intellectuals, and members of the radical middle class. The SZDSZ was the first among the political groups to come up with an elaborate programme, and it accepted the dissidents and the revolutionary heritage of 1956.[11] But it is still unclear if the SZDSZ is a party of

intellectuals, a mass party of marginal strata, or the party of entrepreneurs. The spectacular victory of the opposition resulted in a paradoxical but natural restructuring. The opposition as a group lost some of its
previous importance and found a place within a pluralist society. To be
a dissident does not today imply the lifestyle and moral strength that it
did in the early eighties – today it is just politics. The illegality of the
activities of the old ruling party had resulted in involuntary avant-gardism
in the opposition, which was pushed aside later by the demand for
political skill.

The SZDSZ faced many difficulties before it could step beyond the
intellectual elite circle in which it had started. The alliance decided to be
a mass party rather than an elite party. It gradually found its supporters
– more among the employees than among the entrepreneurs, which
explains the old double nature of the SZDSZ. Leaders of its social
democratic and liberal wings have their differences, but they are tied
together by their common past in the opposition, their long-standing
friendship, and the experience of their 'underground' years. But the co-
existence of the politician-expert-leader-elite (with its academic background) and the simple members whose social emotions are stronger,
would be impossible without conflicts and makes for contradictions on
specific questions. It may be that the SZDSZ is too social democratic for
the entrepreneurs and too liberal for the poor.[12] Still, the SZDSZ is
unique because it accommodates at the same time a liberal economic
concept and a social democratic concept of social justice.[13]

The FIDESZ is marked by its political radicalism,[14] its demand for a
constitutional state, the liberal philosophical basis of its economic
programme, and by the fact that it is free of the 'populist-urbanist'
contradiction which is alive in Hungarian political culture, and which has
divided public opinion in politics and culture since the beginning of the
century. The populists support the organic progress of the nation, while
the urbanists want to imitate the Western European model. In the twenties and thirties, this division was exacerbated by the 'Jewish problem'.
The populists often identified Jews with the urban strata, while the
urbanists labelled the populists' ideas anti-Semitic. This contradiction is
still present as Hungarian political life is being restructured. The FIDESZ
is perhaps the only exception. It has gained an equal place with the other
political parties as a youth organization (the age limit is 35). Its youthful
membership has led the FIDESZ to be notable for its readiness for actions
which have sometimes polarized public opinion, its spontaneity, and its
efforts to reach a new political culture 'with a human face'.

The Hungarian October Party (MOP) and the Hungarian Radical Party
(MRP) have less importance within this group. The MOP, calling itself
'the party of the street', demands a Western system through populist
actions. The MRP's character is similar. The number of their members
amount to no more than several hundred, and they are regarded as
plebeian ultra-radicals. Partisans of this tendency are mainly to be found
among intellectuals living in the big cities, students, employees starting
their careers, some entrepreneurs, and a few from the impoverished strata.

6. Our next political group, the *democratic populists*, believe in the 'third way'. Their ideology is characteristic of countries, regions and societies that have been pushed to the periphery, and it amounts to a proposal for modernization of areas whose social and economic progress has been interrupted. This group often adopts a special political style, appealing not to specific strata or classes, but to the whole 'nation' or 'people'. They do not want to see the nation following global ideas that are alien to its own tradition, but creating an ideology more native to itself, growing from it. They feel that society is basically a moral phenomenon and that moral values must be used to measure economic or political changes. The profound essence of the nation is above and apart from even such important ideologies as liberalism and socialism. The populists, like the reform Communists, want the substance, not just the form, of democracy, and it must be consistent with the national character. But it is a *socialist* democracy for the reform Communists, and a *Hungarian* democracy for the populists.

Democratic populists accept a mixed economy and the market. Their ideal is a 'Garden-Hungary', a country of cooperatives, small landowners, and workers' councils – a society of communities. The multiparty system is necessary but not sufficient. More important is self-government based on local communities. Populists pay a great deal of attention to Hungarian minorities living abroad, mainly to the situation of Hungarians in Transylvania. They are concerned with national identity and human rights, the former being the more important for them. Their relations with every government, as with politics *per se*, are ambivalent, that is, critical and at the same time ready to compromise.

The Hungarian Democratic Forum (MDF) is the most important populist group. It has followed a policy of moderate opposition since it was established in the autumn of 1987. This approach has earned it much recognition.[15] Its emphasis on national issues, consistent middle-of-the-road politics, and a stress on historic traditions are among the reasons for its early popularity. The Forum realized that a national centrist party has always had outstanding importance in Hungarian democratic political life, certainly in the inter-war period. A crucial factor in elections might be the man on the street, i.e. the national petite bourgeoisie. The MDF also realized the importance of the towns and villages, and made an enormous effort to organize country cells. The urban middle class in smaller towns is firmly behind the MDF. From a sociological point of view, the majority of technical workers, intellectuals and teachers, doctors, lawyers, and some entrepreneurs belong to this group: all of whom had no chance of decent careers in the previous political structure, but could not or did not want to join the ruling party and find a place in the cadre-hierarchy. The MDF, as the organization that was founded first, was able to attract the opposition. The crowds that left the MSZMP, unless they joined the MSZP, moved toward the MDF – and towards the Hungarian Social Democratic Party. Some politicians of the MDF could take advantage of the emotionality of politics, always typical of Hungarian political culture. Some MDF speakers were the best at expressing the wishes and demands of the different strata, and could make a strong impact on the emotions of the crowds. At the same time, the question of 'party or movement' and relations between leaders and members have long created tensions in the MDF.[16] Moreover, within the MDF there are various tendencies: alongside the now-dominant 'third way' are representatives of national liberalism and Christian democracy.

Another important representative of the democratic populist group is the Independent Smallholders' Party (FKGP), which was resuscitated in November 1988.[17] This party had already played an important role in the thirties and forties, and became the strongest party in the 1945 elections (taking 57 per cent of the votes). When the Communists seized power the FKGP had to stop functioning. Originally it was founded as an agricultural party of farmers in 1930, but it later became a party of the bourgeoisie. This duality still exists and led to a split within the party in January 1990. Its economic programme is liberal, and its social concept and cultural background are conservative with a Christian-national character. There are many signs that it may become the party of the agricultural elite and of the entrepreneurs. Its historic name will probably attract droves of voters from among the apolitical majority in society, regardless of its programme.

The third important populist group is the Hungarian People's Party (MNP), small in membership and acting as the successor to the National Peasants' Party. The latter fought from a platform of defending the interests of the leftist poor peasants in the forties. Finally, of less significance, the Bajcsy Zsilinszky Friends' Company (BZSBT) may also be classed in this grouping. It was formed in 1936 to keep alive the national heritage of Endre Bajcsy-Zsilinszky, but it became a political group close to the MDF.

Democratic populism is mainly based in the middle class in villages and towns, the entrepreneurs, and in general the population outside the big cities. After the MSZP and MSZDP, the other organizations mentioned can expect the most votes from the strata below the middle class.

7. The last important group is unambiguously right of centre. This is the camp of *populist and religious conservatism*, with a romantic view of nation and community as its central idea. In the rhetoric of its adherents, democracy is replaced with authority and an emphasis on historic traditions. According to them, the various units of society are traditionally collective, and in that setting individual rights have only secondary importance. Nationhood also means a community of values; a nation is a moral unit focused on 'God, Family, Country'. They also find the parliamentary and multiparty system necessary, and they consider the question of Transylvania to be more than a simple minority or human-rights problem – for them this is a crucial matter.

The conservatives' agenda includes: the problems of urbanization; industrialization; the harm done by overwork in the second economy; the ageing and decreasing population; the increasing number of divorces; the problem of abortion; and generally, every social deviancy. To them the main reason for the present crisis is not economic or political, but the collapse of the Hungarian moral character. They regard it as their task to overcome the crisis of values and restore morality. They emphasize the continuity between the present and the historic past (the state concept of the Holy Crown of Saint Stephen), and the importance of Christian ideology in the creation of social integration. They represent, more than any other party, the Christian national ideology, which was the central idea in inter-war Hungary. Sometimes they are characterized by anti-Semitism, anti-Gypsyism, and nationalism.

Of course this tendency is not homogeneous either. There are serious differences between populist and Christian conservatives, but they converge in their conservatism. Here we may mention the right wing of the Independent Smallholders' Party and the MDF. The Hungarian Party for Independence (MFP) also belongs to the right, as they have made abundantly clear.[18] The same can be said of part of the Christian Democratic People's Party, which was resuscitated in the spring of 1989, with its base in the non-urban and less educated strata.

There is no significant difference among these various tendencies when it comes to foreign affairs – except for the extreme leftist conservatives. Practically all Hungarians agree on the necessity of withdrawing the Soviet troops and keeping an Austrian kind of neutrality. But this is regarded as a long-term strategic programme which depends on factors in world politics.

The biggest unknown up to now is the strength of each party's support. The public opinion polls held in Hungary are often contradictory, so we must guess and can be sure only after free elections are held. But the unstable situation can change in several ways before then. Let us examine three of them.

The first is a *conservative counter-attack*, reviving the past – generally called a 'restoration'. This might be brought about by an alliance of the Leninist-Stalinist left wing of the MSZMP with the conformist majority of party apparatchiks worried about their positions, and they can also count on those who have lost their jobs. But this politics, based on 'order', can promise only order – not guaranteed jobs, progress or a better life. Many people know this scenario already – it is not likely to find a role on the domestic scene. The Chinese experience of 1989 is a negative model, as is the closer Polish one with its martial law – in fact, its chances are lowered even more by the recent fall of communist regimes all over Eastern Europe.

In the face of all this, the conservatives may (typically for them) struggle against reforms with delaying tactics or sabotage, in a non-stop fight for positions against the partisans of renaissance. They are betting on the fall of Gorbachev, changes in international politics, and a decline of confidence in the reforms.

The second possible change in Hungary may be a *reform dictatorship*, using the South Korean or Turkish models of economic revision without political reform. The leading elite can then preserve its power, while the country avoids bankruptcy. This can succeed in countries where the work ethic significantly differs from Europe's and where the political system has the means to control crowds, crush opposition and human rights, while it achieves economic liberalization. The Hungarian post-Stalinist systems have not been able to do that. The Messmer government tried before its fall in Poland, and the Grósz government also had some hope of doing it in the first part of 1988. But it did not come together. Still, the idea of a reform dictatorship has not disappeared as an alternative in Eastern Europe, although it has been proven that untrustworthy leaders and a grey technocratic elite are not able to succeed. A populist reform dictatorship, under the aegis of a well-chosen and popular leader, is within the realm of possibility.

Finally, the third scenario is radical reform consistently achieved by a *democratic movement*, which may result in changing the system. This means a revolutionary change at least in its content, if not in its methods. The question is whether a tired, overworked society can be activated by these goals, and if yes, would it be possible to avoid aggression and violence? The mobilization of society cannot be avoided, but a violent uprising would bring unpredictable dangers. Every responsible political organization, so far including the MSZP, wishes a *peaceful* transition. But we know from such examples as the Spanish transition that a party elite that has no authorization from society needs certain guarantees before it is interested in a successful peaceful transition. Therefore, negotiations are needed to reach a series of agreements. The discussions of the MSZP, the opposition round-table, and the 'Third Side' (independent organizations) proved that these groups realize that need. The negotiations are extremely important in the present situation, where there are no legitimate political performers who can get real authorization from society.

The three alternatives are all possible today. The success of a political transition seems more and more likely as elections approach. The most serious question is: what kind of political system and society will exist after the elections? Can a reform dictatorship of legitimate political leaders be avoided in the middle of economic crisis? Will there be a stable government, or will there be several governments, each following in the footsteps of the earlier?

After the elections, a coalition government will probably be formed. We shall see new elites partly tied to the previous ones and partly replacing them.[19] New alliances and new pacts will be made, not only on the political but also on the social scene. One thing is more than probable: the post-communist pluralism about to be born will not be a 'real' bourgeois democracy. It will be, rather, an ambiguous and contradictory, partly corporate and partly populist system in an autocratic and oligarchic society which is slowly losing its feudal character as it embarks on the long road to democracy.

Table 2.1 Political trends in Hungary

Trends	Leftist Conservatives	Conformist Technocrats, Pragmatists	Democratic Socialists, Reform-Communists	Social Democrats	Radicals and Liberals	Democratic Populists	Populist Conservatives
Values	Bolshevik-Stalinist	Value-neutral	Socialist democracy	Welfare state	Civil liberties	'Third Way'	National identity
Issues	centralized planned economy one-party system order (vs. anarchy) COMECON autarky cells in the structure of employment	stability party unity power maintenance democratic centralism	limited multiparty system socialist mixed economy local self-government socialization of institutions 'ideal' (non-statist) socialism	multiparty system mixed economy social policy representative democracy	multiparty system mixed economy human rights representative democracy free ventures social policy social minorities	local communities ('Garden Hungary') multiparty system self-governments direct democracy mixed economy Hungarian minorities	romantic concept of nation and community organic improvement society as a moral phenomenon 'God-Family-Nation' Hungarian minorities traditions collective rights

Table 2.1 contd

Organizations	Ferenc Münnich Society (MFT) MSZMP (Leninist circles)	Hungarian Socialist Party (MSZP)	MSZP Union for Leftist Alternative (BAL) Democratic Youth Alliance (DEMISZ), reform wing	Hungarian Social Democratic Party (MSZDP) Young Social Democrats (SZIM) FIDESZ-SZDSZ left wing	Free Democrats (SZDSZ) Young Democrats' Alliance (FIDESZ) Hungarian October Party (MOP)	Hungarian Democratic Forum (MDF) Hungarian People's Party (MNP) Bajcsy-Zsilinszky Society (BZSBT) Independent Smallholders' Party (FKGP)	MDF right wing Party for Independence (MFP) Christian-Democratic People's Party (KDNP)
Social bases	older party apparatchiks	bureaucracy some former MSZMP members (cadre-elite)	younger generation of former MSZMP members intellectuals	urban middle class working strata	urban intellectuals students private entrepreneurs	countryside intellectuals middle class private entrepreneurs	non-urban strata

Note: This table contains neither the different single-issue movements, nor the large number of trade unions, cultural and other associations for safeguarding the interests of certain strata. Those are beyond the scope of this chapter.

Notes

1. See János Kis,. 'Az 1956–57 -es restauráció', *Medvetánc* 2–3 (1988): 229–277.
2. To my knowledge, the notion of post-Communism was used first by Zbigniew Brzezinski in *The Grand Failure: The Birth and Death of Communism in the Twentieth Century* (New York: Scribner, 1989). In the Hungarian context the term was used first by Ivan Szelenyi in 'Alkotmányozás és a posztkommunizmusba való átmenet néhány dilemmája', *Országgyülési Tudósítások*, 23 March 1989.
3. See Ádám Gere, 'A nagy tévedés', manuscript, 1989.
4. This concept is interpreted on the highest level by Attila Ágh and Mihály Bihari among the thinkers on democratic socialism. See for example Mihály Bihari, *Politikai rendszer és szocialista demokrácia* (Budapest: ELTE ÁJTK, 1985).
5. According to Laslo Sekelj, a Yugoslav sociologist, this one-sided democracy resulted in an anarchic Stalinist system in Yugoslavia.
6. On the transition in Latin America and Southern Europe see Guillermo O'Donnell and Philippe Schmitter, *Transitions from Authoritarian Rule* (Baltimore: The Johns Hopkins University Press, 1986); José Casanova, 'Never Again: Authoritarian Regimes, Democratization, and Collective Learning in Argentina and Spain', (unpublished manuscript, The New School for Social Research, 1987); José Casanova, 'Modernization and democratization: reflections on Spain's transition to democracy', *Social Research* (Winter, 1983): 929–973 etc.
7. On the latent political division of Hungarian society see András Bozóki, 'Kritikai magatartás modellek a fiatal értelmiségiek körében', *Ifjúsági Szemle* 3 (1987):38–49; András Körösényi, 'Vázlat a magyar értelmiség szellemi politikai tagoltságáról', *Válság és reform: A Magyar politikatudományi társaság évkönyve* (Budapest, 1987), pp. 43–58.
8. For a detailed treatment of this issue see András Körösényi, 'A kritikai-ellenzéki értelmiség Közép-Európában', *Századvég* 6–7 (1988): 104–122.
9. The inner splits of the MSZMP are perfectly analysed by László Lengyel in 'Alkonyat', *2000* 9 (1989): 2–6.
10. On the Social Democratic review of the 'historical platform' see György Fischer, 'Apparátcsikok uralma?' *Világ*, July 13, 1989, p. 20.
11. *A rendszerváltás programja*, Budapest, 1989.
12. On the SZDSZ in detail, see András Bozóki, 'A választások és az SzDSz', *Szabad Demokraták* 7 (1989): 3–4.
13. In western countries, a liberal economic policy usually goes with a conservative concept of society, while the social concept of society more often appears with a welfare kind of economic policy.
14. 'A FIDESz politikai programnyilatkozata', *FIDESz Hirek* 4 (1988): 4–6.
15. See 'A Lakiteleki Nyilatkozat', *Magyar Nemzet*, 14 November 1987; 'Az MDF Alapítólevele', *Hitel* 1 (1988).
16. For a more detailed analysis see András Bozóki, 'Földcsuszamlás elött?' *Világ*, August 17, 1989, pp. 16–17; István Csurka, 'A Magyar Demokrata Fórum 88-a', *Magyarország politikai évkönyve 1988* (Budapest, 1989), pp. 304–12.
17. On the announcement of the reorganization of the Independent Smallholders' Party and the outline of its programme, see *Magyarország politikai évkönyve 1988*, pp. 730–33.
18. The draft of the MFP programme was published in their paper, *Ellenzék*, in

April 1989. In their programme they state, for instance, 'Gradually we have to return to the property relations existing prior to 6 October 1944. . . . October 6, 1944 is the turning point, since on that day foreign troops entered our country for the first time. Practically, the deprivation of rights began on that day.' See *Heti Világgazdaság*, 27 January 1990, p. 67, quoted by Mihály Laki. This statement implies that the German troops which invaded Hungary on 19 March 1944, were not foreign troops, and that anti-Semitic legislation, including the confiscation of Jewish property prior to 6 October 1944 (the day when Soviet troops began to enter Hungary) should be regarded as being still in force. This is about the most right-wing political platform articulated to date in contemporary Hungary.

19. There have recently been many analyses of the question of old and new elites in Hungarian sociological literature. See Elemér Hankiss, *Kelet-európai alternatívák* (Budapest: KJK, 1989), Chapter 9, on the 'large' coalition; Erzsébet Szalai, 'Az új elit', *Beszélö 27* (1989): 40–43; József Böröcz, 'Két szék között: motívumok egy társadalomképhez', *Valóság* 11 (1989); Ivan Szelenyi, 'The prospects and limits of the East-European new class project: an auto-critical reflection on "The Intellectuals on the Road to Class Power"', *Politics and Society* 2 (1986–1987): 103–144; Ágnes Horváth, 'Elit és hatalom', (unpublished manuscript, 1988).

3 The character of the political parties in Hungary (Autumn 1989)

László Lengyel

1. The Hungarian Socialist Workers' Party (HSWP)

As the only party in the political arena, the HSWP encompasses the mass of society's unarticulated political values and interests. In this disorganized warehouse you find in one great heap old Marxist-Leninist-Stalinist shelves and flashy social liberal armchairs, with their imported fittings. Tucked away in one corner is the ambitious group of the late Kádár era – this is the upper middle class of society whose members hitched their careers to their entry into the oligarchies of power. Through the HSWP they had access to leading positions in companies, agricultural concerns and the state administration.

Even though they are standing in the corner, they still have considerable economic, political and military weight, perhaps the greatest in the party and the country. They do not have to resort to violence: it is enough to use their economic dominance and the power they can wield through large companies, banks and the state administration against a weak opposition and, which is sadder, a defenceless society.

The other group within the HSWP is, as it were, the intelligentsia. Here you find the liberal socialists, Imre Nagy-style national Communists and reform Communists. These tend to be young, and are more remote from the centre of power. Many of them represent the party opposition of the late Kádár era. Did such a thing ever exist? Perhaps we should talk of party oppositions in the plural, since they never took a united form.

This group represents a large minority in the party today. If a separate movement with its own platform had appeared in Autumn 1988 after the Arad meeting (the unsuccessful meeting between Grósz and Ceausescu), or in early 1989, when 1956 was rehabilitated and a multiparty system recognized, this group would have had a good chance of transforming the HSWP, or of setting up a new party.

Who forms the backbone of the party? Those who joined the party in the middle Kádár era, its period of success. From the 1960s through to the mid-1980s, in their way of life, their values and the relations they developed through family, friends and workplaces, they approved and offered proof of the Kádár policy for the ordinary people: slow but steady growth, pragmatism, less interference in private life, workplace security and social welfare. We should not forget that the party in this period was not an elite party, or the party of bureaucrats, but the party of the 'man on the street'. It was not just Kádár's personal style to express the desires and feelings of the ordinary people, but that of the whole party. These people were attracted to the HSWP in their hundreds and thousands by what the party offered: a flat, a car, travel abroad, a little moonlighting, no social unrest, and a low profile political style. The worker in the big factory and his secretary wife felt at home in the Kádárist party. They could give as much as it demanded, and received as much as they wanted: each left the other in peace.

The heroes of the early Kádár period (1956–1962) formed so scattered a minority that their main role was that of scaremongering. Disappointed ex-party workers and bureaucrats, and cadres who had lived through many a struggle view the present HSWP with understandable bitterness. This diffuse mass bears little resemblance to a movement that seeks the communist Utopia or that is capable of exercising power.

What will happen to the party at the extraordinary congress, and at the elections that follow? Or to put it another way: what will remain of the party? Who can it join in a coalition? Who will accept it as a partner?

One possibility is that the party leadership will maintain the appearance of unity with a new line-up. The bad personnel compromises and informal agreements will continue at the different levels, where each leader hates the other but has to court the favour of the other's group. The Pozsgayists have to win over the king-making oligarchs – county party secretaries, industrial managers, bureaucrats and the little caesars of the media – if they are to stand a chance in the party elections. The oligarchs are looking for a replacement for Grósz, and gritting their teeth they smile at the reformers or flirt with the party of the 'man in the street'.

The leadership understands that any debate about the basic issues will instantly tear the party apart. It will show that party members have less in common with their fellow members than with those outside the party. So no agreement could be based on a real programme. The only point of agreement is what they do not agree on. Party unity that is only based on appearances makes for a party in appearance only: not a movement or a political force, but the remnants of power. In free elections it would be a sure loser. If geopolitical considerations and Western and Soviet pressure resulted in its acceptance as a coalition partner, it would .be treated as surplus baggage, to be jettisoned at the first opportunity.

Let us suppose that the party barons are victorious at the congress. The industrial managers and county leaders will get bored with the meaningless talk of democracy and constitutionality and the liberal/monetarist programmes. They will offer a new agreement. This will consist of index-linked wages and restructuring for workers in large industries, to calm their fears about inflation and unemployment; open inter-company and bank agreements instead of central planning and financial control or free market forces; concessions to middle-class consumers in the form of relaxed customs and foreign currency regulations and work opportunities abroad; and material pay-offs for the opposition parties (premises, telephones, their own newspapers and cars). And they will reach a deal with the local professional elites.

If you want an example of the bad compromises reached by party olig- archies and worker elites, look at Yugoslavia, where the barons at local and republican levels have kept the system running for years. It was the same oligarchy that battled with Rakowski, joining up with the official trade unions, and partly with Solidarity. Li Peng's use of force reflected the interests of the provincial leaders of northern and central China and the rusting Maoist industrial leaders who are opposed to central planning and control, but who would also lose out on the free market.

'If we can, we negotiate; and if not, we slam the door.' 'Factory, land, town and village, and the right to negotiate with foreigners – it is all ours.' Let it be quite clear: we are not talking about the property of a party state, but about the property and power of an elite, which uses the party and state to exercise its rights. If this means the industrial barons have to be HSWP leaders, that is fine. But if they have to join the HDF or the AFD, no problem. The main thing is to maintain the mechanism of privilege, property and power in industry and in the counties.

What if the liberal socialists and the reform Communists win, with the help of a section of the oligarchy? It goes without saying that the victory of reform, market orientation and democratization would be best for the country. Sadly, however, this group lacks any idea of what the future democratic system would look like, what the socialist party's task would be, or even of how any transition might occur.

The oligarchy knows who the factory, the land, the school and the hospital should belong to: to them. The reform circles are still feeling their way on the issue of property and power, who should have them and how they should get them. They are thinking in terms of abstract non- existent state property, which an equally abstract society should manage democratically, according to market rules yet with worker involvement.

This group is little prepared for taking on the giants. It has no mass base, and has nothing positive to offer for the future. Does it dare take on its own oligarchy? It may recruit mass support from the ordinary people within the party, but these are the ones who come off badly at the start of any economic modernization. Support for modernization comes mainly from the intellectuals in the party. Entrepreneurs look to the opposition, or treat the untrustworthy HSWP with suspicion. It is no acci- dent that Imre Pozsgay looks to the Social Democrats and the Hungarian Democratic Forum (HDF) for coalition partners. These are the parties which might attract the mass support that would complement the modern socialist intelligentsia of the HSWP and help them forwards. In this respect, the HSWP's greatest rival is the Alliance of Free Democrats (AFD). The AFD faces a similar problem: its liberal modernization programme has intellectual support but lacks a broader social basis. The

HSWP's liberal socialist wing seeks to win support for a governing coalition from among the more mobile and entrepreneurially minded masses in its own party, who tend more often towards the Social Democrats and the HDF. And the AFD is seeking similar support for an opposition coalition. Without this basis, neither can be an influential party, which is why the fiercest clashes can be expected – and this is already the case – between the radicals of the AFD and the HSWP.

Is there a chance that at the congress the HSWP will become the party of the man in the street – the party that appeals to security and social peace? This is the direction that I see Rezsö Nyers trying to move the party, as it drowns in the flood of talk about reform. He wants to give voice to an HSWP centre-ground that is expecting modernization to proceed in small secure steps.

This is the crowning point in the Kádárist process of turning the party towards social democracy. There are no intellectual fireworks and no overbearing oligarchic self-confidence. It is just hard graft in the workplace party organizations, and an understanding of everyday life. If Rezsö Nyers were to win over the worker politicians, the small entrepreneurs who recognized the positive side of Kádárism in the 1960–70s, he could reshape the party into the party of the small people. The coalition partners he would choose are the Smallholders and the Social Democrats, who are similarly turning towards the ordinary people.

This would turn the party into a broad-based centre party. The technocratic oligarchy and the radical party oppositions would be reduced to small extremes. The HSWP of the man in the street would be a rather old-fashioned, traditional party exercising a patriarchical liberalism. It would slow down the modernization process, but would hope to win over the voting masses.

This party would be a realistic coalition partner. It would continue the Kreisky-style provincial bargaining policy of 20 years earlier, should it have the chance and the time. It would attract the mockery of the intelligentsia, but consequently perhaps the votes of the electorate as well. It could face the voters with a primitively simple policy of offering property to people in their thousands in a cooperative or semi-private form. If it were to pursue a consciously nationalist policy in its relations with the superpowers and its neighbouring countries, it could not be dismissed as a potential coalition partner.

The worst tragedy for Hungary would be if the HSWP were to break up in the middle of the transition. Instead of a peaceful process, we would see first an economic, then a political, and finally a military state of emergency. All three major powers – the Soviet Union, which has the power to wipe Hungary out, the United States, and the emerging United Europe – are interested in a peaceful transition. Any agreement they reach on the future of Hungary will be jeopardized if there is no HSWP capable of participating in a coalition. In the vacuum that would result from the collapse of the HSWP, there would be no political force capable of satisfying all three powers. And a political vacuum cannot last for ever.[1]

2. The Hungarian Democratic Forum (HDF)

The HDF is a child of the late-Kádár era, unlike the 'historical parties' – the Christian Democrats, the Social Democrats, and the Smallholders – which look back to the coalition period of the forties, or to 1956 for their identity; and unlike the Free Democrats, whose reference point is the democratic opposition of the 1970s, which opposed the consolidated world of the middle Kádár period. The HDF was a product of the crisis. From the mid-60s the group of writers who later founded the HDF voiced mounting criticism of the Kádár regime – though their strength and numbers varied. The focus of their criticism was that while there had been improvement in social and economic conditions, the regime had not nurtured moral values – or encouraged others to do so. It had destroyed the traditional communities (communities in appearance rather than in substance) and had prevented open debate of vital national questions, which include the rising levels of suicide and alcoholism, and the failing birth-rate. Furthermore it had not taken responsibility for the Hungarian minorities outside the country.

The death knell of the Kádár era was sounded by the 1985 meeting at Monor. But even at this meeting, in spite of all efforts to the contrary, there were visible splits between the groups that signalled deeper conflicts. It was clear that traditional grievances would not be enough to draw up a programme. In 1986 the populists, lacking a programme of their own, wavered between the democratic opposition, which was capable of formulating a programme but had little chance of power, and the increasingly militant reform Communists and liberal socialists, who had both a programme and a chance of power.

The turning point was 1987. The writers began to sense that the countryside, which had until then seemed unmovable, was at last stirring. But without a programme they were uncertain what stand to take at the head of this awakening. During the first half of 1987 they were in constant talks with the democratic opposition, the 1956 groups and the reform economists over a second Monor meeting which would set out a common programme. But they also kept in touch with the emerging reform wing of the HSWP.

June 1987 was the landmark. György Lázár was ousted, and Károly Grósz arrived as Prime Minister. Imre Pozsgay, whose position had been in danger since November 1986, found himself more strongly placed, with the old Kádárists and the Grósz crowd having to take him into consideration. It was while the talks were going on that the Beszélő group published – without prior warning – a complete programme, 'The Social Contract'. This served as both the pretext and the motive for the populist group to break off the Monor talks. This break was kept secret until September when members of both sides signed an open letter to members of parliament.

Since the Network of Free Initiatives – the democratic opposition, the reform economists, the greens and the 1956-ers – and the Federation of Young Democrats only came into being after spring 1988, and the reformers within the HSWP had no forum of their own, from October 1987 to June 1988 all critical forces lined up behind the Democratic Forum.

The packed Jurta Theatre, and the Lakitelek meeting where the Forum was founded, gave an intoxicating feeling of freedom to an intelligentsia that had been forced through deals, everyday oppression and humiliations. In these months the strength of a movement formed from below was first felt. Another first now occurred, when the HSWP and the government retreated on an important issue: Mátyás Szürös announced that in the future Hungary would take up the issue of the sufferings of the Hungarian minorities outside Hungary.

This change seemed to justify the HDF's policy of exercising pressure to make the state act responsibly. Moreover the HSWP offered martyrs to the cause when it expelled members of the intelligentsia who were in contact with the HDF. These months also saw the HDF hold forums in Miskolc and Kiskunmajsa. This planting of its seed in the countryside turned it into the only truly national movement. Crowning this process in June 1988 was another massive HDF success: the Transylvania demonstration. If in the summer of 1988 the HDF had been capable of working out and presenting an acceptable political and economic programme to the second Lakitelek conference that autumn, it would have become the one rival capable of challenging the HSWP's hold on power.

The HDF leadership failed to produce a programme, for the founders of the Forum did not fully understand the crisis of the Kádár system. The opposition and semi-opposition should acknowledge that it was not the hard blows of the opposition that knocked out the system: it extinguished itself. But why did this collapse happen now? To say that this immoral and dictatorial system was suddenly unable to go on explains nothing. The HDF has still not come up with the answer.

At the 1989 national congress, the membership was, quietly and cautiously, expressing dissatisfaction with the traditional values of the leadership and with the elitist intellectual founders. The new presidium gradually led the loose, uncertain movement that had grown on a personal basis in the direction of a more organized Christian Democratic Party. At the Roundtable talks in the summer of 1989, the HDF was at a disadvantage, unable to match the team of experts representing the AFD and the HSWP. But this was offset by the strength of its membership and by the fact that in most towns outside the capital it was the only challenger to the HSWP.

The Democratic Forum had by now completely broken with the democratic socialist and reform communist principles which it had still been willing to accept at the first Lakitelek meeting. It also distanced itself from the AFD's liberal programme with the vague notion of the Third Road. For a while the HDF found itself restricted to the intelligentsia in the country towns. It was unable to reach the expert office elite and the entrepreneurial middle classes who could be won over by a serious Christian-socialist programme. To achieve such a programme, they needed a team of experts from this elite; yet it was the very lack of this

programme that prevented them from joining. The HDF needs to attract
the support of the higher strata of the villages, but once again some ideas
about property and local government are needed.

The HDF's Protestant character has become diluted, but this could still
prove a disadvantage in a country with a Catholic majority, particularly
if a Catholic party were to emerge.

The danger for both the party and the country is that this movement
will overstretch itself. The voters may use the HDF to punish the HSWP
while the HDF is still without a team capable of governing, and without
the necessary back-up team of experts. The HDF acknowledges these
shortcomings in the direct action strategy it has developed. It discovered
that it can pack not only theatres but also huge squares in the capital and
the country towns, but another danger threatening the HDF is what
happens when there is no national holiday, no reason for a demonstration, and no by-election to organize a campaign around.

The HDF is offering a third kind of system between the state socialism
of the East and the democratic market economy of the West. The existence of this third way has to be proved not only in theory but also in
practice. The new system's political, economic and social picture has to
be drawn. The voters now sense that not only can they destroy a construction that has been developed over the years, but they can also create
one for the years to come. Their fear is that they will not be able to undo
at the next elections what has begun today, uncontrollably and unfore-
seeably. A party that does not present a programme may win the elections, but will be in crisis from the very start of its government.

The hard core of the HDF has two possibilities. The first is to get
together with one or other of the groups within the banking and industrial
elite which is hostile to both the centralized management state socialism
and to the competitive market economy, and would best prefer
monopolistic agreements on prices between managers and employers. The
third road would mean that property which appears to be in state hands,
but is in fact divided between the bureaucracy and the manager
administrators, is passed over to 'nationally minded' company managers
and bankers. By separating the provincial daughter companies and
launching programmes for economic revival, it would hope to develop a
broader property-owning social strata. This of course involves taking on
the local oligarchies, the county and town party organizations, and the
state administration.

'Neither Moscow nor Washington – the Hungarian Road' and 'Neither
Communist nor liberals – just true Hungarians' are slogans which may stir
a section of the middle classes and reveal the aspiring managers.

The second possibility is the relentless struggle against the oligarchs, the
hard and rapid decentralization of the large economic units, the development of new methods of welfare legislation, and populism. This could be
the proclamation of a country of small shareholders and small landowners. The idea of the third road is fed by the belief that Hungarian
society is disillusioned with the present system, but is averse to a
entrepreneurial market economy.

What would be best for the ordinary voters? It would be for the HDF to become a forceful coalition party, in both its mass support and its programme. There is nothing more dangerous in a fragile transition than a major party that is flexible and soft, which takes decisions not according to political considerations but on emotional and moral grounds. This is of particular importance, given the sensitivity of foreign policy issues in the transition. In the eyes of the superpowers which decide Hungary's fate, any future coalition will be measured politically in terms of the predictability and credibility of the parties. To Western Europe and the United States the coalition parties must offer a reliable picture of the economy; and to the Soviet Union, military and security guarantees. The present cautious – and rightly so – statements on foreign policy from the HDF cannot be a substitute for a foreign policy and foreign trade platform. There is no room here for the policy of emotions, moral outcry and illusions. The HDF must understand, as a major coalition party of the future, that Hungary lives in the grip of the superpowers, so the Soviet Union has a central role. If the Soviet Union, which is an empire going through a political and economic crisis, feels itself threatened by events in Hungary, it will find a way to intervene.

In the autumn and winter of 1989 the possibility of insolvency looms before Hungary once again. Without an internationally approved programme and a well-prepared restructuring policy, it will be difficult to get credit. This could lead to a shock similar to – or worse than – that of spring 1982, when the government grabbed in confusion at emergency measures. Today there is unanimous support for an economic policy that maintains the country's solvency at all costs. The difference is that the government does not want to be involved in any discussions over payments. The AFD, on the other hand, has raised the question of cutting or renegotiating the interests which hit the country badly – a tacit form of rescheduling. The merciless demands of the International Monetary Fund would suggest that it will not be easy to convince the creditors. The three choices – complete repayment at all costs, partial rescheduling, or insolvency and open rescheduling – require a programme. Solvency could be one of the big trump cards in the election campaign. The West could play it to help the opposition, by keeping the HSWP government in constant check. But the HSWP could also play it, throwing in the towel. Whatever the outcome, the HDF needs a discussion platform, because it make awake to find it has to manage a country that is insolvent, or is under an unbearable pressure to maintain solvency – or as the constructive opposition, to offer a way out. Will the HDF solve its problems? If the HDF follows the HSWP in breaking up, or proves an unsuitable political partner, the whole of Hungary will feel the effects.

3. The Alliance of Free Democrats (AFD)

If there is one party that is ripe for power, it is the AFD. Yet the party has no real chance of leading Hungarian political life. It has enough experts for three governments, but it is still unlikely that the voters will want them.

The AFD grew out of the group that had come together in the democratic opposition over the previous 15 years. I will not undertake a detailed history of the democratic opposition, but will give here a brief account of the 1980s.

The events of 1980–81 in Poland, in particular the state of emergency, brought the Hungarian opposition into a state of crisis. It brought to an end the human rights strategy that it had pursued until then, and saw the start of the search for an alternative programme and ideology. It had to use this to challenge the government and prove that, in spite of all its concessions, the Kádárist system was a cul-de-sac, and that it was possible – essential – to find a way out.

The opposition had to reach agreement with the 1956 freedom fighters and their heirs, the populist-nationalist writers, and those groups of experts who had become disillusioned with and critical of the late-Kádár system, without considering themselves as an opposition. It was a 'conciliatory' approach that did not constantly pose the question: 'Where do you stand: with us or with the authorities that harass us?' The martyrdom of the movement gave way to the 'equal co-operation of independent minds'. The democratic opposition now took a more long-term approach under the influence of János Kis. Its aim was a more gradual democratic development. One achievement of this more patient policy was the Bibó Memorial Volume. This was the first breach in the wall between the marginalized opposition and influential mainstream professionals. Another was the 1985 meeting at Monor, where for the first time the populist writers could meet the reform economists, the 1956-ers could speak in a relatively open forum, and the democratic opposition could step forward in public.

The discussions raised the idea of a Network, embracing not only those at Monor but also other new groups – the greens, journalists, and independent student and worker organizations. The Network faced a choice as to how it should operate: as a loose front for all democratic organizations, as an alliance of basis groups, or as a party movement with a programme. The first was excluded when the HDF stayed away. The lack of a programme, as well as the fear that a movement would find itself restricted to the democratic opposition, ruled out the second. In the end the Network was formed in spring 1988 as a loose alliance, by which time the Democratic Forum had occupied almost the whole ground of political debate. In its search for a clear profile, the Network lacked not only mass support, but also a programme and means of expression. In autumn 1988, the democratic opposition laid the Network to rest – though not without a struggle – and formed the Alliance of Free Democrats.

The effects of this painful birth on the AFD are clear to see. Although the Network was not operating smoothly in its co-ordinating role, it was far from clear to all its supporters that it should be transformed more rapidly into a party. Many did not like the way the transition was made, particularly as the founders of the AFD were openly proclaiming the party to be a 'return' to the democratic opposition. The Network was treated as if it had simply been the legal cover for the democratic opposition. Consequently, those who had been happy to work in the Network but kept their distance from the democratic opposition now moved away.

But a more important aspect of the change was that the democratic opposition in legality chose to stick together rather than divide up along political lines. Within the AFD numerous political strands come together: liberal conservatives, intellectuals with a Christian slant, the bourgeois radicals, and various shades of social democrats, socialists and greens.

However, instead of the extremes being blunted in a right-wing social democratic direction, which is where the fulcrum of the party lies, one could sense a pseudo-compromise of the extremes, a glossing over of the arguments. Behind the tight coalescence of the AFD was not just a common endangeredness: there is a sense of fate, that 'we have gone through our trials together'. This is strengthened by the opposition's, and now the AFD's sense of vocation. This vocation is to lead society towards the values of Europe; from Eastern Europe to Western Europe, from dictatorship to democracy, from the deprivation of rights to the rule of law, from the planned economy to the market economy. Blocking the AFD's attempt to achieve broader influence is the fact that the HS(W)P sees it as its main opponent, and does all it can to squeeze it into the sidelines. The other parties which lack a programme of their own also, whether cautiously or crudely, draw a line between themselves and the AFD when seeking to make use of the patriarchic relations in the political sphere. What the AFD says may be true and original, but this is of little importance if its rivals are winning over the celebrities of the small towns and villages, and using personal connections to win acceptance and support.

The fundamental problem of the AFD is its minority party consciousness. But would they be a minority if they did not take shelter under one roof? Could they be a majority if they identified with the views of social democracy? Or if they knocked at the door of the Smallholders Party or a liberal free democratic party with their liberal conceptions? 'We expect to be the agile minority, not the majority' is an attitude that arouses suspicion, whether it sets as its aim communist redemption or European modernization. If the AFD freed its own moral hostages, i.e. allowed itself to serve as a moral example to the other parties, then it might not be just a permanent minority but a moral majority of the future. This moral pledge of the minority is sadly reminiscent of the Messianic moral belief of another minority, which, with its Utopian vision of world Communism, chastised a conservative Hungary. That minority saw the cause of its failure either in the inability of the society to recognize the new world, or in a reactionary plot. Today we have a liberal Utopia and a nationalist-communist plot.

The AFD is not an action party, a party of the masses, but a minority party with a programme. It is suited to the period of negotiations and expert talks. It is in its element in the Roundtable discussions, whoever

its negotiating partner. It can show its superiority in its expertise and in
the inexperience and tactical and strategic weakness of the other parties
and movements.

The AFD has two choices. One is to wade into the election campaign
and the coalition negotiations. The other is to take part in the elections
but to prepare its members for the role of the strongest extra-
parliamentary grouping. There is a third choice: the break up of the party
and the crossing of the leadership and membership towards the centre
parties. This, however, is unlikely before the elections.

If the ground for the election is a party battle between the present ruling
party and the united opposition, the AFD can only expect to win seats by
working with the HDF. Since there is little chance of the two groups
putting together a common candidate list, the AFD is unlikely to win with
its own list. In Budapest the AFD candidates have a chance of winning
if they have the support of the whole opposition. The HDF will probably
form a close electoral alliance with the Smallholders and the Christian
Democrats, and a possible coalition after the elections. It may offer
support to the Free Democrats on an individual basis, but the choice of
who it supports will remain with that party. And of course there will be
a bill to pay after the elections for any support given. If the AFD wants
to get into parliament, it must either be dependent on the mercy of the
HDF or must change its strategy.

Could the AFD move towards the HSP reformers? The patient negotiations associated with Járos Kis and the conciliatory approach to both the
communist reformers and the national-populist camp would now be seen
as a retreat. This 'no deals' stand leads to the extreme anti-Communism
and anti-nationalism which the opposition itself recognized as ineffective
in 1982. The effect of fighting with the HDF and the 'national parties' is
that far from giving the AFD the look of a left-wing centre party, it gives
it the image of a party on the extreme right.

So the AFD is not able to move towards the socialists, or even towards
the HSDP. The fact that the party militants are continuously putting the
party on the edge of the political spectrum, with only the Federation of
Young Democrats beyond it, considerably limits the AFD's room for
manœuvre. But AFD candidates getting into parliament with the backing
of a united opposition could get ministerial posts; the AFD could clutch
at a coalition of the present opposition; and the party could participate
in the bargaining surrounding the budget. On the other hand there is the
danger of electoral disaster. To stand in the elections and fail is very
different from staying outside the fight, but remaining a small party. If the
AFD does not want to be a party in quarantine, it must elaborate a
strategy to enable it to survive the fact that its share of the votes will
undoubtedly not match its intellectual power.

One strategy is to maintain a certain distance from the elections, and
prepare for an extra-parliamentary role as the militant opposition. An
expert AFD with little or no role in parliament could constantly draw
attention to pitfalls in government, and to the suspect coalition
programme. It would be free of commitment to the government, and

could, for instance, question the government if it makes big promises to the main interest groups. The government would have more to fear from this vitriolic opposition than from its opponents in the House, for with parliamentary majority it cannot be easily ousted but it can be made to look ridiculous.

An AFD of this kind would not be so much a political party as an independent congregation of experts. It would be a movement which could attract all those who dislike the bargaining and negotiations with local and central authorities. This would prompt the party of programmes to air its ideas. Here its interest would not be in defending a programme and achieving power, but in allowing as many parties as possible to 'steal' from the programme, so that as much as possible could thus be realized. Consequently the party would not attract the careerists and technocrats from the bureaucracy, as the property to be shared out is only intellectual. Furthermore, the party's two great advantages would come to the surface. First, the party's excellent media capability. At any moment it has the choice of a dozen figures who can produce a good public statement. And secondly, its precise knowledge of the rules of the game, which means closely watching your opponents' hand in case they slip the queen back on the board. If the AFD plays this role when it has no direct interest in the tactical warfare, it will be not the judge of Hungarian politics or the prosecution, but the defending counsel.

4. The Social Democrats

During the economic upswing of the Kádár years the workers in the large industrial plants saw a relative improvement in their position. They could rely not only on job security, but also, in certain trades, on high wages in their main employment as well as high supplementary wages in the second economy. In some large companies wages were complemented by allowances from the company itself – flats, holiday homes, social welfare, etc. Most important of all, from the mid-1960s to the early 1980s, the Kádár era gave the workers the goods to spend this wealth on. Skilled workers in the mining, metallurgical, welding and chemical industries could spend their various wages on building houses or on educating their children. The upwardly mobile workforce now had a more secure work environment, civilized living conditions, and a consciousness of quality and – relatively speaking – equality. Social welfare, gradual progress, the sanctity of privacy, and consumerist equality all served to strip off the system's pseudo-communist skin and reveal the socialist or social democratic sympathies underneath.

Additional factors at play were this stratum's isolation from the marginalized poor and the higher elite, its hostility towards the intelligentsia, and its contempt for politics. 'Be master of your trade, have respect for yourself and your mates, maintain solidarity in the workplace, look after the family, and don't let anyone stick their nose into your business.' This workplace democracy determined wages down to the last fillér (penny). No foreman would dare to break the rules of the workplace. It is to this that we owe the co-operative spirit of the workers who help each other out with building their houses. It shapes value judgements about work, managers, engineers and technicians, says what is worth reading in the papers, and what is worth seeing on television. From here come the workers who formed private workplace co-operatives, and these are the workers who fight for wages four times higher than those of lower-middle-class teachers.

The deepest mark left by the Kádár era could be said to be that people achieved what they wanted by economic bargaining, not political struggle. Why bother with political parties outside the workplace when the best way to get a wage rise, to improve working conditions, to get overtime or permission for setting up a private co-operative at work was to talk – formally or informally – to the foreman. This is where the 'Hungarian model' differed most strongly from the Soviet and even Polish models. From the mid-1980s this social group started coming forwards, but it was unlikely that they would start forming parties or even trade unions from below. 'My workplace is my castle' was their line. There was no solidarity between branches of industry because what they had so far achieved, they had achieved individually. The miners and foundry workers had taken on their managers and then the government on their own. Beside this lack of solidarity, there was also the chasm separating the workers and the intelligentsia, hence the natural founders of a social democratic party – workers in large plants and the intelligentsia associating with them – have not appeared.

Can a social democratic party and movement be formed from above by the intelligentsia?

One possibility is a social democratic launch of the democratic opposition. This could have taken place in spring 1987 after the publication of the 'Social Contract' programme. Another possibility is if a section of the HSWP workers should break away, laying claim to the heritage of the social democratization of the Kádár years. If this occurs, the intellectuals would have to go round the factories to bring their social democratic principles into line with the demands for workplace autonomy of the workforce. They would become a party intelligentsia which is in constant search of its own Lech Walesa, and is preparing to govern along the lines of the Austrian Socialist Party 25 years ago. Its base would be corporate interest representation and negotiating parity. This is nothing other than a more credible version of the Kádár bargaining system.

It would have been possible to set up a socialist grouping made up of the worker elite, experts and entrepreneurs, which with a well-defined programme could have fitted in between the Christian and national centre parties, and the communist and/or social democratic parties representing the large factory workers.

But Hungary has no 'national bourgeoisie'. The Hungarian middle class has no thousands of members living off their businesses or capital, or who are freelance or self-employed, whose sense of civic self-awareness is strengthened by the ramparts of their private property – be it in the form of land, business or shares. Instead, its members are semi-dependent citizens with a double income (from wages/salaries and business and capital). The elite worker fits better into this middle class than the teacher. The Hungarian Social Democratic Party (HSDP) set out on a different road, perhaps the worst possible road. The party's greatest problem was the lateness of its launch. By that time, December 1988, the Hungarian Democratic Forum had been around for over a year, and the Network of Free Initiatives for six months, before turning into the Alliance of Free Democrats. When András Révész announced the reformation of the HSDP on 28 November 1988, the political intelligentsia essential to give a party its profile was already (or still) committed elsewhere.

Furthermore it is harder to organize a mass party than a minority party. A mass party must represent some form of continuity with people's earlier lives; it cannot stand for a radical break in their lives. To put it more exactly: it has to do a balancing act between continuity and discontinuity, and that is one of the hardest of political pastimes.

The third problem facing the party is that it has no leaders. The big historical leaders of the past have died. Ten years ago András Révész would have been the ideal party president. Now, sadly, he can only play a honorary role without real influence on the party. There are three potential sources of leaders: the 1953–56 reform Communists, those around Imre Nagy; the democratic opposition; and the HSWP opposition of the 1980s. But they failed to get any one of them. And sadder still, the bickering leaders it does have merely discredit it. Ultimately, it would not matter if its leaders were not colourful characters if they were hard-working party officials who displayed a sense of honour in their work for the party. Even this is not too true of the leaders of the different strands of the party. Instead they display a rigid self-confidence and extreme prejudice. The anger and intrigue are endless.

The HSDP's next problem is its lack of a programme. What is strange is that elements of a social democratic programme are to be found in the AFD and HSP programmes. Since the Social Democrats have not anchored themselves firmly on the left wing, their every sentence is fluid and uncertain. Neither the historical wing, the Renewal group nor the centre have any programme to offer. Their conflicts are not based on programmes but on personal differences. The collapse of the HSWP and the establishment of the weak conglomerate of the HSP have rendered them homeless. (I am talking here about the socialists, not about those who cling on to a long-passed HSWP.) This includes not only the intelligentsia, although they cry out the loudest, but also the workers. They are not represented by the HSP, the HSDP or the ADF. Nor are they national or Christian enough to turn to the 'national centre' parties. The political homeless have three choices.

The first and most obvious choice is to remain outside all parties. This would mean either leaving politics altogether or moving into trade union or local government politics. Workers in large plants might take this choice. The second would be to form a new party before the elections. It would appear that the radical intellectual reformers of the old HSWP who were disappointed by the congress's outcome are leaning in this direction. This little party would not have much chance in the elections; it would shrink into a small club. Of course the need might be there for a left-wing intellectual movement, but that would have quite a different role.

Finally, they could join an existing party. The HSP, which has hobbled its way into power, immediately falls out of consideration. The reformers have tried to win this party to their cause many times, but no more. They might try for the Free Democrats, but the extreme anti-communist slogans coming from the AFD suggest that not only would they repulse any 'left-wing invasion', but would also try to use the structure of the party to stop it. The one remaining party is the Social Democrats. I can hear people whispering that I am trying to turn the HSDP into a crypto-communist organization. Rubbish. It should be recognized that many socialists and social democrats who grew up in the HSWP sincerely want to break both with the Stalinist model and with the Kádárist policy of the middle road as well.

So we have three disintegrated left-wing parties: an unassemblable HSP, a HSWP still in the process of formation, and an HSDP lingering in uncertainty over its future role. A few months after the parliamentary elections will come the local government elections. These are normally fought not along party lines but between local figures and personalities. If this battle is not on an 'out with the communists' platform, but over who is best able to take on the local oligarchy, or who has the best ideas for the town/district, expertise could get a look in. One can imagine the new parliament will be less qualified than the old, but that local government will be more honest and competent. There is work for the left wing to do. At the next parliamentary elections not all socialists, social democrats and radicals will stand with bowed heads. By that time Czechoslovakia may have got started, a country that is more likely to see socialist and social democratic mass movements than Poland. By then Communism as scarecrow will have disappeared.

Translated by Charles Hebbert

Note

1. At the congress, which occurred after this chapter was written, the HSWP broke up into the Hungarian Socialist Party (HSP) and the HSWP, although not with the consequences Lengyel pictured at the time.

4 1989: The negotiated revolution in Hungary*

László Bruszt

Who could have thought even a year earlier that in 1989 Eastern Europe would present a full array of choices on how to topple authoritarian state socialist systems? In April 1989, extorted by the communist Polish United Workers' Party (LEMP), and after LEMP failed to pacify society and to consolidate the economy, the Solidarity Trade Union Alliance compromised and agreed to share power after two months of negotiations. Seeking only the restoration of its legality, Solidarity was forced to agree to run candidates in an election in exchange for renewing its activities. For the time being, the election included an institutional guarantee for a communist majority. Three months after the agreement, with a sweeping election victory behind it, Solidarity established Eastern Europe's first cabinet led by the opposition.

In the second half of the year Hungary was first, and Czechoslovakia second, to open a crack in the barbed-wire fence built around the citizens of the German Democratic Republic (GDR). In a matter of weeks, tens of thousands of persons left the country, but it was inside the GDR that the real effects of opening this 'valve' were felt. In the autumn of 1989 a series of anti-government demonstrations involving hundreds of thousands started an avalanche. In a matter of ten weeks it swept away the Honecker regime.

Barely a few weeks later the old dream of the early twentieth-century radical syndicalists to topple the exploiting system by way of a general strike became a reality in Czechoslovakia, even though in a somewhat different form. A nationwide general (warning) strike completed the call for the overthrow of the old system – of the 'workers' state'. Mobilized by university students and by the classical intelligentsia, workers performed a central role in the Czechoslovakian revolution, and became convinced of the truth of the opposition's watchword: 'As long as we are last, let us be at least the most efficient ones!'

* First published in *Social Research*, vol. 57, no. 2, summer 1990, pp. 365–87.

But they were not to be the last ones in line! At Temesvár [Timisoara] in December 1989 a few hundred Romanians and Hungarians tried to prevent the removal of [Hungarian Protestant] minister László Tökés from the city. He was one member of Romania's handful of opposition workers. The power structure responded with a beastly massacre; violence had to take place before people in Bucharest and in Arad moved to the streets expressing solidarity with the people of Temesvár. Leaders were quickly found, but it took long and bloody fighting before the military changed sides and sealed the fate of Ceausescu's regime together with the 'conductor' – popularly referred to as 'Dracula'.

During the three or four months between the Polish breakthrough and the opening of the Berlin Wall, Eastern European as well as worldwide attention focused on Hungary – making that country the model for Eastern Europe. What happened in Hungary during that period?

What happened?

One should ask first what did not happen in Hungary. Unless one regards the 'sausage strike' organized by the official trade union to protest at meat-price increases as one, there were no significant strike movements. Aside from two important mass actions in March and in June, there were no nationwide anti-government demonstrations involving hundreds of thousands or millions of people as in the GDR and in Czechoslovakia. No violent action took place, and no overt threat of the use of force was made, except for one made by a small-businessman member of the Hungarian Socialist Workers party [MSZMP]. Everyone believed he was a mental retard. Well then, what did take place in Hungary? Negotiations!

Six days after the Polish Communists' embarrassing election defeat a gigantic negotiating machine began to operate in Budapest to establish conditions for free elections. These elections were to be free of compromise, and were to establish a new system of power. In principle, in this system the Communists would have no guarantee whatsoever of preserving even a single morsel of their power. In the framework of 'roundtable negotiations' beginning in June 1989, 50 chief delegates and more than 500 experts of nine opposition organizations, of the MSZMP, and of six organizations that comprised the so-called third side bargained about preparations for free elections in two main committees, twelve subcommittees, and two supplementary committees. The opposition alone presented more than 300 experts in about 200 trilateral conciliatory talks, including expert committee meetings. One should add to this number at least 300 or 400 preparatory negotiations in which leaders and experts from organizations belonging to the three sides reconciled their negotiating positions in advance. This figure includes both the increasing number of MSZMP Central Committee and Politburo sessions, and negotiations at the Opposition Roundtable, often held twice a week. And once we add to this the hundreds of conciliatory talks within opposition organizations and in organizations belonging to the third side, we may count about a thousand meetings or conciliatory talks which were documented in one form or another, and all of which played a role in making the avalanche of three months of negotiations a success.

The number of not documented, closed negotiations and conciliations is not known, but one may assume that their number is no smaller than that of the documented meetings. At these closed meetings, representatives of organizations that took part in the negotiations, often 'talking across front lines' or by striking a small or large coalition, directly or indirectly influenced the agreements. These figures pertain only to the trilateral negotiations, of course. In addition to these there were hundreds of preliminary discussions and negotiations, all of which preceded the 'great national' roundtable negotiation: hundreds of discussions within and among parties and political organizations, in which decisions were reached as to who would negotiate where, about what, and under what authority. The initial negotiating proposals were already prepared in January 1989. Still at that point six months were available to negotiate about 'the' negotiations, and thus also the first half of the year was consumed by feverish negotiations.

All in all, in 1989 Hungary 'negotiated' its peaceful revolution. None of this could be foreseen as of January 1989. What could be seen with certainty was the fact that change was unavoidable, and that it was impossible to stabilize the post-Kádár regime. At that point, however, it was not clear in what form, how fast, and to what extent changes would take place.

The Grósz system was unstable. The 'neo-conservative' cabinet that took power in May 1988 was unable to stabilize the situation, but at that point there was no force to sweep away the old power system in one (or even two) strokes.

At the beginning of the year we found the 'defenders of the castle' on one side. These people were part of the conservative wing of the MSZMP leadership, whose self-assurance was shaken towards the end of 1988 as a result of Gorbachev's consolidation of power. The previous economic year ended with the same catastrophic results as did earlier years. After several years of experimentation, the leadership was consumed by fear rather than being gratified, because in 1988 'at last' (for the first time since the 1950s) they were able to reduce individual consumption.

Disintegration within the power elite became increasingly apparent to the public. Not only a handful of reform Communists played a role in this. Young (or younger) bureaucrats occupied a number of key positions in government. Most of these people were reared by the MSZMP; nevertheless they regarded the party apparatus as their chief enemy because it involved itself in everything. Organizing efforts began against conservative party apparatchiks within the state party, although only quietly at that point. By then several county-level party conferences had been completed, and a few more were in their preparatory stages. At these conferences several 'kingmaker' lordships – conservative county-party secretaries – bled to death. It was around this time that Rezső Nyers, one of the reform

Communist leaders, requested permission from conservative leaders to form an alliance with members of the intelligentsia outside the party, moreover – horrors! – with members of the opposition, in order to pluck the party state's power. Nyers was dissuaded from following through the plan, but by then Imre Pozsgay, another reform Communist leader, established his connections with the 'other' party. He did so with less publicity.

On the other side one could find the fragmented, threateningly silent, silenced majority, a few opposition parties with small memberships, and organizations which embarked on the path of becoming parties. The number of organizations was growing by leaps and bounds however. At this point, taken together, barely 0.5 per cent of the adult population held memberships in independent political organizations. This ratio did not reach 1 per cent even as of September 1989, the time when an agreement was reached in regard to free elections. No one knew then what kind of change the masses would support (and how fast they would want it). At that point the three public power contests of 15 March, 1 May and 16 June 1989 were still ahead.

Perhaps, in those days, the possibility of a forceful reversal still existed and some day we may learn whether secret plans were prepared (e.g., à la Jaruzelski) to liquidate the opposition and to pacify the populace by force, if needed. Although there was no shortage of 'tough' statements and of Workers Guards willing to fight, it seemed that there was no unified bloc within the old power elite brave enough to underwrite the rapidly increasing domestic and foreign-policy costs of this kind of a solution.

On the surface one could take note only of the fact that instead of a murmuring approval by the masses, the conservative first secretary of the MSZMP was forced to make some tormented explanations about a speech he made concerning the threat of 'white terror' (a communist reference to the events that followed the overthrow of the 1919 'red terror'). Accordingly, in the early part of the year the absence of a force capable of driving out the old power structure could be recognized, while the old power structure did not have enough strength left to stabilize its own situation.

The 'need to negotiate' was in the air already in early 1989. But opinions differed greatly as to whom such negotiations should be conducted with and, mainly, under what conditions. In the end, three concepts from among the many that emerged during the first half of the year played a role in the verbal battles of 1989.

The first concept may be characterized as 'defensive political liberalization', a brainchild of the MSZMP conservative wing. (The explanation and interpretation of this concept will be provided later.) This strategy related to a concept of negotiation controlled from the top, a solution that would ensure the MSZMP's dictatorial position.

The second concept came in the form of a proposal to establish power sharing based on compromise. Several alternatives for compromise were provided. By and large, this concept reflected the MSZMP reformers' idea advanced prior to May 1989, and did not suffer significantly from those suggested by several opposition parties prior to March 1989. It carried the assumption according to which the opposition (and other organizations created by those in power) could become direct negotiating partners, and the idea that the MSZMP would be assured of retaining its privileged position.

Finally, the third concept emerged in March 1989. In the end this concept became the unified viewpoint of the opposition in the course of debate within the then-emerging Opposition Roundtable. This concept was called 'one step transition to democracy'. It rejected all intermediate solutions involving compromise, and envisioned as its chief task the establishment of conditions for free elections. Attached to this strategy was a concept that envisioned two negotiating parties – the 'power structure' and representatives of the opposition – sitting at two sides of the negotiating table, with both sides enjoying equal status.

The first concept failed in theory in the aftermath of the February 1989 MSZMP Central Committee meeting which rendered a decision in regard to the acceptance of the multiparty system. In practice, however, elements of this concept continued to play a role in the negotiations all along, until the trilateral agreement was signed. Despite the fact that in late May the second concept was officially removed from the agenda, it reappeared in the course of negotiations and once again played a role in ironing out the final agreement in September, even if in a modified form. The agreement to begin the trilateral negotiations was signed at last on 10 June. It produced a spectacular victory for the third concept, but only on the surface. This, however, should not be understood to mean that the earlier concepts did not play a role in the series of negotiations that were studded with stops and detours. Negotiations stalled several times, and the struggle among advocates of the various concepts continued even after the agreement was reached.

'Defensive liberalization' by the MSZMP played the lead role during the first half of the year. This was a strategy of the 'flexible adjustment of front lines', of a disciplined, slowed-down retreat. The essence of it was to freeze society's political organizing effort, and to establish as many obstacles as possible in the path of organizing, if the freezing effort failed. If it became absolutely necessary to give in, concessions should be made only in regard to matters which did not instantly produce organizations – that is, political parties – which could question the power structure. But if concessions had to be made in regard to matters which did produce opposition organizations nevertheless, this should be done so that those within the power structure retained control of the licensing of the political parties to be established. If they had to give in and political parties were allowed to be freely established, then the maximum concession to be made should be the acceptance of shared power based on compromise, as a result of which the MSZMP would continue to dominate. A variant of the concession scenario called for salvaging at least part of the MSZMP's power.

What was the actual essence of this strategy? In 1988 MSZMP 'hawks' discovered that there were 'loopholes' in the legal system. In the course of the year it repeatedly became evident that virtually all significant, thus-far-unprecedented political events of the year were consistent with Hungarian law. This meant that all of these actions were legitimate to the fullest extent. These included the establishment of opposition organizations, the formulation of independent youth organizations, the establishment of independent trade unions, the organizing of the initial political parties, the demonstrations, the holding of public rallies, strikes at plants which for the first time received great publicity, etc. – in other words, everything that could raise the apparatchiks' blood pressure. (But then, who could have thought in earlier days that there would come a time in which people would take seriously their political rights?)

The task was obvious: the legal loopholes had to be fixed. The first draft of the Law on Associations – permitting groups, societies, associations, federations, and other parts of the social infrastructure to organize – tried to freeze political organizing by the imposition of dozens of stringent restrictions. The first draft of the strike law would have suited even Margaret Thatcher's refined taste. But in 1988 followers of Grósz made a mistake from which they learned their lessons in 1989. The 'mistake' was to permit a full month of public review of the legislative proposal related to associations for purposes of 'societal debate'. As it turned out in the course of debate, the majority felt that the law should restrict the state and not the society. As of February 1989, conservative Communists were still suggesting to workers that they should organize demonstrations outside of working hours if they had problems with the economy. Such demonstrations would be less costly, and workers should really not want to have a liberal strike law. This idea was objected to by the 16 opposition organizations, still devoid of formal power. Responding to mounting pressure, however, the communist-dominated legislature passed a liberal strike law in March 1989, with MSZMP leader Rezsö Nyers claiming that as a class party the MSZMP could not really support a restrictive strike law.

Advocates of defensive liberalization adopted a simple negotiating strategy: negotiations should be maintained within the institutional framework established by the Kádár regime, one that ensured the exercise of unlimited control by the MSZMP apparatus. 'Societal debate' was the institutional framework for exercising such control. As perceived by the Kádár regime, 'societal debate' involved legislative proposals complete with advance conceptual decisions launched by the MSZMP apparatus. Following 'societal debate' both the proposal and the advance decision would be framed into legal paragraphs by the state apparatus. Thereafter the finished draft was to be approved by the MSZMP leadership for presentation to the full parliament for its stamp of approval. Considering the extent of party control exercised in regard to such legislative proposals, it was permissible from the MSZMP standpoint to inject a further series of controlled debates without any risk to the party. This then became known as 'societal debate', perceived to be for the purpose of 'simulating' and/or 'replacing' political pluralism. In the process of 'societal debate' the MSZMP apparatus defined the participants, and determined the time allotted for debate, for the summarizing of proposals, and for the selection to be made from these proposals.

In the course of the year the MSZMP leadership tried to lure autonomous political organizations into this framework with a declining rate of success. Having learned its lessons from the debate concerning the Law on Associations, the power structure now made an attempt to minimize the role of public debate. While in 1988 a full month was granted to opposition organizations to review and debate proposals, in early 1989 this time period was reduced to one week. Moreover, the apparatus offered only one or two days for debating several newly emerging constitutional concepts.

In February 1989, the MSZMP Central Committee adopted as its own the principle of a multiparty system. This took place partly because of foreign-policy considerations and partly because Imre Pozsgay, leader of the reform wing, made a clever move. By bringing the issue of the 1956 revolution before the public, and by relying on public pressure, Pozsgay reinforced the reform wing's position within the Central Committee. But the fact that the conservative wing had a ready-made solution for this turn of events played a role in the Central Committee decision. 'All right', the conservatives said, 'let there be a multiparty system. Let there be political parties!' But the first political parties should establish themselves only if a party law was enacted. Thereafter there would still be time to delay, because registration of these parties would be tied to the existence of a constitutional court, and ample time would be needed for the establishment of such a court. And if, in the end, a multiparty system nevertheless developed, a constitution must be affirmed, one that tied the legitimate functioning of political parties to the acceptance of a vaguely worded concept of socialism. And even then, the acceptance of party registrations would be left to constitutional court judges appointed by the MSZMP. Conservatives reassured themselves that, after all, even North Korea had a multiparty system.

Accordingly, defenders of the castle pursued a dual strategy at the February 1989 Central Committee meeting. On the one hand, they impeded, and took off the agenda, every law that would legally guarantee the political organization of society. On the other hand, they tried to railroad through a parliament each and every new law that would conserve the largest possible part of the MSZMP's power.

These tactics did not work well, however. Opposition organizations became more vocal in their attacks on the government, on the MSZMP, and on parliament because of the newly introduced ideas and the shortness of time allowed for debate. Even parliament, the good old voting machine, was no longer what it used to be. More than once during the February and March sessions it surprised the representatives of the power structure.

And then in March 1989 the Opposition Roundtable (EKA) was established. The creation of the EKA nullified the conservatives' calculations to divide the opposition by way of 'dialogue' to be conducted separately with each of the various parties. The EKA emerged as the unified representative of the opposition, and rejected the strategy devised by MSZMP conservatives. The EKA called for bilateral negotiations between the power structure and representatives of the opposition, rejected all legislative proposals that would remove from the hands of a future, freely elected parliament, the opportunity to formulate a state and a social system, and declared a willingness to enter into negotiations only in regard to laws directly related to the holding of free elections. MSZMP conservatives responded with dilatory tactics. They stressed their willingness to negotiate, but meanwhile declared the opposition demands to be unacceptable, and submitted counterproposals which minimized the opposition's role in negotiations and which would have ensured the MSZMP's dictatorial position.

But time did not work in favour of the MSZMP. Essentially the two-month tug of war appeared on the surface as a struggle between new and old political organizations in regard to the question of which group of organizations possessed even the smallest degree of legitimacy. From the outset the opposition questioned the legitimacy of parliament, of the government, and of the MSZMP. In return, representatives of the power structure questioned the legitimacy of the opposition. In the second round the opposition raised questions about the legitimacy of the third side – organizations established by the party state – the MSZMP wanted to seat at the negotiating table. Quite naturally there came an immediate response to this.

The opposition did not offer excuses for a single moment; moreover, it emphasized that the lack of legitimacy was of the essence. No one represented anyone, no one had legitimacy to accomplish anything, or more accurately: at best, everyone could speak only on behalf of their respective organizations, or the members of their organizations, while no one could speak on behalf of 'the' society, and no one could claim any special authority. This was more or less the outcome of two months of wrestling in the mud. In a paradoxical way, there could have been no better preparation for the great national summit. The issues were compelling. No one held legitimate power in a country rapidly sliding downward in the direction of economic chaos. No one represented 'society', and no one was authorized to enunciate the 'public will'. Under these circumstances the *sole* possible solution became obvious. The apparent crisis could be resolved only by establishing legitimate power, one that possessed appropriate authority. The sole possible path by which this could be accomplished was the holding of free elections.

There was no possibility for democratization based on compromise! Any compromise solution would only have reproduced the problem of legitimacy, and together with that it would render management of the deepening crisis impossible. In other words: the agenda was complete. Negotiation was necessary concerning every issue which served as a precondition for, and permitted, the holding of truly free elections, elections that provided equal chances for each of the competing parties, and an opportunity for voters to become freely informed. On the other hand, no negotiations could take place concerning issues which would restrict to any extent the possibility of placing the country into the hands of a freely elected parliament.

The great national roundtable negotiations began against this background, six days after LEMP's election fiasco, and six days before the reburial of Imre Nagy and his associates, the executed leaders of the 1956 revolution. The MSZMP agreed to the agenda proposed by the EKA, agreed that parliament would not consider the issues subject to negotiations prior to reaching agreements, and agreed 'to do everything possible' to get parliament to approve the agreements. In exchange, the MSZMP included in the negotiations a third side composed mostly of organizations established by the party state (such as official trade unions), but it was declared that the 'third side' would have less authority than the two chief negotiating parties.

Just what convinced representatives of the power structure to agree to negotiate? Several factors played a role. The EKA's united stance convinced the MSZMP leadership that except for organizations created by itself, it would have no one to negotiate with unless it accepted, at least nominally, the principle of the opposition that the crisis could not be resolved unless legitimate power was established. In reality, of course, the opposition was able to convince fully only the reform Communists of the need to negotiate, and they amounted to only one wing of the power structure. The conservative wing of the apparatus ground its teeth when it agreed to join in the negotiations, and the progression and speed of negotiations was determined primarily by the changing power relationship between conservatives and reform Communists.

By then, however, the conditions of power increasingly favoured the reform Communists. Although temporarily the conservative Grósz-Fejti line was able to slow down negotiations, by late summer the circle was closed around the MSZMP apparatus, even if one had to wait until the MSZMP's October congress for full disarmament. The ring was formed as a result of the co-operation of several forces. On the one hand, in the course of negotiations, informal, unofficial co-operation was going on among several opposition organizations and the reform Communists led by Imre Pozsgay. News and rumours were passed along. Much of this was officially announced at the EKA level, but the public was not informed about most of the negotiations.

Informal collaboration existed by now between government bureaucrats and the Pozsgay wing on the one hand and EKA experts on the other. Although weighing less, the government's Young Turks themselves joined the ring. They played a role in accomplishing the fact that even before the negotiations began, the party abolished the so-called *nomenklatura*, that is, the MSZMP apparatus's legal authority to appoint managers in various government offices. (The Polish Solidarity trade unions were unable to accomplish this fully even in the course of roundtable negotiations.) Then, in mid-1989, they pushed through parliament the introduction of the vote of confidence, signalling to the opposition in legal terms that the government did not – or, more accurately, did not want to – depend on the MSZMP.

The final element of the ring that surrounded the conservative wing was provided in the form of collaboration among reform circles organizing within the MSZMP on the one hand and reform communists in top MSZMP leadership positions on the other. From the outset, reform circles undermined the power of the MSZMP apparatus at its foundations, and it took great effort and strong arguments for the opposition to convince reform-circle representatives not to want to join the EKA. Let them stay within the MSZMP instead, at least until the agreement was signed. Let them weaken the apparatus from within. Opposition leaders claimed that it would be tragic to increase the number of EKA member organizations by just one other powerless organization, while leaving the exclusive authority over organizations which enforced the party's power in the hands of the conservative wing, which was 'left to its own'.

But there is yet another factor to be recognized in order to understand just how the seemingly protracted MSZMP-EKA wrestling in the mud was suddenly disrupted in early June, and just why representatives of the power structure were willing to take their seats so speedily at the table with the agenda proposed by the EKA. In 1989 the revolution of 1956 once again became an issue in Hungary. This occurred for the first time in February, when Imre Pozsgay suggested a compromise to the party apparatus regarding the reassessment of the revolution, simply referred to before as the '1956 events'. In the long term the message concerning the proposed compromise was rather simple: there would be nothing to negotiate with anyone if the reassessment called for the term 'counter-revolution', because 'we' would be sitting down with the descendants of the same 'counter-revolutionaries' to reach an agreement, thus spitting in our own faces. If the reassessment deemed the 1956 events a 'revolution', once again there would be nothing to negotiate with anyone, because in that case 'we' served the counter-revolutionary regime for 35 years, and would have no right whatsoever to play any political role in a democratic regime. Accordingly, let us take a middle-of-the-road approach. Let it be a 'popular uprising'. This would enable at least some subsequent historical adjustment, and what is important, it would also enable a solution based on compromise. 'We' did not break down the popular uprising, it was 'they' who did it, and it was 'they', not 'we', who forced this system upon society. Just who were included under 'they'? Well, the Muscovites, the conservatives, and the enemies of reform. 'We' tried to manage appropriately the power granted by them and by Moscow, and now that the opportunity has emerged, 'we' return power to the people.

The 1956 revolution played a central role for the second time in 1989 on the occasion of Imre Nagy's reinterment. By this time the Kádár era's consciousness of the national 'we' based on the principle of mutual non-interference was seriously threatened for the first time. More accurately, by May it became clear that the funeral, which was being elevated into a national cause, would, for the first time in a long time, redefine the categories of 'we' and 'they'. At the same time, the opposition proclaimed that the funeral represented the burial of state socialism, and from the standpoint of MSZMP reform Communists their own 'presence' at the funeral gained fundamental importance. It meant that they could not be regarded as part of the 'they'. And even if only in the end, and only after lengthy negotiations with the opposition, were reform Communists allowed to be present at this mass movement of several hundred thousand people which was televised throughout the day, it became clear who would be on the 'they' side. Those who still did not permit popular sovereignty to prevail at a time when Hungary was no longer Moscow's captive, when even in the East they were giving voice to the fact that the 'Brezhnev Doctrine' was no longer valid, and when Eastern European countries were permitted to decide their own fate.

In the end at Imre Nagy's funeral there was no clear delineation between 'we' and 'they'. Negotiations commenced six days prior to the funeral, and Károly Grósz was first to speak. Throughout the negotiations the Communists succeeded in isolating the opposition from the greater public, and a majority of the people were unable to identify either the parties or the front lines, even at the conclusion of negotiations.

Lessons learned

One may assume that future studies to be written about the peculiar features of the Eastern European transition to liberal democracy will rediscover evidence to prove that a uniform state-socialist model never existed, and that individual countries deviated to a significant extent from the basic theoretical model. Differences in their transitions to democracy were also determined primarily by these deviations, above all by substantial differences between the internal power structures of individual party states, and by differences in the ways in which societies of individual Eastern European countries became 'normalized' and consolidated. The fact that these differences played a decisive role may be attributed greatly to changes in the Soviet Union.

In Hungary, just as in other Eastern European countries, the dramatic change in the external environment enabled factors within the country to play a decisive role in formulating the system. For the first time since 1948 an opportunity presented itself to suggest openly a change in the model, and for the first time it became possible to make a fundamental change in the power structure. While previous Soviet leadership groups almost instantly sanctioned any deviation from the basic model by way of direct and indirect pressure and interference, the new leadership under Gorbachev let it be known to Hungarian leaders that its primary objective was not to upset social peace in Hungary, and that it regarded social stability as more important than adherence to the Soviet model.

During the first part of the transition, Hungarian domestic political events followed the shifting power conditions in Moscow with the sensitivity of a seismograph. Thus, for example, in the autumn of 1988 when Ligachev's coup against Gorbachev almost produced success, in Budapest, just two days before the dramatic Central Committee meeting in Moscow, the MSZMP Central Committee also held a meeting. At that meeting hard-liners sharply attacked the reform measures and the idea of liberalizing the system, claiming dissatisfaction among rank-and-file party members. János Berecz, a leading conservative, went so far that in an interview he called himself the 'Hungarian Ligachev'. Later on, after it became evident that Gorbachev had succeeded in repelling the conservative attack, power conditions within the MSZMP also changed, and chief anti-reform spokesmen were forced to depart.

Another fundamental and peculiar feature of the 1988–89 Hungarian events was the fact that while the potential scope of internal political activities significantly increased, at least in so far as (tolerance manifested by) the East was concerned, the country's sovereignty, its ability to chart the direction in which its own development takes place (primarily in regard to the economy) plummeted to a minimum. This phenomenon was linked primarily to the dangerous acceleration of indebtedness to Western creditors. During 1987 and 1988 the Hungarian leadership 'managed' to double the country's indebtedness repayable in dollars, and while the threat that Hungary could become insolvent appeared every day, Western creditors gave increasingly direct indications that they would be willing to continue financing the Hungarian economy only in exchange for significant changes in that economy. In other words, as Gorbachev stabilized his position, a situation evolved in which Hungary was subject to simultaneous pressure from both the East and the West. Pressure from the East aimed for political changes to prevent societal crisis, while the forceful 'pull' from the West called for a radical transformation of the economy, also implying changes in the political structure.

From among the internal conditions for change, disintegration of the party state, and with that the emergence of open conflict within the political and economic elite, played the central role in Hungary. The above-described changes in the external environment, primarily the change in the external economic environment, played a role in the disintegration of the party state. The latter was highly unfavourable from the standpoint of the inflexible and obsolete structure of the Hungarian economic system. Series of liberalizing, decentralizing, and centralizing government policies which followed in close sequence served only to deteriorate the condition of the economy. The drying up of external resources needed to sustain the economy heightened internal tensions in an economic system in which each actor in the economy expected to receive its resources from the central government. But the process of 'softening' the party state which had begun much earlier also played a role in disintegrating the system. Among all state-socialist systems it was Kádár's system that removed itself most from the basic model established in Stalin's time. Kádár's 'soft-authoritarian' system tried to sustain a monopoly of power in harmony with the maintenance of social peace by providing solid economic prosperity to citizens. At the institutional level the softening of the 'model' manifested itself primarily in the fact that the previous single-centred power structure – while preserving its fundamental hierarchic character – was transformed into a bargaining system with many actors, one that was hardly transparent and was difficult to control even from the top. In many respects, this softened system of power resembled an anarchistic feudal system of power. The distribution of resources, moreover, even the rules for distributing resources, were no longer determined at the centre, but by 'princedoms' that evolved on the basis of regions and the various branches of the economy, and by the outcome of battles fought and coalition agreements reached among the 'estates of counts' established on the basis of subordinate branches of the economy and by regions. A bargaining system like this will rapidly fall apart as soon as the resources subject to bargaining dry up, and if only the losses may be distributed within the system.

Beginning in the second half of the 1970s, the ever-increasing economic and social tensions presented a choice to the MSZMP leaders. Although the alternative of 'hardening up' the system – that is, a return to the Ceausescu or Husak type 'raw authoritarian' model – was brought up repeatedly within the party, the Hungarian communist leadership opted for attempts to escape by making advances in the economy. It did so without strength, and without success. Subsequently, towards the end of 1988, at a time when the transition had already started, Grósz's party leadership made a weak attempt at 'reversal'. By that time, however, the party state had fallen apart to an extent that not even within the party was it possible for conservatives to 'scratch up' a sufficiently significant base for such a political change. The heightening and overt appearance of tensions within the economic and political elite accompanied the ever-increasing economic and social tensions. Heads of large state enterprises – the 'red barons' – declared war against the government during the first half of the 1980s, and so did the technocrats of the state apparatus against the party apparatus and against large enterprises intertwined with leaders of various branches of the economy, as well as reformers against conservatives, etc.

The rifts within the various elites prepared the ground for the second condition of transition, notably for the establishment of an informal alliance between reform Communists and the organized forces of civil society. A meeting of forces that were to play a fundamental role in subsequent changes took place as early as 1987 at Lakitelek. Various alternative ways out of the crisis were discussed there. Reform economists, representatives of populist writers, Imre Pozsgay – leader of the then-still-weightless reform wing of the MSZMP – and a few representatives of the democratic opposition were present. The most important leaders of the democratic opposition were not invited to the conference. Later, this fact played a role in the division of autonomous political forces. At the same time, however, the 1987 meeting played a fundamental role with respect to changes that were about to occur, notably in the establishment of the Hungarian Democratic Forum (MDF). The informal alliance that came about at the meeting played a role in the struggle for the broadening of political rights, as well as in the negotiations conducted in the interest of changing the political system.

Subsequently, the alliance against the party state was joined by so-called reform circles organized within the MSZMP. They declared war against the conservative wing of the party apparatus. Disintegrating the MSZMP from the inside, they stood up in the interest of democratizing the

MSZMP and for the adoption of opposition demands. The technocrats in the state apparatus strengthened the tightening ring around the party apparatus. Their primary purpose was to render economic management independent from the party apparatus. 'Young Turks' within the apparatus, characterized among others by Prime Minister Miklós Németh, recommended in 1989 that negotiations be held with the opposition. And while they fought for the independence of government from party head-quarters, they also wanted to establish the government as the central point of negotiations regarding political transition. And although the Opposition Roundtable rejected this idea by claiming that they wanted to negotiate with the real 'power', that is, with representatives of the MSZMP Central Committee, in several subcommittees of the trilateral negotiations representatives of the opposition and of government technocrats belonging to identical friendly or intellectual circles played the decisive role. In the end, an informal alliance, which in its range encom-passed the radical wing of the opposition, the reform circles, and the technocrats as well as the reform Communists, 'encircled' and neutralized the previously omnipotent party apparatus. Within this 'alliance' the apparatus technocrats played a decisive role in achieving that even before the trilateral negotiations for 'pacification' and 'disarmament' – that is, the separation of the party apparatus from the state bureaucracy – began. In early 1989 the technocrats achieved the institution of a vote of no confidence in parliament. In a formal sense, this rendered the government and the individual ministries dependent on parliament. In addition, the technocrats played a role in the abolition of the MSZMP apparatus's authority to make leadership appointments, that is, of the *nomenklatura*. In September 1988 for the first time they abridged the party apparatus's authority to appoint leaders. Then, with the progressive disintegration of the party state, the apparatus itself did away with the remnants of the *nomenklatura* in the spring of 1989, even before the trilateral negotiations began.

The third internal condition for transition was to 'take the lid off' the authoritarian system, that is, to attain and to defend the political rights of civil society. From early 1988, small groups of intellectuals – jurists, sociologists, historians, philosophers and artists – established an increas-ingly large number of autonomous political organizations. These played a decisive role in this respect. In a majority of the cases the emergence of these groups meant no more than taking seriously political rights which existed already on paper, assuming the existential risks that came along with taking human rights seriously in Eastern Europe. These autonomous political groups organized the struggle against a new deprivation of political rights, and in the course of struggling against repeatedly renewed restrictive legislative proposals there came about informal relationships which enabled the opposition to take a joint stand in March 1989: the establishment of the Opposition Roundtable.

The fourth condition for transition was the accomplishment of a radical change in the political orientation of society. In contrast to the rest of the Eastern European countries, mass movements did not topple the old system in Hungary, and in the course of the Hungarian transition it was not so much the mass support enjoyed by the opposition but rather the passive rejection of the old system that played the decisive role. Towards the end of 1988 the conservative wing of the MSZMP attempted to acquire a mass base by invoking the threat of 'white terror', but as the great assessments of the year 1989 proved, only the opposition was able to take masses of people to the streets. Such assessments were provided by the demonstrations held on the occasion of the 15 March national holiday, in the course of which far more people appeared at celebrations organized by the opposition than at officially organized events. Above all, the reburial of the 1956 revolutionary leaders in June served as such an assessment. Despite the above-mentioned sizing up of strength, political organization within civil society was rather low throughout the transition period. Even in September 1989 when an agreement was reached to call free elections, the ratio of the adult population organized as part of the autonomous political organizations did not exceed 1 per cent.

Translated by George K. Horvath

5 Political transition and constitutional change in Hungary*

András Bozóki

In Hungary the process of systemic change began in 1987. It is approaching completion in the political sense and in terms of public law after the free elections, with the new government having been formed, whereas it is just at the beginning in the economic sense. A generally accepted set of conceptions and a scientific paradigm of the post-communist transition are not yet available, though an increasing number of social scientists experiment with the theoretical explanation of the transformation of the post-totalitarian system. The Hungarian social scientists have done a great deal in the theoretical mapping of the earlier system, one should only remember the concepts of *redistribution*,[1] *bureaucratic co-ordination*,[2] *cycle theory*,[3] *dictatorship over needs*,[4] and of the *dual society*,[5] or the studies of the political system[6] and of East Central European modernization.[7]

However, the theoretical approaches of political *transition* have so far been based on those experiences which have been produced by the South European, Latin American and South-East Asian transitions: on transition from authoritarian rule. O'Donnell and Schmitter's four-volume work[8] has created a conceptual network for the interpretation of such transitions by social theory, besides the empirical analyses. The authors differentiate between liberalization and democratization, between gradual and continual transformation, and they describe in detail the stages of the dissolution of regimes based on the principle of authority: the internal struggles (hard-liners versus soft-liners), the nature of political opening and political pacts. Consequently they have isolated the following grades of transition: 1. autocracy (dictatorship), 2. liberalized autocracy (dictablanda), 3. limited political democracy (democradura), and 4. political democracy.[9]

The works of Juan Linz,[10] Larry Diamond,[11] José Casanova[12] and others also represent a significant contribution to the description of such

* First published in *Südosteuropa*, no. 9, pp. 538–49.

transitions. The question is, however, how far can these theories of transition for the analysis of the democratic transformation of societies be applied to those having a different historical tradition and political culture in other regions of the world, in this case the study of the East Central European revolutionary changes of 1989–90? After all here the nature of the fallen system was different from those in Latin America and Southern Europe, and it must be taken into account that the evolving new set-up would also be different. The above theories of transition, however, even if they cannot be applied for the post-communist political transition in every respect, offer a significant basis of comparison, hence the similarities and differences can be better highlighted.

The East Central European transitions have not followed a single pattern, and have taken and take place in a different manner in almost every country. In Poland a uniform opposition (the Solidarność) faced a relatively uniform authority, and their political struggles took place at roundtable conferences, the outcome of which was a pact allowing for elections of restricted freedom. In Czechoslovakia and the GDR the pressure of the bloodless mass movement ended the communist system, thus the system fell before the legal framework of the new set-up had evolved. In Romania the bloody anti-totalitarian revolution was victorious over the living spirit of totalitarianism and parallel to it a coup-like change of power took place.

In Hungary systemic change took place in the following three phases. The *first phase* (from 1987 to February 1989) was characterized by the appearance of *autonomous initiatives* within the state party, by the internal disintegration of the system, by the civic social initiatives outside the party *growing into a movement*,[13] *being politicized and finally transformed into parties*. At that time the internal disintegration was only sensed by a relatively narrow circle of political public opinion; and the various autonomous political organizations began to turn towards party-like activities only towards the end of the period. The taboo of the multiparty system fell only between November 1988 and February 1989. What characterized the strategy of the state party and the initiatives of the opposition during that period?

After the May 1988 party conference of the Communist Party (HSWP), the leadership had already put constitutional reform on their agenda, but wished to keep the process of liberalization, within the framework of the so-called *socialist pluralism*, under their control. Their idea of 'socialist pluralism' was to allow only those non-political and social organizations which had not endangered monopoly rule, with the exclusion of rival political parties and trade unions, and to allow for a limited expansion of the space of 'social dialogue' in the interest of achieving the 'national consensus' advocated by reform rhetoric. However, the actual acceptance of some elements of democracy led to consequences contrary to the intentions of the party leaders: it was not the post-totalitarian dictatorship which was democratized, but rather a process was started which fundamentally challenged the framework of the one-party system. This could have been stopped only if reform politics had been violently turned back, but it would have only further deteriorated the crisis situation in Hungary. And neither the HSWP, nor the government or parliament had the social legitimacy which would have been needed to 'control' reform.[14]

The first meaningful legal change took place with the amendment of the *Act on Associations*. This Act created the legal frame of reference for the evolving political organizations. Though there had been no legal barrier to the setting up of political parties, anyone who wanted to organize such a thing could expect police harassment. Naturally the executive organs of dictatorship did not stand on the liberal interpretation of law, according to which 'everything was allowed that was not forbidden by law', therefore the 'provocative' exercise of human rights declared by the Constitution and based on legalism was enough to cause the suspicion of 'anti-state conspiracy'.

The creation of the Act on Associations was immediately followed by its broader and narrower political and legal interpretations. According to the broader interpretation, the sphere of the right to association included also the right to organize political parties – in other words, the legal conditions of a multiparty system were created. In fact all the old parties (Independent Smallholders' Party, People's Party, Social Democratic Party), reorganized between November 1988 and January 1989, referred to it as well as the new parties growing out of social movements (Hungarian Democratic Forum, Alliance of Free Democrats, Federation of Young Democrats), as a consequence of which a *de facto* multiparty situation evolved within the institutional framework of the one-party system.

According to the narrower interpretation of the Act on Associations – represented by the hard-liners of the party, and the then Secretary General – the political parties were to be taken out of the validity of the Act on Associations, and and Act on Parties to be made at a later date was to regulate these political organizations.

At that stage the strategy of the opposition aimed at the expansion of social space, the broadening of the opportunities for political communication between individuals and groups. As the Hungarian opposition was divided right from the outset because of historical reasons, it chose different methods in the pursuit of its objectives. The first moderate opposition group, the HDF, made efforts to cooperate with the reform wing of the state party, and located itself *between* the government and the opposition. On the other hand, the radical – liberal opposition organizations (AFD, FYD) were committed to the principle of human rights and defined themselves unambiguously as in *opposition*, rejecting co-operation with the Communist Party leadership. Their activities helped to create that *critical publicity* which radically transformed the language of political discourses in comparison to the traditional party jargon, hence it significantly increased the role that critical intellectuals played in the transition.[15]

The *second phase* of political transition (March–October 1989) was characterized by *negotiations* between the state party and the opposition.

The significance of the phase is also indicated by the fact that a number of social scientists call the Hungarian transition 'negotiated revolution'.[16] It was at that time that the process of law-making dictated by the state party could be stopped and the opposition succeeded in making parliament pass only those laws to which the Communist Party and the opposition had previously agreed.

In late January 1989 the reform wing of the party took an offensive posture; Minister of State Imre Pozsgay presented a reassessment of 1956 to the public, classifying 'counter-revolution', considered to stand above all challenge in communist phraseology, as a 'popular uprising'. As a result of the ensuing internal struggles, the Central Committee of the party politically accepted the multiparty system in mid-February, and gave up the ideological dogma of the leading role of the party. Simultaneously, however, such steps were taken by which it hoped to safeguard the longer term leading position of the party. In this strategy a key role was allocated to the planned new Constitution, in which the just-accepted multiparty system was supposed to be curtailed. The 'socialist' nature of the system was intended to be safeguarded in the new Constitution too, thus only those parties could function legally who had programmes that confirmed to it. The new Constitutional Court that it was planned to set up was supposed to control it. Naturally the party leadership wanted to avoid the risk of free elections, and they envisaged a negotiated sharing of the mandates by the representatives of the parties instead of open competition. The strategy of the Communist Party aimed at keeping the still embryonic opposition divided, and in this spirit negotiations were conducted separately with these organizations in February and March. The leaders of the state party proposed entirely free elections only for 1995.

Meanwhile a negotiated type of transition was launched in Poland with the participation of the most important political forces. The Polish pattern seemed to be suitable to be followed both by the Communist Party as well as by the opposition proto-parties, though each of them considered widely the different elements of the pattern to be followed. The objective for the HSWP – once it had to accept the multiparty system – was to reach a compromise similar to the semi-democratic achievement of the Polish roundtable talks, hence retaining the decisive traits of state socialism; whereas the divided opposition forces realized that they were weak and unorganized in themselves, and that they could not hinder the efforts of the HSWP. The danger even emerged of a transformation where the HSWP would dictate the reform steps and the tempo of transformation, within the framework of the existing system, utilizing the chances offered by the fact that the opposition had not formed a single anti-totalitarian organization along the Polish pattern, but had developed towards pluralism. In this case the reforms and the necessary new laws would not have meant systemic change but the renewal of the system. The rallying of the divided opposition forces became necessary. On 21 March 1989 – only a few days after the great opposition demonstration brought about by the 15 March holiday – the *Opposition Roundtable* was set up with the theoretical and practical help of opposition lawyers.[17]

The new situation was unpleasant for the HSWP, as its leadership wanted to co-opt some of the new organizations into power, hoping that they could then always depend upon their loyalty. The united opposition, however, meant a much greater danger. The Opposition Roundtable did not yield to the renewed dividing efforts of the HSWP, and did not attend the negotiations of 8 April, to which not every party of the Roundtable was invited. While the HSWP encouraged roundtable talks where the parties of opposing interests would have been seated side by side, the Opposition Roundtable insisted on an angular negotiating table so that the representatives of authority and of the opposition could sit face to face with each other.

After months of bargaining the parties agreed upon a triangular table: the organizations of interest representation, known as the satellites of the party state, were to be seated along the third side, while the two others were to be occupied by the HSWP and the Opposition Roundtable respectively. Thus after a tenacious struggle the Opposition Roundtable was able to retain its unity and became a participant in real negotiations from June 1989 onwards.

The meaningful phase of the trilateral negotiations lasted from 13 June until 18 September 1989, and the issues of political as well as economic transition were equally dealt with.

Initially the Opposition Roundtable thought that only the key issues, constituting the pre-conditions of peaceful and democratic transition (electoral law, the amendment of the penal code, act on information, etc.) should be negotiated, whereas the HSWP proposed the discussion of all political, economic and social issues considered important by that party. The essence of the argument of the Opposition Roundtable was that the national assembly elected in 1985 was not legitimate, therefore no fundamental issues, otherwise directly unrelated to transition, should be left to them. This is why the negotiations on Constitution-making, the topics of the institution of the President of the Republic and that of the Constitutional Court were opposed by the Opposition Roundtable. The introduction of these legal institutions became important for the HSWP because it had become clear by early summer that the party was unable to realize the February plan of negotiated elections. Thus it was forced to withdraw again, which was accompanied by the loss of influence of the intra-party conservative forces. The party had to accept the fact that there would be free elections in Hungary and was thought to have a last chance for the partial control of transition, provided a popular candidate of the HSWP acquired the presidential position and provided it succeeded in incorporating the features characteristic of the social system of socialism into the amended Constitution.

Finally the parties agreed on discussing the political issues in six subcommittees. The subcommittees were the following: 1. the amendment of the Constitution (President of the Republic, Constitutional Court, etc.); 2. law on parties and the financing of parties; 3. electoral law; 4. principles of the amendment of penal law; 5. publicity, information policy; 6. safeguards on the non-violence of transition.

In this chapter I am going to deal only with the negotiations related to the topic of Constitutional amendments.[18] The Opposition Roundtable – if it was forced to negotiate despite its original intentions – strove to supervise the entire Constitution item by item, sentence by sentence. Though already at that time the opposition held the view that the Hungarian Constitution of 1949, following the pattern of the Soviet constitution of 1936, could not be reformed, and that the newly elected national assembly was to create a Constitution new even in its structure, the amendment of the Constitution was, however, started within its original framework, thus significantly contributing to the completion of the 'Constitution of transition'.

The parties agreed upon calling Hungary a Republic instead of the earlier 'People's Republic', however a heated debate ensued while the content of the term was being defined. The HSWP applied the definition 'independent, democratic socialist state based on law', whereas the Opposition Roundtable wanted to eliminate the ideological elements from the Constitution, and proposed the formula 'independent democratic state based on law'. After long disputes, the terms 'bourgeois democracy' and 'democratic socialism' got into the text of the Constitution with equal weight, in keeping with the September agreement. Accordingly: 'the Hungarian Republic is an independent democratic state based in law, where the values of bourgeois democracy as well as of democratic socialism have an equal standing.'

The negotiating parties amended the Constitution so that it would be suited to representing the multiparty system. Accordingly, in Hungary political parties can be freely formed and can function freely, and though they cannot directly exercise public authority, they may participate in the shaping and expression of popular will. Incompatibility was also stated in the Constitution in the interest of separating the political parties from public authority.

The amended Constitution which was passed in October 1989 as a result of the trilateral negotiations, had provisions for the setting up of the Constitutional Court, the commissioner of citizenship rights in parliament (ombudsman) and the State Audit as the economic and financial control agency of the national assembly, as new legal institutions.

The greatest debate ensued around the issue of the one person Head of State, the institution and competency of the President of the Republic, who was to replace the earlier Presidential Council. According to the argument of the HSWP, such a Head of State, directly elected by the people and hence having a strong legitimacy, was needed in a situation where the political legitimacy of parliament could be challenged, and would safeguard the continuity of the authority of the state; whereas the Opposition Roundtable held the view that only a freely elected new national assembly had the authority to decide upon the introduction of this institution, as neither the then-existing assembly, nor the participants of the trilateral negotiations, had adequate authorization to introduce such a fundamental legal institution.

This is how the problem of *legitimacy* became a key issue. It became obvious that an *ex lege* situation had evolved in the political sense of the term: the bodies representing political authority already did not have, and the opposition organizations still had not acquired, the political legitimacy needed for Constitution-making, as it could derive only from popular will expressed by free elections in democracies.

Nevertheless the Opposition Roundtable agreed to have a provision on the institution of the President of the Republic in the Constitution amended by them. But it also succeeded in having the principles of Act I of 1946 accepted for the definition of the competency of the President. It meant that the President was 'weak' as far as competency was concerned; the nature of the presidential role was one of balancing between legislative and executive authority, and did not mean an autonomous power centre. The President was not above the branches of authority and could exercise his powers only through the responsible government. The parties agreed upon the Speaker of the national assembly to exercise the rights of the Head of State temporarily.

However, no agreement was reached on *who* should elect the President (either parliament or the people), and *when* the President of the Republic should be elected (before or after the parliamentary elections).

The HSWP held the view that the President of the Republic should be elected *directly* by the people. It had primarily political reasons, namely: The Communist Party had a popular politician (Imre Pozsgay), whereas the potential candidates of the opposition were almost totally unknown by the population due to one-sided information being put out by the mass media.

The initially uniform stand of the Opposition Roundtable was that a parliamentary democracy and not a presidential system should be built in Hungary, because this is what can offer safeguards against a one-man rule. The competency of the President would be 'weak' in vain if he had a stronger legitimacy than the legislators because of direct elections; in such a case the danger of Bonapartism cannot be excluded, and a situation like that which led to the fall of the second French republic in the last century could evolve. The Opposition Roundtable held the view that the election of the President by *parliament* was the constitutionally acceptable solution in a parliamentary system.

In relation to the time of the presidential election, the HSWP stressed that it should take place as soon as possible, in other words, *before* the parliamentary elections, so that the stability of public authority may be retained. But the Opposition Roundtable was of the view that the situation was not unstable and so would not be stabilized whether a presidential election were brought forward or not. The opposition was also worried that a presidential election held before the free parliamentary elections would influence or simply rig the competition of parties and the elections, and would offer an opportunity to the Communists to save their power partially. The Opposition Roundtable wished to avoid the Polish pattern and thought that the dismantling of the old system would not be complete if a President of communist past became the Head of State at an early date.

The opponents agreed in that the election of the President should not be left to the then-existing parliament. The HSWP, however, did not want to grab the post of President temporarily: therefore the breaking up of the unity of the Roundtable and the acceptance of its stand became an issue of survival.

Only the historians of the future can find out if contacts were established between the HSWP and some moderate opposition parties, and if so, in what form. But it is a fact that, overthrowing the originally uniform proposal of the Opposition Roundtable, first the Christian Democrat People's Party and next the Hungarian People's Party proposed the election of the President by plebiscite at an early date in July 1989. They were joined by the Bajcsy-Zsilinszky Friendship Society and the Independent Smallholders' Party, and there was a great pressure on the Hungarian Democratic Forum, acting in this issue as the 'pointer of scales'. According to some parliamentary sources, the HSWP would have been inclined towards a bargain, in which it would have given up the Workers' Militia functioning as the paramilitary unit of the state party in exchange for the post of the President. In mid-August, one member of the Third Side, the DEMISZ (the former League of Young Communists), started a campaign of signature for the early presidential elections. Though the HSWP disassociated itself from this action, the Opposition Roundtable assessed it as the overthrow of the agreement constituting the basis of negotiations.

Finally the HDF also changed its stand. Though theoretically it agreed to the election of the President by the new parliament, it regarded the first occasion as an exception and agreed to the election of the President by plebiscite before the parliamentary elections.

Thus the Opposition Roundtable was practically split over this issue: the Four were left in a minority (FYD, HSDP, Trade Union League, AFD), as against the Five, who insisted upon the original agreement; thus there was a rift between the moderate and radical wings of the opposition.

As the Opposition Roundtable was based on the principle of consensus, no decision could be reached for a long time because of the different views of the organizations constituting the Roundtable. The Roundtable kept on postponing a definite stand at the trilateral negotiations, rolling the issue like a snowball to newer and newer talks. It went on until 18 September, the last meaningful round of talks, as it became clear later on.

In the third month of the talks tension grew among the parties of the Opposition Roundtable as well as at the trilateral negotiations. At last political public opinion wanted to see results, and the HSWP was also inclined towards minor allowances in order to enforce its concepts in the basic questions left pending. Certain people in government circles also informed the opposition that law-making procedures could not be slowed down and that government would enter their bills in parliament even without consensus. The reform wing of the HSWP also urgently needed an early agreement so that it could be successful at the approaching party congress in October on the basis of these achievements.

The Five within the Opposition Roundtable held the view that the results hitherto accomplished should not be risked, and despite the difference of views in even the most important issues the agreement had to be signed with the Communist Party. In contrast to them, the Four thought that no democratic state could evolve if the Workers' Militia survived, if the election of the President preceded the parliamentary elections, if the HSWP did not give an account of its wealth, and if it did not leave the places of work; therefore they did not wish to enter into the bargain. Thus the minority of the organizations constituting the Opposition Roundtable did not sign the pact at the 18 September plenary session, but giving up their right to veto they did not hamper the other organizations in signing it. On that day the real history of the Opposition Roundtable came to an end, and the meaningful phase of the trilateral talks was also terminated.

The third *phase* of the political transition lasting until the free elections (October 1989–April 1990) was already characterized by the *participation of the society*. During the weeks after the partial signing of the pact on 18 September, the AFD campaign of signatures for the settlement of the still-outstanding issues and subsequently the plebiscite of 26 November which sharply marked the split between the radical and the moderate opposition. In the meantime the old HSWP ceased to exist at the October party congress and it was replaced by the significantly lighter Hungarian Socialist Party (HSP).

The divisions of the opposition cannot be considered unfortunate from the angle of the success of political transition. The signing of the pact safeguarded the agreements reached until that time, so the cardinal Acts, including the electoral law, could be passed in October itself. On 23 October 1989 the Republic was proclaimed and the national assembly passed the Constitution of the transition.[19] Refraining from signature, however, enabled the Hungarian opposition to avoid entering into a temporary pact with the Communists similar to the Polish one which did not allow for entirely free elections. In 1989 the success of Solidarity was limited by the previously reached agreement, which is a telling example of the limitations of a purely negotiated type of transition. It became clear that no real systemic change was possible without the participation of the society. It was a characteristic feature of the Hungarian political transition that it went along the *path of negotiations* as far as it was possible, but it did not halt at that point, and, going beyond the Polish example, the society itself could close the chapter of the past at the plebiscite initiated by the organizations which did not sign the pact, and by the Smallholders' Party which joined them. This fact is not altered by the hasty decision of parliament in three issues out of the four already put for the plebiscite during the campaign of signatures: it obliged the successor party of the HSWP to stop organization at workplaces, to give an account of its wealth, and the Workers' Militia was dismantled. It was the plebiscite of 26 November which ultimately removed all the obstacles in the way of free elections and made possible what the parties of the Opposition Roundtable were not strong enough for: the completion of the dismantling of the party state so that preparations for the elections could start.

The plebiscite decided that presidential elections could take place only *after* the parliamentary elections, thus the new Republic would be a parliamentary and not a presidential one.[20]

However, despite the clarified constitutional situation, the series of constitutional amendments were not completed even at the time of the election campaign. One of the last decisions of the old national assembly was a political time bomb ruling that the President of the Republic should always – even after the parliamentary elections – be *directly* elected by the people, in contrast to the spirit of the earlier agreement. With this decision the old parliament created such a situation that the newly elected parliament had to start its operation with the debate of a new Constitutional amendment in the interest of the governability of the country.

After the elections

A six-party parliament was established after the elections in Hungary: the Hungarian Democratic Forum, the Independent Smallholders' Party and the Christian Democrat People's Party forming the governing coalition, and further, the Association of Free Democrats, the Hungarian Socialist Party and the Federation of Young Democrats as opposition parties. Of them only the HSP insisted upon supporting the idea of a directly elected President.

The largest party of the government coalition (HDF) and the largest opposition party (AFD) reached an agreement on the principles of the amendment of the Constitution on 29 April 1990.[21] Both parties have realized that the political compromises of 1989 reflected an earlier phase of the process of systemic change, when the strategy of the opposition aimed at the reduction of the weight of the communist executive power and the increase of the authority of legislation. In the meantime they also tried to settle those issues on which no agreement had been reached during the trilateral talks, such as, for instance, the political and legal settlement of the situation of the national media, which had not been done and which thus threw some shadow on the purity of the election campaign. In the agreement the parties declared that:

- they aimed at the establishment of party-neutral national media;
- they would abolish the legal institution of the 'Acts of Constitutional force' requiring a two-third majority vote, and instead they recommended the enumeration of all those issues in an Act which would require a two-third parliamentary majority confirmation, but they wished to restrict the sphere of such laws considerably;
- they would restore the original status of the President of the Republic, in keeping with Act I of 1946.

The latter proposal was passed by the large majority of the national assembly and Árpád Göncz was elected interim President, in keeping with the logic of the parliamentary system.

The agreement between the HDF and the AFD already consists of such elements which aim at building the new institutional system instead of pulling down the old one.[22] Here the increasing role of the executive and a better balancing of the branches of authority should be mentioned in the interest of governability indispensable to crisis management. This is why the introduction of the 'constructive no-confidence motion' established in the FRG among others was proposed. The essence of it is that no-confidence motions cannot be presented against individual ministers but only against the Prime Minister, and further, that the government can be toppled only if a new Prime Minister is simultaneously accepted.

The objective of the two largest parties in these measures was to avoid the 'dictatorship of the legislature', which could paralyse the government and evoke a situation such as that which led to the fall of the fourth French Republic. The strategic programme of systemic change was the demand for a 'strong parliament and weak government', which is understandable after 40 years of dictatorial government. But even after the dismantling of the old system, those fears had to be overcome which derived from the negative experiences of the earlier dictatorship against the strengthening of executive power.

In the summer of 1990 the minority parliamentary party (HSP) initiated a campaign of signatures in the interest of electing President by plebiscite. Nevertheless, the 29 July plebiscite on the method of presidential election became invalid because less than 15 per cent of the voters had taken part in it. With this invalid plebiscite, initiated by the former Communist Party, the question of presidency could be constitutionally solved on the basis of the majority of the parliament. From 3 August the former AFD representative, Árpád Göncz became the first President of the Republic.

The process of constitution-making is still going on. It has again become clear that the introduction of the democratic system of institutions in itself does not guarantee the unfolding of political democracy, though it is undoubtedly a pre-condition of it. Today it is not yet clear whether the nascent post-communist system will be a liberal democracy or a corporatist-populist set-up. One can only answer the question of whether the new Constitution and system of public law will correspond to the political and legal culture of the country after several years of tested experience.

Notes

1. Konrád, György, and Szelényi, Iván: *Az értelmiség útja az osztályhatalomhoz* (Intellectuals on the Road to Class Power), Budapest, Gondolat, 1989.
2. Kornai, János: *A hiány* (The Economy of Shortage), Budapest, KJK, 1980.
3. Bauer, Tamás: *Tervgazdaság, beruházás, ciklusok* (Planned Economy, Investment, Cycles), Budapest, KJK, 1979.
4. Fehér, Ferenc, Heller, Ágnes, and Márkus, György: *Dictatorship Over Needs*. Oxford-New York, Basil Blackwell, 1983.
5. Hankiss, Elemér: *Kelet-európai alternatívák* (East European Alternatives), Budapest, KJK, 1989.

6. Bihari, Mihály: *Politikai rendszer és szocialista demokrácia* (Political System and Socialist Democracy), Budapest, ELTE ÁJTK, 1985.
7. Kulcsár, Kálmán: *A modernizáció és a magyar társadalom* (The modernization and the Hungarian Society), Budapest, Magvetö, 1986.
8. O'Donnell, Guillermo and Schmitter, Phillipe: *Transitions from Authoritarian Rule* Volumes I–IV. Baltimore, Johns Hopkins University Press, 1986.
9. O'Donnell, G. and Schmitter, P.: c.f. Vol. IV. *Tentative Conclusions about Uncertain Democracies.*
10. Linz, Juan: 'An Authoritarian Regime: Spain' In: Allardt and Lithuen (eds) *Mass Politics*, New York, Free Press, 1970; 'Transitions to Democracy' *The Washington Quarterly* Summer 1990.
11. Diamond, Larry: 'Strategies for Democratization' In: Brad Roberts (ed.): *The New Democracies*. Cambridge Mass. MIT Press, 1970.
12. Casanova, José: 'Never Again! Modernization and Democratization: Reflections on Spain's Transition to Democracy' New York, New School for Social Research, manuscript, 1987.
13. See Bozóki, András: 'Critical Movements and Ideologies in Hungary', *Südosteuropa*, 7–8/1988.
14. Faragó Béla: 'Mi történik Magyarországon?' (What is happening in Hungary?) *Századvég*, 1–2/1989.
15. Szelényi, Iván: 'Polgárosodás Magyarországon: nemzeti tulajdonos polgárság és polgárosodó értelmiség' [Embourgoisement in Hungary: National Bourgoisie and Civic Intellectuals] An interview of András Bozóki. *Valóság*, 1/1990.
16. See e.g. Bruszt, László: 'Tárgyalásos forradalom' [Negotiated revolution] In: *Magyarország Politikai Évkönyve*, [Political Yearbook of Hungary], Budapest, 1990.
17. On the role of the Opposition Roundtable see: Richter, Anna: *The Opposition Roundtable*, Budapest, 1990; Bozóki, András: 'Út a rendszerváltáshoz: az Ellenzéki Kerekasztal' [The Way to the Change of System: Opposition Roundtable]. *Mozgó Világ*, 8/1990.
18. On the negotiations in detail see: Bozóki, András: 'Az Ellenzéki Kerekasztal [elsö] története' [The (first) History of Opposition Roundtable], *Beszélö*, March 3, 10, 15, 24, 31 and April 7.
19. Act on Constitution XXXI/1989.
20. Faragó Béla: 'Gondolatok a magyarországi alkotmányozás folyamatáról' [Thoughts on the process of Making of Constitution in Hungary] *Századvég* 1/1990.
21. Act on modification of Constitution of Hungarian Republic XVI/1990.
22. The HDF-AFD Treaty. See *Beszélö*, May 5, 1990.

6 The Hungarian parliamentary elections, 1990*

András Körösényi

1. Re-emerging pluralism in Hungarian politics: The character of the political parties

In a smooth transition lasting 30 months, the decay of the Communist Party and the emergence of the opposition parties made it possible for Hungary to have free parliamentary elections in March 1990.

The communist regime looked stable until the mid-1980s, then the decay of the regime began fast. The first signs of the crisis had already appeared in 1985, when 40–45 independent candidates were elected at the last one-party general elections. The years 1985–87 were still the golden age of communist reformism. The reforms, however, failed to preserve the one-party system: the opposition entered the stage very soon. The years 1988–89 can be characterized by a two-sided process: a rapid decay of the Communist Party and a slow, gradual rise of the opposition. There were no two strong, determined and self-confident characters in this political drama, like Solidarity and the Communist Party in Poland, but several hesitant second fiddlers. The Communists resigned under rather weak pressure, because even they themselves had lost their belief in the legitimacy of their rule as well as their self-interest in maintaining it. The succession crisis and the embittered battle between reformers (I. Pozsgay, Gy. Horn) and hard-liners (K. Grósz) also weakened their position. The name of the party was changed to the Hungarian Socialist Party (HSP), but that was not enough to gain the confidence of the public. After the simultaneous abolition of the *nomenklatura* system and other privileges of the Communist Party, the regime collapsed by the autumn of 1989, before the opposition could take power. Since no political power stood behind the government and the legislature, a real power vacuum came into being, which lasted until the March/April 1990 parliamentary elections.

The political basis for the 1990 elections had developed by the beginning of 1989. There were no big 'umbrella' organizations, both the ruling

* An earlier version first published in *Electoral Studies*, vol. 9, no. 4, 1990, pp. 337–45.

Communist Party and the opposition were divided. On the opposition side, the Hungarian Democratic Forum and the Alliance of Free Democrats were the most influential parties. The *Hungarian Democratic Forum* (HDF) was founded in September 1987 as a national-populist political movement, occupying a 'centrist' position between the ruling Communists and the radical opposition groups. The political character of the Forum had changed significantly by the end of 1989: it had moved away from its populist standpoint, broken with the reformer Communists and built up a Christian-democratic image. This shift was due to Jozsef Antal, the new president of the HDF, who shaped the Forum to be the Hungarian counterpart of the German CDU/CSU and the Austrian Volkspartei.

The other major opposition party, the left-liberal *Alliance of Free Democrats* (AFD) was formed by dissident intellectuals and human rights activists, who made up the radical opposition to the communist regime. Its closest political counterparts in European politics, in programme and political philosophy were perhaps the British centre parties, but in the final six months there was a shift towards a much more Thatcherite economic stance. The Hungarian dissidents did not have a single, charismatic leader, like Vaclav Havel in Czechoslovakia.

The other radical opposition party, the *Federation of Young Democrats* (FYD) was originally founded in March 1988 as a youth organization. The FYD became well known and popular because of the radical speeches of Viktor Orbán, who was the only charismatic figure in Hungarian politics, and because of radical political actions, such as collecting tens of thousands of signatures to force hard-line communist MPs to resign. They had a political philosophy similar to that of the Free Democrats, but by the pre-election period they had successfully moved away politically from the AFD; this was crucial – it kept their sympathizers as voters and it reshaped the image of the party from militancy to moderation and thoughtfulness.

The *Independent Smallholders' Party* (SHP) was originally founded in the inter-war period, and was then the major opposition party. It was the party of the peasants with landed property. As the single anti-communist party which took part in the 1945 contest, it had taken all the votes of the right (57 per cent) and won the parliamentary elections. At the end of 1988, former Smallholders MPs began to reorganize the party, but it then became entangled in an ongoing leadership crisis. However, the party survived, and by raising the question of landed property, it became popular in rural Hungary by the pre-election period. (It claimed back the collectivized land of the peasantry.)

In the beginning of 1989, old social democrat politicians also tried to reorganize the Social Democratic Party, which had fused with the Communists in 1948. In the inter- and post-war period, the *Hungarian Social Democratic Party* (SDP) was the party of the working class, based on trade-union member factory workers. The new SDP, however, did not turn back to this tradition, but tried to build up a left-liberal middle-class party. The SDP also suffered from an ongoing leadership crisis, which damaged the image of the party.

On the other side of politics, the ruling Communist Party was in decay. The internal struggle within the Hungarian Socialist Workers' Party finally led to an open split in October 1989. The reform wing, led by I. Pozsgay, pushed K. Grósz and the hard-liners out and reshaped the party under a new name as the *Hungarian Socialist Party* (HSP), under which title they kept their governing position until the 1990 elections. The HSP reformers tried to build up a new, social democratic image, but were not able to stop the decline in their party's popularity.

The hard-line communists tried to revive the old *Hungarian Socialist Workers' Party* (HSWP). Though they had the highest number of party members in the pre-election period, their political influence did not extend beyond their own rank and file.

2. The electoral system

The electoral system was a product of a political compromise. It was discussed and decided upon by the main opposition parties and the ruling Communist Party during the 'roundtable negotiations' in August and September 1989.

The historic parties (Smallholders, Social Democrats, Christian Democrats) favoured proportional representation (PR) with county-based party lists, which was used in 1945 and 1947. However, the general mood in the country, especially among the MPs in the parliament, made it impossible to abolish the existing local constituency representation. Since there were no huge popular movements behind the new political parties, their legitimacy was limited. The local notables and the citizens did not want to let the whole nomination process be controlled by party bureaucracies. The long debate and the general mood made it impossible to introduce any election system based on a single principle. Therefore, the electoral system became a combination of different principles and techniques.[1] The 386 seats of the unicameral Hungarian parliament were divided into three categories: 176 were to be elected in single-member constituencies (SMC), 152 from regional party lists, and 58 from national party lists.

The country was divided into 176 SMC (single-member constituencies) and 20 regions, i.e. multi-member constituencies (19 counties and the capital, Budapest). The voters had two votes, one for an SMC candidate, and one for regional party lists.

In the 176 SMCs there was a two-ballot system. In the first ballot there was a majority rule: if one candidate gained an absolute majority, he or she took the seat. Otherwise, the first three candidates could enter the second round, plus any other candidates who got at least 15 per cent of the votes cast in the first round. In the second ballot, there was a 'first-past-the-post' system: the plurality of the votes was enough to gain the seat.

The second votes of the electorate were cast for regional party lists. Each region had a number of seats in the parliament, in proportion to the

number of its residents. The smallest region, Nográd county, had four
seats, the largest, Budapest, had 28. The seats in each county were
distributed by PR among the parties.

There were 58 additional seats for a national pool. These were
distributed among the national party lists in proportion to their residual
votes. (Votes which are not enough to gain a seat either in an SMC or
in a regional contest are regarded as residual votes.)

The combination of three different channels made the Hungarian election system more 'balanced', and safer for the major and medium-sized
political parties. There were four built-in obstacles in order to hinder the
tiny splinter parties: 1. the strict regulations of the nomination process;
2–3. the criteria for putting up regional and national party lists; and 4.
the 4 per cent threshold. More detail on these points follows:

1. According to the regulation of the nomination process, anyone
   (whether a party member or an independent politician) who wanted to
   be a candidate in an SMC, had to gain support and collect the
   signatures of at least 750 local residents.
2. A party list could be nominated in a region if the party was able to
   put up candidates in a minimum of at least a quarter of the SMCs in
   that region.
3. A national party list could be set up if a party was able to put up at
   least seven regional lists.
4. A party could not gain any seats from its regional and national lists
   unless the votes for its regional lists exceeded 4 per cent of the total
   votes cast for regional lists.

3. The election

The transition process might have been too long for the Hungarians,
because they became rather bored by the time of the electoral campaign.
The campaign did not make the country very excited and the first post-
communist election turned out to be a choice without enthusiasm. The
turn-out was rather low, compared with the East German or Czechoslovakian: 65 per cent in the first round and 45 per cent in the run-off. The
explanation might be found in the peculiarity of the Hungarian transition
process. Whereas in Poland, East Germany and Czechoslovakia the transition was a consequence of huge mass movements, in Hungary it was not
preceded by a popular revolt. The collapse of communist rule was much
more an outcome of a struggle between small elite groups of the regime
and the opposition, than the result of mass pressure from below. The
opposition parties altogether did not have more than 100,000 members in
the pre-election period. People in the street followed the process of transition with approval, but without participating in it.

3.1 The official campaign period and the nomination process

The official election campaign had two parts, each one month long. The first half of the campaign was closely linked with the nomination process. According to a multiparty agreement, each of the registered 54 Hungarian political parties had the right to advertise its political programme on the main TV and radio channels.

Due to the strict regulations of the nomination process, most of the 54 parties were de-selected; 28 political parties were able to put up candidates in SMCs, and 19 of them on at least one regional party list. But only 12 parties were able to put up seven or more regional lists and thus gain the right to put up national lists and take part in the distribution of the 58 seats reserved for the regional votes. All the other parties lost their right to win seats even from their regional party lists, as well as their access to the main media sources in the second half of the campaign, where time was reserved for party political broadcasts. Otherwise, there were no limitations on access to media sources, so the political programme of the parties got good publicity. The political broadcasts of the main TV and radio channels were controlled by a multiparty committee, which successfully maintained 'fair play' in the distribution of the party political broadcasts.

The whole campaign and the election itself took place in rather 'fair' circumstances. All political parties, who had candidates, sent representatives to the electoral committees, they checked the process of vote casting and counting, and no serious incidents were reported. Unlike East Germany, the election campaign was dominated by internal political contest in Hungary: the outside influences were marginal. After the pre-selection process of the nomination, the political scene became much clearer for the second half of the campaign: 12 national parties remained on the stage and competed for the votes. There were no political surprises in this pre-selection process.

3.2 The first round

The first round of the elections clarified the political scene and brought three minor surprises. First, the turn-out: 5,093,119 citizens cast their ballot, which meant a relatively low (65 per cent) turn-out[2]. Second, the 4 per cent threshold reduced the number of relevant parliamentary parties to six, as Table 6.1 shows.[3]

The HDF gained a plurality of the votes, but the Free Democrats were close behind them. The Forum was ahead by 3.3 per cent in the national total of votes cast for regional party lists – a wider margin than had been predicted. The Socialist Party and the Young Democrats achieved the result predicted by the opinion polls. The real surprise lay in the poor results of the Smallholders, in the collapse of the Social Democrats and in the advance of the Christian Democrats.

In the regional distribution of these votes, the Forum got the plurality

Table 6.1   The votes cast for regional party lists (in %)

1. Hungarian Democratic Forum (HDF)	24.71
2. Alliance of Free Democrats (AFD)	21.38
3. Smallholders' Party (SHP)	11.76
4. Hungarian Socialist Party (HSP)	10.89
5. Federation of Young Democrats (FYD)	8.94
6. Christian Democratic People's Party (CDPP)	6.46
7. Hungarian Socialist Workers' Party (HSWP)	3.68
8. Hungarian Social Democratic Party (HSDP)	3.55
9. Agrarian Alliance (AA)	3.15
10. Party of Entrepreneurs (PE)	1.89
11. Patriotic Electoral Coalition (PEC)	1.87
12. Hungarian People's Party (HPP)	0.76
+ others	0.96
total	100.00

Source: Magyar Nemzet, 28 March 1990, p. 1

Note: Table 6.1 shows the distribution of the political preferences of the electorate. The 386 parliamentary seats were distributed through three different channels: 1. 120 among regional party lists by proportional representation; 2. 176 by single-member constituency (SMC) contest; 3. 90 by national list (in proportion to the residual votes from the first and second channel).

of the votes in 15 regions, the Free Democrats in four and the Smallholders in one, out of a total of 20 regions.[4] Since the 152 seats of the regional party lists were allocated by PR, the actual distribution of these seats among the six national parties was: Forum 40, Free Democrats 34, Smallholders 16, Socialist Party 14, Young Democrats 8 and Christian Democrats 8 seats (see Table 6.4). The rules defined by the electoral law and the distribution of the votes made it possible to distribute only 120 out of the 152 regional seats. The remaining 32 increased the seats in the national pool from 58 to 90.

Among the 176 single-member constituencies[5] there were only five where the final result (i.e. clear majority) emerged in the first round. Three of these seats were won by the HDF and two by independent candidates. In general, the Forum took the lead in 80, the Free Democrats in 63 and the Smallholders in 11 constituencies. The lead of the Forum was significant, but not overwhelming. In 171 constituencies the second round was to be decisive. Uncertainty about what the voters of the de-selected parties would do, as well as the confusion of the local and national electoral pacts, made the results unpredictable. The general trend of these pacts, however, suggested the likely pattern of coalition making. The HDF–CDPP and the AFD–FYD alliances were confirmed, but the Smallholders' Party was divided on what it should do.

Table 6.2 The changing positions and the final distribution of the 176 single-member constituency seats

	1st round	2nd round
HDF	80	114
AFD	63	35
SHP	11	11
HSP	3	1
FYD	3	2
CDPP	4	3
AA	2	2
PEA	1	–
J	2	2
I	7	6
total	176	176

I = independent candidates
PEA = Patriotic Electoral Alliance
J = joint candidates of different parties

Source: Calculated by the author

3.3 A landslide in the second round[6]

The second round produced a landslide for the Forum. The HDF gained 41.2 per cent of the votes and won altogether 114 out of the 176 seats which were contested. (Three of them had already been won by the Forum by absolute majority in the first round.) In the first round they had taken the lead in 80 constituencies, and now they not only won those 80 seats, but gained a further 34 victories. The Free Democrats turned out to be the big losers in this landslide. They lost 28 places out of the 63 where they had secured a plurality of votes in the first round, and won only 35 of the 176 single-member constituency places. The Smallholders stood their ground in their strongholds and won 11 constituency seats. (See Table 6.2.)

4. The role of the election system

The victory of the HDF in the run-off elections was much higher in terms of seats gained than of votes won. The SMC electoral system gave an advantage to the party which got the highest number of votes at the expense of all the other parties. As a consequence of the first round and of the electoral pacts (a couple of candidates stood down in favour of their allies), in the 171 SMCs, where the run-off was held, the HDF was left with 154 candidates, the AFD with 135, the SHP 69, the HSP 58, the CDPP 21 and the FYD 12. Table 6.3 shows the number of votes cast in the second round and the distribution of the 176 SMC seats (five of them

Table 6.3 Votes cast in the second round* and the distribution of the SMC seats

Parties	Votes		Seats	
	number	*(%)*	*number*	*(%)*
HDF	1,460,838	41.22	114	64.77
AFD	1,052,096	29.69	35	19.89
SHP	376,988	10.64	11	6.25
HSP	219,024	6.18	1	0.57
FYD	76,279	2.15	2	1.13
CDPP	130,903	3.69	3	1.71
independent	103,922	2.93	6	3.41
others	123,791	3.50	4	2.27
total	3,543,841	100.00	176	100.00

* = the Table contains the figures of five SMCs, where, in fact, absolute majority, and therefore final result were achieved in the first ballot

Sources: Magyar Hirlap, 1990 április 10, pp. 4–5, and *Beszélö*, 1990 április 14, p. 22

Table 6.4 The distribution and sources of seats

Party/	SMC	regional	national	total	%
HDF	114	40	10	164	42.49
AFD	35	34	23	92	23.83
SHP	11	16	17	44	11.40
HSP*	1	14	18	33	8.55
FYD	2	8	12	22	5.70
CDPP	3	8	10	21	5.44
AA	2	–	–	2	0.52
I	6	–	–	6	1.55
J	2	–	–	2	0.52
total	176	120	90	386	100.00

SMC = single-member constituency
I = independent candidate
J = joint candidate of different parties

Source: Magyar Hirlap, 10 April 1990, p. 1

Note: As there is more specific information about the real party alignment of the joint candidates, the figures are slightly corrected by the author.

had been already won in the first round). Table 6.3 also shows how effectively the different parties transformed their votes into seats in the SMC contest.

The third channel of the electoral system, however, slightly decreased the defeat of the Free Democrats and the other four parties who could

Table 6.5 Distribution of seats by national and regional PR (%)

parties	national PR	regional PR
HDF	29.37	33.33
AFD	25.41	28.33
SHP	13.98	13.33
HSP	12.94	11.67
FYD	10.62	6.67
CDPP	7.68	6.67
total	100.00	100.00

Source: Calculated by the author

Note: The 'regional PR' column shows the actual distribution of the seats by regional proportional representation in the Hungarian general elections.

gain seats in the national pool. The number of the 'lost' residual votes became especially important after the 32 seats were taken from the regional seats and added to the national pool, where the available number of seats therefore increased to 90. These 90 seats were distributed in proportion to the residual votes of the parties. In spite of that, the Forum finally gained 164 out of the 386 parliamentary seats (42.49 per cent), while the Free Democrats won 92 seats (23.83 per cent), the Smallholders 44 (11.4 per cent), the HSP 33 (8.55 per cent), the Young Democrats 22 (5.705 per cent) and the Christian Democrats 21 seats (5.44 per cent). Table 6.4 shows the distribution of seats.

The following conclusions can be drawn about the role of the electoral system:

(a) The overwhelming victory of the HDF was only partially counter-balanced by the proportional distribution of the regional and national list system.
(b) The final results of the AFD and the SHP, which were able to take part effectively in the SMC contest, were close to their proportion of the national votes.
(c) The last three parties, which were unsuccessful in the SMC contest (none of them gained more than three constituency seats), suffered heavily from the SMC part of the electoral system.
(d) Compared to a nationwide PR, the regional version of PR also 'distorted' the result slightly. In the relatively small multi-member constituencies the distribution of seats diverged slightly from the national proportion of votes. It favoured the two major parties (the HDF and the AFD), while the others lost by it. (See Table 6.5.) The regional PR had two consequences: first, the smaller a party the larger was its loss; and second, the more evenly distributed the votes of a (smaller) party, the more serious was its loss (in the latter case, the FYD fell back to the level of the CDPP, in spite of its better average).

5. Patterns of contest

In the 176 SMCs, 1,623 candidates took part in the first ballot contest, i.e. 9–10 candidates in a typical constituency. As a consequence, only five candidates secured a majority of the votes and became MPs on the first ballot. In the other 171 constituencies, second ballots were held with the participation of 496 candidates. In five out of these 171 constituencies the turn-out was under 50 per cent of the first ballot, so here all the candidates had the right to participate in the second round. In the other 161 constituencies between two and four, but usually three, candidates contested the seats on the second ballot. The election was dominated by the competition between the HDF and the AFD; most of these constituencies (105 out of 161) were characterized by four different patterns of contest depending on which party was the third participant in the second ballot in addition to the HDF and AFD candidates. The pattern of party contest in the run-off elections had a strong regional character.

(a) In rural Hungary the SHP did well and took part in the tripartite contest in 29 SMCs.
(b) In the purely Catholic regions the CDPP became the member in the triangle contest in 12 SMCs.
(c) The HSP was usually the third participant in Budapest, where the SHP and the CDPP were weak, and in the heavy industrial region of Borsod. So a HDF–AFD–HSP contest marked 39 SMCs.
(d) In 25 constituencies, where electoral pacts were made between the two ballots and candidates stood down in favour of another one's, (especially in Budapest and in Pest county) there were many HDF–AFD single combats.

Notwithstanding these different patterns, all but three of these 105 constituencies were won either by the HDF or the AFD.

6. The achievement of the parties

What explains this electoral/political landslide in the second round? What kind of constituencies did the parties have? What were the social and regional backgrounds of the parties? A look at the parties themselves may answer these questions.

The Hungarian Democratic Forum

It seems that the Forum was able to become a 'catch-all' party, appealing to voters from all social groups in all regions in Hungary. In the second round the Forum was backed by most of the voters of other, de-selected parties. There were constituencies where the Forum increased its votes by 50 per cent or even doubled them in the second ballot, in spite of the

Table 6.6a Party alignments and residence

	Budapest	Towns	Villages	Total
FYD	22	44	34	100
SHP	12	31	57	100
CDPP	13	36	51	100
HDF	26	40	34	100
HSP	31	40	29	100
AFD	32	43	25	100
average	22	40	38	100

Table 6.6b Party alignments and age-groups

(Age: years)	18–33	34–49	50–65	over 66	Total
FYD	56	30	10	4	100
SHP	15	27	36	22	100
CDPP	7	21	33	39	100
HDF	21	38	27	14	100
HSP	10	37	20	23	100
AFD	28	40	22	10	100
average	23	34	26	17	100

Table 6.6c Party alignments and education

(Classes)	under 8	8	C	D	E	Total
FYD	5	25	20	35	15	100
SHP	31	27	17	20	5	100
CDPP	29	27	18	18	8	100
HDF	10	24	17	31	18	100
HSP	21	22	15	20	22	100
AFD	8	22	20	35	15	100
average	16	24	18	28	14	100

under 8 = unfinished primary school; 8 = primary school; C = technical education (for skilled workers); D = grammar school; E = university degree (BA or MA).

Note: Tables 6a, b and c are calculated by the author, using the results of an MKI opinion survey: *Magyar Hirlap*, 28 March 1990, p. 5

Table 6.6d Political preferences of income groups

	poor	middle	well-to-do
CDPP	4.5	5.5	1.6
FYD	5.3	5.5	5.3
SHP	14.0	6.8	7.0
HSP	5.7	8.7	5.8
HSDP	1.5	4.0	5.3
HDF	12.5	18.0	23.9
AFD	20.8	16.8	28.0
don't vote	6.8	3.3	2.1
others	28.9	31.9	21.0
total	100.0	100.0	100.0

Source: GALLUP–Budapest, Research Report, 20 March 1990

lower turn-out (45.5 per cent). In general, the HDF and the AFD showed differing capacities to increase their votes in the second round. In those 125 SMCs where both of them took part in the second round, the HDF candidates gained an average 29.1 per cent and the AFD candidates an average 5 per cent increase in their votes. Opinion polls[7] in the pre-election period showed that the main strongholds of the Forum were the country towns, while the Free Democrats were strong in Budapest, and the Smallholders in the villages. The first round proved this prediction correct; however, the Forum finally overtook the Smallholders' Party in most of the villages and was not even defeated by the Free Democrats in Budapest. The supporters of the Forum were slightly over-represented among the middle-aged, and the well-educated people, and under-represented among the under-educated citizens. The HDF drew vast support from the middle-class Hungarians (see Table 6.6).

The Free Democrats

In general, the constituency of the AFD was among the well-educated urban population in the young and middle age-groups (see Table 6.6). The November 1989 referendum showed the crucial role of the Budapest votes (the Budapest votes decided the referendum in favour of the Free Democrats), and Budapest was regarded as the main stronghold of the Free Democrats. The results of the first round, partly, justified these expectations: they took the lead in 20 out of the 32 Budapest constituencies, and gained the 27.1 per cent of the votes on the Budapest regional list (5.8 per cent above their average). But even these good results were not enough for victory. The Forum did much better than was expected: it won the competition of the regional lists by 28.4 per cent of the votes and took 11 out of the 20 seats where the Free Democrats had the leading position at the constituency level, winning 23 out of the 32 Budapest

Table 6.7 Voting pattern by regions. The difference from the national average

	HDF	AFD	HS(W)P*	SHP	CDP	FYD
metropolitan Budapest	+ 3.6	+ 5.7	+ 2.5	− 5.0	− 0.7	+ 2.6
industrial north-east	− 2.2	− 4.2	+ 3.9	− 3.1	+ 5.0	− 0.9
rural–protestant 'Tiszántul'	− 2.3	− 4.2	+ 1.9	+ 5.9	− 3.9	− 1.6
rural mid-south	+ 0.9	− 2.1	− 2.5	+ 2.7	+ 0.2	− 0.4
urbanized north-west	− 2.5	+ 4.8	− 2.9	− 0.9	+ 0.7	0.0

* = HSP and HSWP votes together

Source: Calculated by the author

single-member constituency seats altogether. But still, in Budapest the Free Democrats did much better than their national average. In general, the Free Democrats did well in the developed, more urbanized north-west Hungary and in the metropolitan area of Budapest, but got below their national average in the rural areas (see Table 6.7). The Free Democrats were also able to increase their votes in the second round, but much less so than the Forum.

The Smallholders

The Smallholders' Party was disappointed by the result: they ended 4–6 per cent below the final opinion poll forecasts, getting only 11.7 per cent of the votes. In addition, there was not the slightest electoral shift towards the Smallholders' Party in the second round. The party was 'frozen' into its limited, sectional electorate. It was not able to break away from its 'single-issue' character (the SHP claimed the collectivized land should be returned to the peasantry) and to develop any appeal for the electorate beyond its sectional voters.

The constituency of the Smallholders' Party was the poorly educated, old age-groups of the rural areas (see Table 6.6). The party is more popular among men than among women. All six counties where they did much (more than 4 per cent) over their average[8] belong to the rural '*Tiszántúl*' and mid-south Hungary (see Table 6.7), where the Smallholders have had strong political traditions since the inter-war period. By winning 44 seats (11.4 per cent), however, the Smallholders were able to keep their 'centre' position between the two main opposition parties; without them neither a 'centre-right' nor a 'centre-left' government could be formed.

The Christian Democratic People's Party

To pass the 4 per cent threshold and get into the parliament was a great success for the newly reorganized CDPP. They got 6.5 per cent of the total votes cast for the regional lists although they did not have regional lists in five counties. The typical Christian Democrat voters were the elderly, poorly educated, female (mostly church-going) citizens in villages or provincial towns. In Budapest the party won only 5.7 per cent of the vote. The strongholds of the CDPP are the Catholic regions of north-west and north-east Hungary. In most constituencies in the Protestant 'Tiszántúl' (east Hungary) the CDPP could not even put up candidates (see Table 6.7).

The Hungarian Socialist Party

In general, the result of the HSP (national average: 10.9 per cent) was about what was expected, as far as the regional lists were concerned. But the failure of all but one of its individual candidates was a humiliating defeat. Beside M. Szürös, the interim president of the republic, only M. Németh, the popular Prime Minister, could win in his constituency, but as an independent (non-party) candidate. The poor electoral result of the party was first of all not a judgement on the current HSP government, but rather a referendum on the four decades of the one-party system. Combining the votes for the two heirs of the Communist Party (the HSP and the HSWP), it is plain that they did best in Budapest, in the industrial and in the Protestant rural area ('Tiszántúl').

The Federation of Young Democrats

The FYD, gaining 8.9 per cent as a national average, was able to keep most of the electorate recorded by the opinion polls since the spring of 1989 (it was permanently between 8 and 11 per cent). The FYD have gained 22 parliamentary seats. As a small party with evenly distributed regional results (see Table 6.7), it got 20 of its seats from party lists. One of its two constituency victories was a victory over Pozsgay, the number one politician of the reforming HSP. The FYD got many more votes from the young voters than from any other age-group; otherwise, a slightly higher support from the urban well-educated electorate. The regional distribution of its electorate was similar to that of the AFD.

7. Conclusions

The elections were partly a referendum on the falling one-party regime (which explains the poor result of the HSP), but were as much, especially in the second round, a choice for the future: a decision on who should form the government, the moderate centre-right HDF or the radical left-liberal AFD?

The election turned out to be a victory for the *right*. The HDF–SHP–CDPP coalition got 42.9 per cent of the (list) votes, and with the landslide HDF victory in the SMC run-off, they gained 229 out of the 386 seats (59.33 per cent), a strong majority in the parliament.

The humiliating failure of the socialist *left* was a consequence of various factors:

(i)   The defeat of the incumbent HSP and the HSWP, which were blamed for the past 40 years.
(ii) The fragmentation of the left. All three socialist parties (HSP, HSWP, HSDP) refused to form an alliance with any of the others.
(iii) There was a striking phenomena – the absence of a traditional social democratic party, with strong blue-collar and trade-union backing. The HSDP got 3.6 per cent – insufficient to secure even one parliamentary seat.

The voting patterns showed a remarkable regional character. The geographical distribution of the (list) votes revealed five distinct regions. In the metropolitan area of Budapest (which contained one-fifth of the total electorate), the HSP and the new parties, especially the Free Democrats, won more than their national average, while the Smallholders had a poor result. The industrial (and Catholic) north-east region turned to be a stronghold for the (ex)-communist HSP and HSWP and for the Catholic CDPP. In the rural (and Catholic) mid-south the Smallholders did best, while in the rural and Protestant 'Tiszántúl' the SHP and the (ex)-communist parties had votes above their national average. The most urbanized (and Catholic) north-west became the strongholds of the Free Democrats and the Christian Democrats (see Table 6.7).

In general, the political scene has developed towards a *tripolar* structure: with a governing centre-right HDF–SHP–CDPP coalition: with a fragmented and discredited socialist-left (HSP, HSWP); and with the left-liberal AFD–FYD (which was the radical anti-communist opposition of the former ruling HSWP/HSP).

Notes

1. 1989 Electoral Law, *Heti Világgazdaság*, 1990 március, *Választási Különszám*, p. 17–29.
2. The registration of the electorate was made by the local administration automatically and without any registration fees. Discounting minor administrative mistakes, the whole adult population was registered, therefore the turn-out figures express the proportion of the voters in the adult population.
3. The de-selected parties still had a chance to gain seats in SMCs. However, only the Agrarian Alliance could gain two seats.

4. *Magyar Hirlap*, 1990 március 28, p. 1.
5. The source of the SMC results of the first round: *Népszabadság*, 1990 március 31, p. 28–31.
6. The source of the following figures of the second round: *Magyar Hirlap*, 1990 április 10, p. 4–5, and *Beszélö*, 1990 április 14, p. 19–22.
7. The source of the following figures on the social composition of the constituency of the parties: surveys made by the Gallup and the MKI (Magyar Közvéleménykutató Intézet):*GALLUP-Budapest, Research Report*, 20 March 1990; and Lechmann Hedvig: 'Kik szavaztak a pártokra?' *Magyar Hirlap*, 1990 március 28, p. 5.
8. Votes of the parties by regions: *Népszabadság*, 1990 március 31, p. 31.

7 Hungarian transition from a public choice perspective

László Urbán

Introduction

The recent transformation of the East-Central European communist regimes[2] towards becoming multiparty democracies has generally been a peaceful transition in the sense that no bloodshed has occurred. However, the Hungarian transformation was exceptionally peaceful, even compared to the other examples of the region. Not only has violence not occurred, but anti-communist demonstrations or general strikes were also absent, unlike in Poland, Czechoslovakia or East Germany. Why? This is the question this chapter tries to answer.

The main thrust of the explanations provided by political scientists for these transitions tends to be conflictual. They focus on the forces and constraints which made the controlling elite of the communist regime tolerant of the emergence of the opposition and accepting of its increasing dominance. The role of these forces in explaining how these transformations could come about is certainly essential. But if it was solely a matter of force, one would expect some resistance on the side of the major beneficiary groups of the old regime, especially if we take into consideration the fact that they unquestionably controlled the armed forces and the bureaucracies not only before but even during the first phases of the transition. Why didn't they shoot?

The sequence of events is certainly relevant. There was a domino effect. However, Hungary was in the forefront of the transition, ahead of East Germany and Czechoslovakia, and, after March 1990, even ahead of Poland, but still without major conflicts.

One can observe a common characteristic of all the above-mentioned transitions: that at a certain point, the ruling communist leadership concluded an agreement with the representatives of the opposition. Why?

In the remainder of this paper the author will provide two different explanations: conflictual and co-operative.

Conflictual versus co-operative approaches

James Buchanan (1990)[3] distinguished between the perspectives of *constitutional economics* and *constitutional politics*, as two distinct kinds of reasoning – being *co-operative* and *conflictual* respectively. From a conflictual perspective, politics seems, by its very nature, to involve conflict between and among individuals and groups within a polity. However, even if we do regard politics as a distributional game or enterprise, it need not be a zero sum game. Actually, the public choice perspective, or the economics of politics, is based on a different assumption. 'A necessary condition for cooperation in social interaction is the prospect for positive expected gains by all parties, or in the gainer-loser terminology, the prospect that there be no net losers.' (Buchanan, 1990, p. 9)

Professor Buchanan also distinguishes between two levels of politics. *Constitutional politics* refers to the choices among alternative sets of basic rules within a society, while *ordinary politics* refers to the conflictual struggle within a particular framework. He suggests that the basic nature of *constitutional politics is co-operative*, because the definition of the rules for ordinary politics may embody positively valued prospects for all members of the polity. The transformation in East-Central Europe undoubtedly changed the political system of these countries on the constitutional level as well. What can we learn from a co-operative kind of reasoning?

Conflictual explanations

What influenced the communist leaders to tolerate the emergence of the opposition and later even to negotiate an agreement with them? The answer from a conflictual perspective is: they had no other choice, they were forced to do that. Several factors can be listed as to why that was the case.

1. Economic crisis

The first factor to be mentioned is the economic crisis which became quite obvious by the time the political transformation started. The survival of the existing economic system did not have much benefit to offer, not even for the political elite. Reform within the framework of the one-party system resulted in important changes, but the Hungarian experience during the two decades of economic reforms made very clear the limits of the impact of such reforms. However, the economic crisis itself can not explain the breakthrough, since it was much less severe than in the other countries of the region.

2. Gorbachev no longer backed up the old guard communist leaders

Gorbachev certainly deserves a credit for not keeping the incumbent communist leadership of the small East-Central European countries in power with his support. However, he was unable to replace any of the old guard leaders, like Eric Honecker in the GDR or Milos Jakes in Czechoslovakia, even if they opposed his new concepts. Gorbachev certainly did not force these leaders to give up their dictatorial positions, although he removed an important source of strength behind them when he abolished the Brezhnev doctrine.

3. Importance of the reputation in the West

The economies of the region have been heavily depending on good trading relations with the Western countries. In addition to this, some of them have been so indebted that they could not risk a potential break with the West. In order to avoid economic bankruptcy, they needed to maintain good relations with the West, so they could not order a bloody crackdown. The economic isolation of communist China after the Tienanmen Square massacre proves that economic backlash was a real threat.

4. Danger of popular uprising

If the communist leaders had not realized that they were forced to tolerate the emergence of the opposition movements and later to negotiate and conclude an agreement with them, they most likely would have been swept away by popular unrest. The opposition parties were ready to negotiate and were willing to make compromises, and this flexibility made them an acceptable partner for the communist leaders.

My opinion is that, although Hungary was far from potential unrest, in the mind of the Kádárist communist leadership the memory of the 1956 uprising was still very vivid and they were concerned about a repeat scenario of that kind. However, this fear in itself does not provide a sufficient explanation, because it had been ever present throughout the previous three decades.

With the above-mentioned factors, how satisfactory can the explanation be that is provided by a conflictual approach? On a relatively high level of generalization, the major threats and forces seem to be listed here. Of course the list is not exhaustive, but my purpose was only to provide a summarizing outline.

My concern here is whether the co-operative perspective can refute or add something to the conflictual explanation.

Co-operative explanations

As already mentioned above, the classical co-operative kind of explanation is based on the assumption that the whole game is not zero sum, so all the players can become net gainers (with different shares of benefits, of course).

1. Role of the reformers

A special case for this kind of reasoning could be based on the role of the so-called reformers within the Communist Party. At least in the Hungarian case, the role of this group within the party and governmental leadership was very important during the whole transition period. At the beginning, they assisted in the removal of János Kádár, who became the major obstacle of the necessary adjustments by the early 1980s. Later, within the new Politburo they (Imre Pozsgay and Rezsö Nyers) counter-balanced the anti-opposition sentiments of the new party leader Károly Grósz. In February 1989, Pozsgay pushed through the Central Committee of the Communist Party a resolution that recognized the 1956 revolution as a popular uprising and granted formal approval of multiparty competitive elections. In March 1989 the Communist Party pragmatic-conservative leadership (Károly Grósz, György Fejti) initiated negotiations with the representatives of the opposition parties. The negotiations between the Communist Party and the opposition started in June. The communist delegation was led initially by Fejti and they did not make much headway during the summer. However, in September Pozsgay became the leader of the Communist Party delegation and he concluded the agreement with the representatives of the opposition by the end of the month. During the next period, the government, headed by another reformer, Miklós Németh, played a crucial role in maintaining peace and balance until the free elections were held in March 1990.

What happened during the summer? In late June Grósz as party leader was replaced by a four-member group as the presidency of the Communist Party: Németh, Pozsgay, Nyers and Grósz. The reformers clearly took the lead during the summer. How could they do that without any resistance?

A potential explanation can be derived from the role of the reformers. If at the beginning of the transformation, the intention of these people was already to institutionalize a multiparty democracy and if they controlled the Communist Party during the transition, then it is no surprise that the transition was peaceful and they deserve the credit for it.

However, both of these assumptions are questionable. The views of the reformers themselves changed during the transition, and it is very difficult to clarify whether this was a cause or a result of the ongoing events. Let us not question the good intentions of the reform leaders. Even they, however, would not claim that they were in control of the Communist Party during the transition. So, the question remains: why did the reformers gain control gradually within the Communist Party and within the government, and why were they not blocked and replaced by conservatives who resisted the transformation? The short answer is that the reformers took over the lead easily because the pragmatic conservatives let them do that. Why? Because the potential supporters of the pragmatic conservatives, the rent-seekers of the old regime, had their own business to take care of, which offered high positive returns for them as opposed to organizing political resistance against the transformation of the system.

2. What about the rent-seekers of the old regime?

The question is especially relevant in the light of an argument provided by Jan Winiecki (1990).[4] He applies a property rights-based analysis, stressing modes of rent maximization by the ruling groups as a crucial variable in explaining why economic reforms fail in Soviet-type systems. His major point is that it is the apparatchiks and bureaucrats of the communist regimes who gain most from maintaining the institutional status quo, and they are the groups which resist change most strongly. 'Given the key positions of these groups in the STE (Soviet-type economic) system, we may predict a very high probability of failure of decentralizing, market-oriented, efficiency-increasing reforms.' (Winiecki, 1990, p. 204).

Winiecki's argument is very persuasive, so we have to raise the following question: why did the apparatchiks and the bureaucrats, as major beneficiaries of rent-seeking activities within the framework of the old regime, allow the reformers to gain control of the Communist Party which finally resulted in the systemic transformation?

This is the point on which a public choice kind of reasoning can be useful.

3. Peaceful transition and 'spontaneous privatization'

Isn't it possible that the expected benefits within the framework of the new regime, or new structure of property rights, were larger for the major groups of rent-seekers than the rents they could acquire within the existing property rights structure? In the Hungarian case it was possible!

In 1985, the property rights of the majority of the enterprises in the public sector were decentralized and largely delegated to the firms themselves. The so-called enterprise councils received most of the property rights. Half of the members of an enterprise council of a firm were representatives elected by the employees of the firm, the other half were delegated managers. However, in practice, the top managers almost always controlled this body. The original intention of those who supported this reform was to take the property rights out of the hands of the governmental bureaucracy which always sabotaged and distorted market-oriented reforms, as explained by Winiecki.

As a result of the deregulation efforts of the government, from 1987 the state-owned enterprises had the right to establish corporations together with outside investors. Since most of the large enterprise were heavily indebted by that time, the typical form was that a portion of the assets of the enterprise was provided as an in-kind contribution to the new corporation and the outside investor was a bank. This kind of reorganization speeded up in 1988.

In 1988 the old Hungarian parliament passed a legislation on the new forms of business associations, and the government created a rather favourable environment for foreign direct investments. From that year, parallel with the political transformation, a transformation (corporatization) of the forms of the business companies in the public sector started. In the typical case, a large company in the public sector transformed itself into a centre of a number of smaller joint stock companies, or limited liability companies, or formed joint ventures with a Western investor, or with other outside investors, e.g. with a bank or another company. The top managers of the former state-owned companies became top managers of the new companies, which were then no longer exclusively state-owned enterprises. These are companies partly owned by different institutional investors or foreign private owners, so they are part of the private sector. This is the so-called 'spontaneous privatization' process, with the help of which many apparatchik and bureaucrat beneficiaries of the old regime found legal opportunities to establish a solid economic basis for themselves within the framework of the new regime, capitalizing on their control over state property and access to information.

These people faced the prospect of being laid off after the political transition was completed, but instead of using their influence to slow down the transformation, the most competent, well-positioned and clever individuals, who could have been the organizers of such a possible resistance, found individual ways to establish themselves within the new framework.

This spontaneous privatization did not prove to be very efficient from an economic point of view. These managers were not interested in making the best deals as real individual owners, they merely used the delegated property rights in order to create safe and well-paid positions for themselves in the private sector.

As the transition was going ahead, the process increasingly frustrated more and more people, and after the free elections the new government practically stopped it for a while. However, this process of 'spontaneous privatization' proved to be very beneficial politically during the earlier phases of the Hungarian transformation, because the prospect of gaining personally changed the attitude of influential segments of the major beneficiary groups of the old regime towards the whole transition, letting the Hungarian transition be an exceptionally peaceful one.

After the free elections the new government created the State Property Agency (SPA) as the representative of the state as owner during privatization. This agency has to approve any privatization transactions, but Hungary is the only country where the managers are still playing a very important role as initiators of the transactions. They are acting as agents of the SPA, being controlled by it. This involvement of the management is the major reason behind the fact, that far more privatization trans-actions have been completed in Hungary so far, than in Poland or in Czechoslovakia, where the management is regarded with suspicion and their involvement is politically not acceptable.

In addition to the above mentioned major institutional factors, I can add other methods which worked to bring about similar results. For example, as a gesture to the international monetary institutions, the state had already liberalized the pre-conditions for running small-scale private enterprises in 1983. After a couple of years, for many governmental and party bureaucrats, a private business owned by someone in the family became a popular way of earning extra revenue, and it very often became the major part of the family income. Understandably, they did not oppose the new system as fiercely as they would have, had their office been their only source of income.

During the transition period, it was the policy of the Németh govern-ment to send hard-liner and mostly unqualified people from the military, police and other bureaucracies into early retirement with a decent pension. Buying them off this way proved also to be very beneficial from the viewpoint of the peaceful transition in Hungary.

Conclusion

In explaining the transition in East-Central Europe, in addition to the conflictual arguments – emphasizing the forces and constraints which forced the leadership of the communist parties to tolerate the emergence of and the peaceful takeover by the opposition – a co-operative kind of reasoning also has something to add to the picture.

In the case of the Hungarian transition, two different co-operative kinds of explanation have been provided here. One emphasized the special role played by the so-called reformers within the Communist Party. The other was a public choice kind of explanation of the role of 'spontaneous privatization'. This provided ways for many people from the major beneficiary groups of the old regime to join the new system as net gainers.

In the opinion of this author, these factors are deemed to be responsible for the exceptional peacefulness of the Hungarian transition.

Notes

1. The author thanks Professor Richard Nunez for correcting the English in this paper.
2. Countries of the former communist Eastern Europe can be divided into two major groups according to their previous history. Czechoslovakia, East Germany, Hungary, Poland, Slovenia, Croatia and the Baltic states are referred to here as *East-Central Europe*, distinguished from the rest of the countries which are called *Eastern Europe* in the narrower sense. The major difference

between the two groups is cultural and goes back to the early Middle Ages, when East-Central Europe became Roman Catholic while the rest followed the Byzantine orthodoxy – see Szücs, Jenö (1983): *Vázlat Európa három történeti régiójáról* (Outline on the Three Historical Regions of Europe), Budapest, Magvetö, 1983. According to this understanding of the term, the bloody transformation of the Romanian regime was not an East-Central European case. Moreover, the ultimate outcome of that transformation is still unclear. This paper deals with the experiences of the East-Central European countries only, comparing the Hungarian transition with the Polish and the Czechoslovakian.

3. Buchanan, James (1990): 'The Domain of Constitutional Economics', *Constitutional Political Economy*, Vol. 1, No. 1, pp. 1–18.
4. Winiecki, Jan (1990): 'Why Economic Reforms Fail in the Soviet System – A Property Rights-Based Approach,' *Economic Inquiry*, Vol. XXVIII, April, pp. 195–221.

8 From Communism to democracy in Hungary

George Schöpflin

The reason why Communism fell apart in Hungary, according to the usual Budapest version, is that it rotted away. Like every truism, this contains an element of truth and begs a number of questions as well. Above all, it demands almost insistently, why? The answers are partly to be found in the remote past, in the origins of the Kádár regime and in the way in which that system was put together after the revolution of 1956, and partly in the very particular circumstances of the mid-1980s, when the system ran out of steam and cried out for a new infusion of energies, but this could not be arranged because of the way in which it had been put together. Crucially, Kádár's own role as a conservative innovator who could not move with the times when the need arose requires particular scrutiny.[1]

After 1956, Kádár had to re-establish his power, reorganize the Communist Party that had fallen apart in the revolution, break down the resistance of the population, end the general strike and liquidate the institutions that the revolution had generated. He could not be too fussy about the means and he did not have much of a choice either. Kádár's tactics were to use every possible lie and all forms of coercion in destroying the opposition to his rule. By the early 1960s, Hungarian society was thoroughly cowed.

Kádár, however, was not Stalinist himself and he did not want to rule over a country run solely on the basis of terror, always assuming that this is possible at all. Pivotally, he drew the lesson from the 1956 revolution that the people were not to be trusted with power. If they were given a choice, they would not exercise it in the way that he wanted; on the contrary, all sorts of undesirable political goals would be pursued, like a multiparty system, workers' self-management and spontaneity. In Kádár's view – and this can be deduced from the kind of political system that he subsequently established – political choice was to be the preserve of the few, of individuals like himself – 'honest socialists'.

Depoliticizing society

From that time, Kádár's tactics could be described as having evolved towards a strategy – depoliticize society and keep the population sweet through economic concessions. To this end, the system needed both economic and administrative adjustments, many of which had political implications. The Communist Party would continue to insist on its monopoly of power, but this would no longer be defined in Stalinist terms as an absolute monopoly, but would become discretionary. This dispensation was arrived at in its final form more by good luck than by design, but it proved to be a most successful one from the party's standpoint.

It offered a considerable flexibility in dealing with society, in the management of power and in the routinization of administration. Essentially it gave the power elite wide-ranging discretion in the exercise of power – there were no fixed criteria for anything. This meant that each and every concession remained a concession and could not be transformed into a right. It provided opportunity for pragmatism – much admired by those in the West who entirely failed to understand the true nature of the system – and created just enough social space for different social groups to find satisfaction.

The trouble with this degree of discretion was that it gradually but irremediably undermined the system of power itself. A power elite is not a small club of people who know each other personally, but a complex organism and, as such, it requires some basic ground rules, some relatively clear and understandable criteria for the exercise of power and a legitimating ideology. In Hungary, as in other communist countries in the 1970s, the official ideology lost this cementing quality and it was not replaced by anything other than the ideology of power itself, coupled with the external threat of Soviet intervention.

The party offered a deal to intellectuals and the intelligentsia – the former create values, the latter administer them as teachers, lawyers, managers, engineers etc. – that went to the heart of the Kádár system. One of the roles of intellectuals in one-party systems is to act as the mirror in which the ruling elite sees itself reflected; the elite's self-confidence and morale depend crucially on this, in the absence of genuine legitimation through elections. Kádárism sought to incorporate these social-professional groups in order to use their talents.

The co-optation of the creative intellectuals was problematical, but here the system hit upon a brilliant device. Instead of being forced to stand up and proclaim, as they had been in the 1950s, that 'socialism was the most marvellous system in the world', they could say, in effect, 'the system that we have here in Hungary is full of defects, it does not work very well, it is open to criticism on a whole variety of grounds; but it is the best that we can hope to have.' This formula completely demobilized crucial intellectuals and built self-censorship into their public utterances.

The character of the system was, then, deeply opportunistic. There were no fixed standards, everything was subject to the needs of the day, decided on by a political leadership that had largely lost its vision. It knew it wanted to hold on to power, but it could no longer justify it in any terms other than those of power. The ideals of equality, modernity and rationality – central to the Marxian idea of the future – were gradually lost as power-holders and intellectuals recognized that the system could not be adapted any further to meet these goals.

This left the party with the threadbare proposition that it was the agent of a 'revolution', which no one took very seriously, though it did make it impossible for Kádárism to come to terms with the (genuine) revolution of 1956. For Kádár, the events of that year were forever a 'counter-revolution', because it had defined its own foundation myth in having seized power as a Marxist-Leninist party against the anti-Communists. That was the limit to the Kádárist integration strategy.

Declining legitimacy

As far as justification by power was concerned – 'we rule because we rule' – this was vulnerable to any direct challenge to that power or threat of a challenge. Essentially, legitimation by power alone was a dangerously thin support, because any loss of power would weaken the core of the party's rule, as eventually happened. Buying peace through economic expansion proved to be exposed to economic failure, hence the successful management of the economic system was crucial for keeping the system together.

Once that failed, as it did in the mid-1980s, it was evident, though few accepted this in public, that as long as Kádár remained at the helm, the system could only disintegrate from within. The external proprieties were maintained, but by the mid-1980s the stagnation was unmistakable. Kádár, from having been a conservative reformer, had become an opponent of all change, a true reactionary. That was the moment when Kádárism lost the backing – political, intellectual and psychological – of those supporting intellectuals who had played such a vital role in sustaining it from the early 1960s onwards.

Because the process in Hungary was a gradual one, there was no clear visible dramatic moment from when it is possible to date the beginning of the end. Nevertheless, the last months of 1986 saw increasing signs of the growing alienation of the previously supportive intellectuals from the regime. By the beginning of 1988, it was widely accepted that a change was essential, but the way in which this was to happen remained contested.

The central issue was, of course, the decline of the economy and the growing recognition that economic reform on its own was not enough. The political impediments to change would have to be removed and that obviously meant that the party's control over the political system and power would have to be loosened. The recognition of this was the key element in the changing consciousness of the intellectuals. There were two broad strands in this – the work of the party reformers and that of the democratic opposition.

Opposition within and opposition outside

The loose current known as the party reformers were historians, jurists, sociologists and political scientists, with official posts, who had for some time been calling for a transformation of the party's political monopoly into something more responsive to public opinion. The democratic opposition, on the other hand, had consciously taken a stand outside officialdom and chose marginalization.[2]

At more or less the same time, both the democratic opposition and the party reformers launched a concept that has come to be known as 'constitutional Communism'.[3] The idea behind this was that of one-party pluralism. The Communist Party would retain power, but this would no longer be absolute or a monopoly; rather, it would be circumscribed by legal and political constraints, thereby enabling the market to function in the economy and the political leadership to gain greater legitimacy. The key document from the democratic opposition was entitled 'Social Contract' and it came from the group around the samizdat journal *Beszélö*. Its most striking feature was a ringing call for Kádár to go; without Kádár's removal from the leadership, the document recognized, no change was possible. The party reformers were more circumspect in this respect, but they too pushed for a political system with constraints on the power of the party. Both currents proved to be influential, especially on sections of the party itself, which was not, of course, immune to the growing ferment in the country.

By the early months of 1988, the tight control by the party over intellectual opinion was a thing of the past. The Hungarian Democratic Forum, set up by the populist current, was only one of dozens of discussion groups. They were a part of the opposition, but were in many ways more ready to deal with the party than the democratic opposition proper, something which resulted in constant tension between the two. Both were committed to democracy, but the language of the populists was more nationalistic and more concerned with returning to true Hungarian traditions than the democratic opposition liked.

The social background of the two groups also set them apart. The democratic opposition was drawn primarily, though not exclusively, from the urban, Budapest, Jewish middle class and intelligentsia; quite a few of them were the children of established communist figures and had had a communist background themselves. They had sloughed this off by the time they moved into the opposition, of course, and were committed to human rights and democracy. The populists, on the other hand, were generally from the country, of a more humble background, for the most part non-Jewish and had had no part in Marxism at all. This socio-cultural difference also contributed to the tension between them.

By the spring of 1988, the situation in Hungary was widely described as 'fluid' and 'decaying'.[4] The party leadership, above all Kádár himself, had no response to the increasing ferment, except to make threatening noises. In effect, the leadership was not leading and the ferment in intellectual life was beginning to affect the party membership, which was far from unaffected by the country's problems and the changing mood. The personality of Kádár became another important factor in this complex. Born in 1912, he was 75 years old at this time and was manifestly losing control. His obstinate refusal either to change or to go evidently persuaded his opponents in the party to prepare a coup for his removal.

The Fall of Kádár

The Kádárist leadership was forced to make the concession of permitting the convening of a party conference – an event where all the party bodies are represented, but without the weight of a party congress – and this was duly scheduled for May 1988. Kádár's opponents used this to remove him. The new leadership, however, turned out to be much weaker and more divided than expected. It looked afterwards as if removing Kádár was the only point on which they agreed. Károly Grósz, the new party leader, essentially looked towards some kind of an authoritarian model of economic efficiency and high levels of coercion; Imre Pozsgay and the party reformers, on the other hand, were increasingly attracted by an open, democratic system. For all practical purposes, the outcome was a stalemate.[5]

Grósz did nothing during the summer months, while Pozsgay accepted that the media could widen their already extensive freedom to comment, so that the stand-off and hesitancy in policy persisted. The months between the beginning of September and the end of November 1988 represented the watershed. In September, with a more determined leadership, the Communists might just have been able to seize the agenda and push through a reform programme of their own. By the end of November, it was too late. During those weeks, Hungarian society became aware of the weakness of communist rule and of its own mounting political weight. Besides, the conservatives' last redoubt, the Soviet Union, had also disappeared. In the past, the hard-liners had always been able to eliminate criticism by referring to Soviet disapproval. This pretext for doing nothing had gone as Gorbachev's reform programme progressed.

From the end of November, overtly political organizations began to spring up. Hungary had begun to assume the appearance of a multiparty system. The Hungarian Democratic Forum had already moved into the public arena in September. The democratic opposition established itself as the Alliance of Free Democrats at this time and the so-called nostalgic parties, the Smallholders and the Social Democrats, which had taken part in the post-1945 coalition and briefly revived in 1956, once more returned to the political stage.[6]

The party loses control

Inside the party, however, the contest continued. The reformers argued that change was urgent and would only work if pluralism was accepted, otherwise Hungarian society would not accept the authority of the political leadership and hence its energies could not be mobilized. The conservatives disliked this, but were stripped of all counter-arguments by their fear of popular upheaval *à la* 1956 and the fact that they did not have an intellectually viable alternative strategy. The break-up of political monopoly was merely a question of time.[7]

In the summer of 1989, the party finally sat down with the opposition parties at a roundtable – in reality, the two sides sat opposite each other – to try and work out the method of handing over power and to construct a new political system. Work on drafting a new constitution had been going on for some time in the Ministry of Justice, but the political sanction came from the roundtable agreement in September. This sanctified a political structure with an over-strong parliament and weak presidency. The thinking underlying this was the expectation that the Communists would retain much of their strength even after the forthcoming elections, so that the position of the government *vis-à-vis* parliament should be a weak one.[8]

No one actually expected what happened in October – the complete collapse of the party-state, the communist system in its entirety. The Communist Party held a congress at the beginning of October and was deeply split between reformers and conservatives. A dubious compromise was patched up, by the terms of which the party reconstituted itself as the Hungarian Socialist Party. This appeared to break the spell and the control exercised through the *nomenklatura* system vanished. Party discipline over parliament and government went too, so that on the 23 October, the anniversary of the outbreak of the 1956 revolution, Hungary was formally declared to be a 'Republic' and no longer a People's Republic. Communist rule was over.

Between October and March 1990, the time was spent in a long-drawn-out election campaign. The chief antagonists did not include the successor to the Communists, the Hungarian Socialist Party, but were the Forum and the Free Democrats. The conflicts of the past now bore their fruit in the bitter and often vindictive hostility between the two. The Free Democrats discovered that they could widen their appeal by offering the voters a radical anti-communist programme, based on the rapid introduction of a market system. At the same time, the Free Democrats also included a strong Social Democratic element, offering social protectionism; how these two were to be reconciled was never made clear. The Forum, representing provincial, small-town middle classes and petty entrepreneurs, as well as a strand of Christian Democracy, also had to contend with the national radical populists in their ranks. In this sense, both parties were conglomerates, incorporating contradictory political currents.

In the elections, which were held under an unbelievably complex voting system, the Forum emerged decisively as the largest single party and the Free Democrats failed to match the promise of their vote in the first round of polling. This left the Forum with the task of forming the government.

Table 8.1   The results of the 1990 general elections[9]

Name of party	Percentage	Seats
Hungarian Democratic Forum	42.49	164
Alliance of Free Democrats	23.83	92
Independent Smallholders	11.40	44
Hungarian Socialist Party	8.55	33
Federation of Young Democrats	5.44	22
Christian Democratic Party	5.44	21
Independents	1.55	6
Agrarian Alliance	0.26	2
Joint party candidates	1.04	2

The parliamentary elections produced the distribution of votes and seats that are shown in Table 8.1.

On 2 May, the newly elected parliament assembled for the first time and learned that the Forum and the Free Democrats had reached a deal over a wide range of issues on the running parliament and political life.[10] They agreed that the president of Hungary would be elected by parliament and that it would be a noted Free Democrat, Árpád Göncz; there was agreement too on the personnel of the ten permanent and five special parliamentary committees; on establishing an independent body to supervise radio and television; on limiting the range of issues for which a two-thirds majority vote was required to basic laws affecting the system itself; and one or two other, lesser issues.

Antall emerged as prime minister designate, as the leader of the largest party, and he successfully persuaded the Smallholders and the Christian Democrats to join him in a coalition. This gave the government a comfortable majority. While the composition of the Forum's parliamentary faction was partly populist-radical and partly Christian Democrat, the wing of the Forum to which Antall belonged, the government was dominated by the Christian Democrats.

The new government was announced on 16 May. Eight portfolios went to the Forum, including interior, foreign affairs and defence; three to the Smallholders; one to the Christian Democrats; and three independents were invited to take on finance and foreign trade. Antall stressed that the government would pursue a policy of introducing an all-encompassing marketizing reform, whereby the share of the state in the economy would decrease from 80 per cent to an eventual 20 per cent, though this would take time. In this process, the Hungarian government looked to participation by foreign capital. The emphasis was on gradual rather than sudden change. Both the new government and its programme were approved by parliament by 218 votes in favour, 126 against and 8 abstentions.

The background to the new system

Both the government and the opposition were feeling their way rather gently into the new political system, which was untried and run by individuals who were relatively inexperienced in politics. After the general elections of March–April, the coalition took office in May. However, the key event was not so much the new government, but the behind-the-scenes compact between the leader of the Forum and Prime Minister, József Antall and the leadership of the main opposition party, the Alliance of Free Democrats.

This deal essentially excluded the smaller parties and, indeed, there was some hostility to it within the Forum itself, but the pre-eminence of the leader of the Forum, József Antall, was sufficient to overcome this. Furthermore, a section of the Forum, the national radical populists, also regarded the compact with some disfavour. On the other hand, without a deal of this kind, running Hungary would have become extremely difficult and the opposition could well have degenerated into sterile criticism. On the negative side, the compact drew the opposition into co-responsibility with the leadership of the Forum without any countervailing access to power, and it showed up the relative fragility of the Forum itself. Seeing that Antall's control over the Forum was imperfect, some analysts suggested that political stability would, in effect, be safeguarded by a tacit alliance between the government and the main opposition party. This was positive in the short term, but in the longer term it could give rise to a tradition of closed deals and would impede the opposition in its true task of opposing the government.

The Hungarian system was put together in some haste and through a series of last-minute deals during the roundtable negotiations of the summer of 1989, and the opposition groups represented there assumed that the Communists would continue to be a major force in politics. Hence they established a system in which parliament was strong and the government relatively weak. The system was unicameral, there being no second revisory chamber. The constitutional court was still untried; it was unclear how much influence it would have over the system. The presidency was weak, largely ceremonial, and though individual incumbents might be influential behind the scenes, this was not, say, the United States or French system of a strong presidency. The entire edifice was further weakened by the institution of the referendum, which allowed issues to be brought before parliament by as few as 100,000 signatures. The potential for mischief was considerable, at least in the longer term. On the other hand, the attempt by the (ex-communist) Hungarian Socialist Party to organize a referendum on the presidency in July turned out to be a complete fiasco, with a turn-out of only 14 per cent, as a result of which it was declared invalid.[11]

The government itself very largely excluded the populists and drew on the Christian Democrat and liberal reformist currents within its ranks, as well as on its Smallholder and Christian Democratic Party allies. Antall's programme, as announced on 22 May, was more a kind of statement of general principles than a detailed, step-by-step blueprint for change. The Antall programme enunciated four basic principles, viz the government intended to pursue a strategy of freedom, rule of law and the room for individuals to fulfil their aspirations; it would be a government of the entire people and would look to winding up the remnants of the previous regime and to creating a framework for freedom. Second, its aim was that the state should be seen as an enabling body, rather than viewed as an oppressive one. Third, as far as economic transformation was concerned, the government was fully aware that the worst still lay ahead. The government was going to establish a record of the situation and look for remedies with the criterion of a social market economy. And last, in foreign affairs, but with broad cultural and social implications, returning to Europe would be the watchword.

Antall referred specifically to the heavy burden of the past – a demographically poor situation, low life expectancy, poor public health etc. This would require a complete overhaul of the health and social services, but in order to pay for this the economy must be turned around as without economic growth no changes were possible. The housing situation would also have to be completely reshaped, as well as education. And the legal system required considerable adaptation.

Prospects of political stability

The success or failure of Antall's government would depend in the first place on whether or not the economy could be revitalized – that, after all, was why the communist system collapsed and a democratic one was installed. The political context of the new system was far from negligible. On the positive side, there was universal agreement that democracy was the best possible system for the country, so that authoritarianism had a very little base. Equally, the election of a legitimate government would be enormously helpful in securing popular confidence in that government and the self-confidence of the rulers.

As for the actors themselves, both parties and politicians were inexperienced. The same went for the electorate. They would all be learning on the job, sometimes with quite unrealistic expectations of what democracy could achieve. The Forum, as mentioned, was divided. While the Christian Democratic and liberal reform wings could co-operate effectively, the influential populists could make considerable trouble. The Forum's allies, especially the Smallholders, were an unstable element, elected on the promise of returning all land to the peasantry, as in 1947. The Christian Democratic Party was rather backward-looking and amateurish. The strains on the coalition were already in existence by mid-July. The suggestion that religious instruction be made compulsory in the schools caused a furore and had to be withdrawn, for example, with the Christian Democrats broadly in favour and the liberals uneasy.

At the outset, the opposition seemed more cohesive and more professional. The Free Democrats were strongly led and the Young Democrats,

FIDESZ, was an original and energetic group. The Hungarian Socialist Party, the legatee of the Communists, was highly experienced. Nevertheless, the Free Democrats were not entirely convinced that their role was to give off-stage support to the government and it was in any case divided between a neo-liberal free market current (in the ascendant) and a Social Democratic current.

The problems of being a conservative

The difficulty of the emergent right in Hungary was located in the 40 years of Communism, as was so much else. The communist period eliminated the first few halting post-war attempts to create a conservatism more modern than what had existed between the wars and subsequently, any idea that conservatism might undergo a rethinking was moonshine as long as the Communists were in power. The consequence of this was that when Communism collapsed, the new government had very few ideas of what defined it.

The problem was what exactly being right-wing or conservative meant in these circumstances. In this sense, the newly fledged right was not only untried in terms of administrative experience, but equally had very little in the way of ideas from which to derive a strategy for how it intended to govern. This operated on two levels – it lacked the broad ideas by which to define conservatism at all and it was not well placed to formulate the specific strategy for transforming a communist into a democratic order.

In Western Europe, conservative parties had undergone an altogether different experience and they had emerged as two broad streams – a traditionalist current, which emphasized religion, the family and tradition as its primary intellectual sources, and neo-conservatism, which was much more dynamic and looked to free markets and individual enterprise. Their Hungarian counterparts, on the other hand, had not been able to undertake this modernization. Under communist domination this was inconceivable, indeed the very idea of conservative thought was inconceivable and, for that matter, ineffective politically, because only ideas which could engage in a dialogue with the rhetoric or contents of the official doctrine could offer a challenge.

Religion and nationalism

Neither religion nor nationalism was effective in mobilizing opposition to the existing regimes, neither was able to make a serious dent in the Communists' self-legitimation, which was the most effective weapon in the old system's arsenal. For the most part, the Communists were successful in containing the challenge of religion. It had had its teeth drawn by a mixture of blandishments and threatened coercion. Much the same could be said for nationalism. The Communists could never hope to be accepted as the legitimate agents of nationhood – the communist and nationalist agendas were too far apart for this – but a sort of *modus vivendi* from which both benefited could and did come into being. In effect, therefore, two of the sources from which conservatism might have grown were diverted into less dangerous terrain by the Communists.

Consequently, when the right emerged blinking into the sunlight after the collapse of Communism it did so naked. Being right-wing was, evidently, anti-Communist, though seeing that everyone condemned the communist period, including the newly minted socialist party that sprang into existence on the ruins of Communism, this did not mean very much. It was hard to put together a conservative agenda in any positive sense, and in this connection, the lack of time did not help.

From one particular perspective, the conservatives of Hungary were in genuine difficulty. In order to be conservative, they have to an extent been forced into a paradoxical radicalism – the rejection of the last 40 years. Ideally, they would like to return to the pre-communist period and do away with everything that Communism wrought as alien and repellent. This, of course, was an impossibility and there were aspects of the communist revolution, which however partial and distorted it might have been did constitute a social revolution that could not and would not be undone. Some of these irreversible effects of Communism included the ending of the peasant problem of rural over-population and low agricultural output; the corresponding rise of urbanization, the growth of an urban proletariat and the spread of industrial working methods; the near universal demand for modern citizenship and democratic rights; the widespread acceptance of Western consumerist aspirations; and the disappearance of the pre-war elites with their traditional legitimation.

The unviability of this anachronistic conservatism lay in the fact it simply sidestepped the enormous changes in social structure, political attitudes and values that had taken place since. In effect, the right was reconstructing itself on the basis of a pre-modern conservatism that was appropriate to the pre-modern semi-authoritarian system of the inter-war period. The implication was that conservatism in Hungary was sliding towards intellectual irrelevancy at a time when new ideas were badly needed.

The failure or weakness of conservatism could also be attributed to the limp response to the new situation by the intellectuals of the right. Instead of trying to assess the situation in its real terms, the right-wing intellectuals – the populists – preferred to continue as they had always done, to refer to their mission as the spokesmen of the nation and to try to encompass what was happening by traditional, affective means, rather than modern rational ones. The weaponry of the right was fiction and poetry, rather than statistical tables; the 'true son' of the nation, it is said, can 'understand the tragedies of his people from within' and has no need of dry, academic argumentation. This reliance on the affective dimension left those with the task of governing dangerously exposed to making the decisions by no rational criteria – assuming they were listening to their intellectuals at all.

The pre-modern values articulated by the intellectuals of the right clustered around nation, religion, tradition and family, which, of course, the old right also espouses in the West, but does so in conjunction with at least a readiness to discuss neo-conservative concepts of individualism and markets. This latter appears to be rather weak in Hungary on the right. The fact that these ideas are central to the programme of the Free Democrats illustrates the confusion between left and right.

The populist mind-set

In summary form, the populists begin from the proposition that the nation is the pivot of existence, that it is an organic community held together by affective bonds that are threatened by alien, modern practices. For the populists, the nation is also a moral category, so much of their discourse is couched in heavily moralizing language, which can often be highly manipulative – unavoidably so, when the affective dimension plays so salient a role in their world-view. In this perception, individual choice and personal accomplishment must be subordinated to the collective good, so consumerism is condemned as selfishness.[12]

Somewhere at the back of the populist mind-set is the ideal of the self-reliant, largely autarkic clearly patriarchal peasant family, which is the repository of the finest values of the Hungarian nation, to which the money-using economy is alien, and agricultural activity is patrimonial rather than orientated towards commodity production. Because the peasant barely exists in contemporary Hungary, the populists' ideal-type has tended to focus on the stable family, with two or three children, modest aspirations and relatively low educational levels, but who is superior to the lumpenproletariat, not least because the term 'lumpen elements' tends to be a codeword for Gypsies, who, naturally, are outside the Hungarian nation. In effect, the populists articulate the apprehensions and desire of the lower-middle and upper working classes, many of whom are first generation and are fearful of the challenge of competition, democracy and modernity.

Anti-Semitism is not an automatic corollary of this set of attitudes, but the Jewish question has inevitably become linked with the role of the populists because, as a result of the very particular patterns of Hungarian history, Jews were among the primary modernizers in the nineteenth century and came to be seen as the bearers of the alien values of modernity. Some, though not by any manner of means all, of the populists have brought anti-Semitism back to the political agenda, by, in effect, arguing that Jews cannot become members of the Hungarian nation, so that their ideas in politics are suspect and alien.[13] Thus there is an unmistakable hint in some of these ideas that the establishment of a liberal democracy in Hungary is tantamount to an attempt by Jewish liberals 'to "assimilate" the Hungarian nation to its style and thinking'.[14]

The foci of conservatism

While the ruling coalition, to be fair, did not accept the remedies of the populists, it did little to distance itself from them either. In essence, it appeared to have four major reference points in formulating a strategy. The first of these was the '*nation*'. Using the nation as a legitimating principle is, of course, perfectly proper, but this would involve a wide-ranging open debate about the redefinition of nationhood, its functions and its objectives in the 1990s. The nearest the government came to this was the declaration that the prime minister of Hungary was the prime minister of all Hungarians, i.e. those living in the successor states as well as in Hungary.

The second reference point was *religion*, which had a concrete expression, for example, in the proposal to introduce optional religious education in schools.[15] This encountered wide-ranging protests and was amended. In broader terms, religion was the basis of a social protectionist attitude, that the state had far-reaching responsibilities for the welfare of the nation and that, in turn, could be utilized to legitimate an *étatist*, interventionist strategy.

That leads directly to the third reference point, *étatisme* itself. To judge by the policies of the government, it was reluctant to accept the introduction of the market, and, indeed, was elected on a 'moderate' platform that promised slow movement towards marketization. Rather than contemplate a big bang approach to privatization, the policies of the government tended to favour a privatization from above, with considerable powers being given to state agencies. It was inevitable that this would reproduce some, though not all, of the worst features of the communist party-state and would give rise to the standard problems of patron-client networks, the parasitism of the state on society, the blocking of initiatives and energies and the restriction of choice.[16]

The fourth reference point concerned the *language of public discourse* and the debates themselves. The coalition found itself in a difficult position as far as the media was concerned. The media were overwhelmingly populated by individuals whose thought-world and attitudes were far more open to liberal-rational ideas than the 'Christian middle course' professed by the government. This was not necessarily because journalists and communicators were, as the government tended to believe, in the pocket of the main opposition party, the Free Democrats, but more because the views of the communicators tended to coincide with the Free Democrats' philosophy.

As a result, the government came to feel that it was not treated even-handedly by the media, that the media were dominated by a liberal intellectual hegemony which excluded alternatives like its own and hence its sensitivity to media treatment grew by leaps and bounds. This was no doubt made worse by the lack of experience of the government and its ministers of criticism *per se* and the frequently personalized and moralizing tone of media comment. Demands for tighter government control of the media, with an unmistakenly authoritarian flavour, began to be heard as a result, especially from among the populists.[17] This liberal hegemony was a serious handicap in fostering the modernization of Hungarian conservatism.

The hesitations of conservatism in Hungary had a further, undoubtedly unintended, consequence – to an extent it was beginning to pull the liberal opposition on to its own ground. In part, this was virtually automatic, in as much as the government sets the agenda in all political systems and the opposition responds to it. If that agenda was primarily concerned with questions of what constituted the Christian and European values of Hungary, then the opposition was bound to become involved.

The Free Democrats regarded themselves as the protagonists of liberal European values. Where they were weak, however, was in formulating a conception of the role of nationhood in politics. If anything, they tended to dismiss it uneasily as an irrelevant leftover from the past, which was manifestly a mistake. The result seem to have been that the main opposition party felt itself vulnerable on the national issue and reacted – even over-reacted – when the government made reference to it. If the Free Democrats were definitively to be trapped in this intellectual blind alley, then it would do little to enhance the parliamentary process.

The long-term problem was that when a political party or government coalition relied on categories that were of limited value in drawing the cognitive map by which the real political situation could be understood, its solutions would be ineffective or counter-productive. In the medium term, a major economic crisis could easily leave the government stripped of its legitimating ideology and find its self-legitimation undermined.[18] In a relatively untried democracy like Hungary's, the question under this scenario was whether a collapse of this kind would bring down only the government or the system as a whole.

Notes

1. The nature and characteristics of the Kádár system have generated an extensive literature in Hungary, notably László Lengyel, *Végkifejlet* (Final dénouement) (Budapest: Közgazdasági & Jogi, 1989). See also László Bogár, *Kitörési kisérleteink: egy modernizációs csapda anatómiája* (Our attempts to break out: the anatomy of a pitfall in modernisation) (Budapest: Közgazdasági & Jogi, 1989).
2. On the background to the democratic opposition, see George Schöpflin, 'Opposition and Para-Opposition in Hungary', in Rudolf Tökés (ed.), *Opposition in Eastern Europe*, (London: Macmillan, 1979).
3. See, for example, Mihály Bihari, *Reform és Demokrácia* (Reform and democracy) (Budapest: Eötvös, 1990); also István Schlett, 'Közelitések a politikai rendszer reformjához', (Approaches to the reform of the political system) *Az opportunizmus dicsérete* (In praise of opportunism) (Budapest: Magvető, 1990) and Béla Pokol, *Politikai reform és modernizáció* (Political reform and modernisation) (Budapest: Magvető, 1989).

4. Personal recollection.
5. George Schöpflin, Rudolf Tökés and Iván Völgyes,'Leadership Change and Crisis in Hungary', *Problems of Communism*, 37:5 (September–October 1988), pp. 23–46.
6. Rudolf Tökés, *From Post-Communism to Democracy: Politics, Parties and the 1990 Elections in Hungary* (Bonn: Konrad Adenauer Stiftung, 1990).
7. Several of the contributions to the *1990 Yearbook of Politics* in Hungary are relevant here, see notably Attila Ágh, 'A pártosodás éve: válságok és szervezetek', (The year of party formation: crises and organisations), Mihály Bihari, 'Egy pártkongresszus szociológiája', (The sociology of a party congress), István Kukorelli, 'Az Országgyülés a többpártrendszer elsö évében', (The legislature in the first year of the multiparty system) all in Sándor Kurtán, Péter Sándor and László Vass (eds), *Magyarország politikai évkönyve 1990*, (Budapest: Aula-OMIKK, 1990).
8. On the roundtable negotiations, see András Bozóki, Út a rendszerváltáshoz: az Ellenzéki Kerekasztal' (The road to the transformation: the Opposition Round Table), *Mozgó Világ*, 16:8 (August 1990), pp. 23–38.
9. Table taken from András Körösényi, 'Pártok és szavazók – Parlamenti választások 1990-ben' (Parties and voters – parliamentary elections in 1990), *Mozgó Világ*, 16:8 (August 1990), pp. 39–51.
10. The text of the agreement was in *Népszabadság*, 3 May 1990.
11. It was held on 29 July. Legislation on referenda required a 50 per cent turn-out for validity.
12. The second issue of *Századvég* 1990 is devoted entirely to the question of populism. See in particular the article by Mária Heller, Dénes Némedi and Ágnes Rényi, 'Népesedési viták 1963–1986' (Debates on population growth 1963–1986), pp. 69–105.
13. See the writings of István Csurka, passim. Sándor Csoóri, in many respects the most prestigious spokesman of the populists, has also implied that Jews are outside the definition (his definition) of Hungarian culture, see his 'Nappali hold (II)', (Daylight moon), *Hitel*, 3:18 (5 Sept. 1990).
14. Csoóri, ibid.
15. There was an interesting parallel here with Poland, where, it was reported, the Senate had passed a law outlawing abortion, *The Independent*, 2 October 1990.
16. On some of the consequences of state-directed privatization, see Kálmán Mizsei (editor), *A privatizációs kihivás Közép-Kelet-Európában* (The challenge of privatisation in Central-East-Europe), (Budapest: MTA Világgazdasági Kutató Intézet, 1990).
17. Csurka, again, made repeated calls for government control over the electronic media.
18. On legitimation crises, see Andrew C. János, *Politics and Paradigms*, (Stanford: Stanford University Press, 1986), pp. 142–146 and the literature reviewed there.

9 Revival of the past or new beginning? The nature of post-communist politics*

András Körösényi

The collapse of Communism and the first free elections gave room for the emergence of multiparty systems in East-Central Europe. A wide range of political parties have been flourishing and new political regimes have been established. The post-communist transition did not follow a single pattern: three major types of regimes had emerged by 1990. Dominant non-authoritarian party systems, led by the 'national liberation movements', had emerged in Poland, Czechoslovakia, Croatia and Slovenia; dominant authoritarian party systems had been revived in Romania and Bulgaria; and competitive multiparty systems came into existence in Hungary and East Germany.

Political dominance of 'national liberation movements'

In Poland, Solidarity, being deeply rooted in the movements of 1980–81, has overwhelmingly dominated the political scene and remained an 'umbrella organization' of the opposition (then of the government). None of the political parties – Social Democrats, Christian Democrats, Nationalists – could win any seats against the candidates of the Citizens' Committee, which was backed by Solidarity at the 1989 general election. The role of Solidarity, the 'umbrella organization' of the anti-communist opposition, is similar to the 'national liberation movements' of the de-colonization period in the developing world. The Polish Solidarity, or the Civic Forum in Bohemia, absorbed all the political forces of the opposition, as did the Indian Congress Party, and they were also led by charismatic leaders (Walesa, Havel). These movements did not have any specific policy orientation or electoral programme beyond a general democratic and Western-looking attitude and reform programme. With their 'aggregative' character they won the elections with an overwhelming majority and became dominant ruling parties.

* First published in *Political Quarterly*, vol. 62, no. 1, January–March 1991, pp. 52–74.

The Czechoslovakian development of the party system produced an intermediate position between the Polish and the Hungarian patterns. The Czech Civic Forum and the Slovakian Public Against Violence dominated the political scene, but could not become the 'melting pot' of all the non-communist political forces. Therefore, the Czech, the Slovak and the Federal parliaments developed a multiparty character.

Revival of authoritarianism

In Romania and Bulgaria authoritarian regimes and dominant authoritarian party systems emerged.[1] In Romania, the nationalist and semi-communist National Salvation Front, successfully creating an image of the leading force of the December 1989 revolution, was able to preserve the power and the monolithic character of the regime. In Bulgaria, the reform-wing of the former Communist Party, by changing the name of the party to Socialist and promising free elections and other reforms, won the multiparty elections. It is characteristic of the new Romanian regime that the strongest opposition party in parliament is organized along ethnic principles by the Hungarian minority. The two revived historic parties, the National Liberal Party and the National Peasant Party, achieved a rather poor result. In Bulgaria, the coalition of the opposition parties did much better, but the former ruling party, renamed as Socialist, won an absolute majority of the parliamentary seats.

In Romania and Bulgaria the (ex-)communist ruling elites were able to win the multiparty elections and preserve their political power. In spite of the personal continuity, the character of the regimes are different from their predecessors. The Romanian National Salvation Front does not have a distinct ideological orientation, but has become a rather pragmatic political party. However, it preserved the nationalist character of the Ceaucescu regime, as the anti-Hungarian and anti-Gypsy pogroms showed (the National Salvation Front either inspired or did not condemn these violent actions). Beside its nationalism, the Front has a *populist* character. The mobilization of the working class (miners) against the democratic political opposition gives a Latin-American Peronist character to the new Romanian regime.[2] Though this kind of violence did not happen in Bulgaria, the overwhelming electoral victory of the ex-communist Socialist Party is due to its strong rural and working-class constituency.

The Serb Republic also belongs to the group of new post-communist authoritarian regimes, though there were no multiparty elections there. Serbia, under the rule of the populist nationalist S. Milosevics, became one of the first among those countries to begin to transform their communist one-party system into an authoritarian one-party regime. It was the success of the populist-nationalist appeal which made it possible for the Serbian ruling elite to avoid free elections for a long time.

This remarkable success of the (ex-)Communists, and the authoritarian character of these regimes (especially of the Romanian) can be explained by historical factors:

1. In these countries there were no dissident or opposition movements under communist rule. The Ceaucescu regime was overthrown by a spontaneous mass revolt, while the Bulgarian was reformed by the ruling elite itself. The opposition in Romania appeared only after the revolt, at the end of December 1989, and in Bulgaria in the second half of 1989. Neither of them was well established, well known or organized. Neither of them had for longer than half a year been active before the elections.
2. These countries do not have strong parliamentary traditions with free elections.
3. The political culture of the population, with the categories of G. Almond and S. Verba, is traditionally a 'subject' rather than 'participatory' one.[3]

Beside these similarities, the Romanian and Bulgarian political regimes have different prospects for the future. While the Romanian could easily slip into a pure one-party authoritarianism, where no legitimate political opposition exists, the politically more balanced Bulgaria has greater potential towards becoming a representative multiparty system.[4] In Serbia the regime probably could keep its authoritarian character, even if it could not avoid holding multiparty elections.

Competitive multiparty systems

While in Poland or Romania the new political regime has a secular one-party character, in Hungary and in East Germany the emerging political scene became more pluralistic. In East Germany, though various political parties were able to take part in the first multiparty elections in March 1990, the political agenda, and therefore the new political scene, was dominated by the manner and speed of unification. The new East German politics were very much influenced by the West German political parties. In Hungary, the new party system developed much more from internal political sources. The lack of a revolution or a strong popular movement left room for a gradual and smooth political development, marked by the slow decay and split of the ruling Communist Party on the one hand, and by the groupings of the opposition along various political traditions and orientations on the other hand. A wide range of political parties developed and stabilized themselves on the political scene, and no room was left for any 'umbrella organization' of the opposition forces. Therefore, in Hungary, a moderate pluralism emerged with a representative party system; various political parties appeared with specific ideologies, policy orientations and constituencies. Both in Hungary and East Germany the elections were dominated by the contest of the emerging new parties, which produced clear-cut policy alternatives. These countries have the best prospects for the development of an alternative government and of a West European-type multiparty democracy in the post-communist East Central Europe.

Table 9.1 Types of post-communist party systems

Party system	COMPETITIVE MULTIPARTY moderate pluralism	DOMINANT single-umbrella organization	AUTHORITARIAN reshaped ruling party
Character of the party system	representative, with policy alternatives	aggregative, no policy alternatives	aggregative, no policy alternatives
Ruling elite	new	new	old
Parliamentary tradition	strong	strong	weak
Political culture	participant/ subject	participant/ subject	subject
Countries	Hungary East Germany Czechoslovakia*	Poland Croatia Slovenia*	Romania Bulgaria Serbia

* Slovenia and Czechoslovakia can be regarded as mixtures of competitive and dominant party systems.

The collapse of the one-party regimes and fast transition to the first post-communist parliamentary elections raises a series of questions for political scientists. What issues appear on the political agenda? What factors explain the new party formation? What are the roles of political traditions and of the new issues? What characterizes the voting behaviour of the newly enfranchised citizens? What political preferences or cleavages exist after a four-decade-long attempt at political neutralization and social homogenization? What kind of party systems emerge in these countries?

This paper is an attempt to discuss these questions and use mainstream methods and approaches to analyse the moderate pluralism which developed in politics and the party system in Hungary.

The nature of Hungarian politics

In Hungary, a two-year-long transition process took place before the March 1990 parliamentary elections. The first opposition movement appeared in the autumn of 1987, and by the time of the 1990 elections 12 political parties were able to set up a nationwide organization network. Six of them passed the 4 per cent threshold and became parliamentary parties, as is shown by Tables 6.1 and 6.4 on pages 77 and 79.

As to their origins, the six parliamentary parties fall into three categories. The first is constituted of those parties which developed out of the dissident movements of the 1970s and 1980s: the Hungarian Democratic Forum (HDF), the Alliance of Free Democrats (AFD) and the

Federation of Young Democrats (FYD). The second category is that of the revived historic parties, which had their origin prior to the Second World War: the Smallholders' Party (SHP), the Social Democratic Party (HSDP), the Hungarian People's Party (HPP) and the Christian Democratic People's Party (CDPP). They had dominated the political scene with the Communist Party in the last two multiparty elections in 1945 and 1947. The third category contains the two heirs of the former ruling Communist Party, the hard-line Hungarian Socialist Workers' Party (HSWP) and the moderate, reform-oriented Hungarian Socialist Party (HSP).

The origin of the new Hungarian parties

The first striking feature of the electoral results was the dominance of the *new parties*: the proportion of the total votes for them (HDF, AFD, FYD) was over 50 per cent. (55.3 per cent.) In fact, the competition of the two major opposition parties, the HDF and the AFD, defined the political agenda in the pre-election period, and their split determined the emerging left–right dimension of Hungarian politics. It is a peculiarity of the new Hungarian political scene that the two main parties, the HDF and the AFD, grew from two small groups of intellectuals into dominant political parties.

The AFD was formed around a dissident group of 'urbanist' intellectuals which had existed since the mid-1970s. They formed the dissident 'human rights' opposition of the communist regime. Ideologically they came from the left (many of them are ex-Marxists), but developed towards a left-liberal middle-class radicalism by the mid-1980s. The recent involvement of leading economists gave a rather libertarian character to its economic programme.[5] The HDF was formed in 1987 around the traditional 'national-populist' group of intellectuals, whose ideal was a 'third road' (neither communist nor capitalist), genuinely 'Hungarian' future. They were less hostile to the existing regime, and had contact with the reform wing of the ruling Communist Party.[6] By the autumn of 1989, however, the HDF had developed towards a Christian-democratic character.

The division of the Hungarian *intelligentsia* into 'urbanist' and 'populist' groups has historical origin. This historical split can be explained first of all by political and ideological factors, but sociological factors play some role as well. These two tiny subcultures have deep-seated roots and some continuity since the 1930s.

The 'urbanist' intellectuals[7] of the 1930s received inspiration from the nineteenth-century liberal tradition and from the development of democratic political institutions in Western Europe. The 'populists'[8] were inspired by nationalism and by the anti-capitalist left as well. Both were 'democratic' and opposed the authoritarian conservative Horthy regime, but in very different ways. The political target of the 'urbanists' was the *political* emancipation of the lower classes, universal and secret franchise, right of assembly, trade unions rights, etc. Democracy has a *procedural* meaning for them. In contrast, the 'populist' intellectuals, although they never rejected democratic ideas, concentrated on a programme of *social* emancipation of the under-classes (first of all the millions of landless peasants). Therefore land reform and other social reforms were in the centre of their political programme. Populist thinking had a rather anti-elite and anti-establishment character. They criticized the ruling elite, the gentry and the Christian middle class as well as the liberal urban bourgeoisie. They stood for the creation of a new social elite, recruited from the peasantry, which was regarded as the only embodiment of the genuine Hungarian character. For the 'populists' democracy had a *substantive* meaning, i.e. democracy meant a certain social arrangement rather than institutional setting and legal procedures. Therefore, unlike the 'urbanists', they were much more interested in the output (policies) than in the input side of politics.

The political and ideological differences were strengthened by social factors. While 'urbanist' liberalism was associated with the Budapest Jewish intelligentsia and middle class, the 'populist' approach was favoured by the reform-oriented 'Christian' middle class (professionals, civil servants, intellectuals).

The split was a consequence of the peculiar pattern of capitalization and embourgeoisement in late nineteenth-century Hungary. Lacking a 'Hungarian' urban middle class, the Jews dominated the emerging bourgeoisie. Therefore, liberalism and capitalism were associated very much with the Jewish social elements of society. While the failure to create a pure nation-state strengthened nationalism, the social tension produced by rapid economic modernization boosted modern anti-Semitism. These two tendencies fused very much by the inter-war period and had an influence on 'populism' as well.[9]

The populist tradition remained continuous in the post-war period and under communist rule among intellectuals, especially in Hungarian literature. In fact, the revolt of the 'populist' writers at the 1986 Congress of the Writers' Association against the cultural policy of the Kádár regime was one of the antecedents of the foundation of the HDF. On the 'urbanist' side of the Hungarian intellectual tradition, direct continuity was broken in the 1950s. The generation of the 1930s was dispersed: some of them emigrated, others became victims of the Holocaust. Survivors of the war who stayed in Hungary were either imprisoned or silenced under the Rakosi era of the 1950s. The following generation, especially those who were of Jewish origin, became Communist in the post-war period. They regarded Marxism as the only progressive idea and remedy against anti-Semitism and nationalism. Under strict communist control and censorship of cultural life, the internationalist 'urbanist' and the national 'populist' attitude was expressed in literature and in the esoteric debates of historians.[10] The split between 'progressives' and 'nationalists' never disappeared in twentieth-century Hungarian political thinking. The revival of urbanist political thinking began with the appearance of the dissident Marxist philosophers at the end of the 1960s (the 'Lukács school'). By the end of the 1970s, the urban wing of the intelligentsia, leaving Marxism behind them, switched towards the liberal and radical political tradition of the inter-war period. The traditional political split evolved again. By the 1980s, two tiny but influential groups had evolved in Hungarian intellectual life. Having their historical prejudices, they regarded each other with resentment and hostility.

The traditional and mutual prejudices of the urban and populist wings of the Hungarian intellectuals explain to a great extent the divergent character of the evolving political pluralism. The subcultural hostility between the two elite groups strengthened their ideological differences, and determined the *left–right* scale.

Does the left–right dimension exist?

The second striking feature of the electoral results was the victory of the right, and the failure of the left. But who is on the left and who is on the right in Hungarian politics? Do these categories matter at all on the new political scene?

To answer these questions, the following questions should be taken into consideration. What kind of issues appeared on the Hungarian political scene? Are they really separated into coherent 'groups' of issues along the left–right division? What are the main differences between the character of the left and right? Let me list a series of these characteristics of left and right in terms of some dichotomies[11] (Table 9.2) and attach those parties to each (in brackets) which have a specific alignment with those characteristics.

Table 9.2   Characteristics of Hungarian political parties

Left	Right
International (AFD, FYD, HSDP, HSP) (HWSP)	National (HDF, SHP)
Secular (FYD, AFD, HSDP, HSP)	Denominational (CDPP)
Urban (FYD, AFD, SDP)	Rural (SHP, HDF)
Industrial (HSDP)	Agrarian (SHP)
Unions (HSDP, HSP)	Business
Neutrality (FYD, AFD)	Defence (HDF)
Civil rights (AFD, FYD)	Social order
Liberal	Authoritarian
'Liberal' (FYD, AFD) (pro-abortion)	'Conservative' (CDPP) (anti-abortion)

The characteristics of the right can be attributed more to the HDF, the CDPP and the SHP, while those of the left rather better to the AFD, FYD, HSP (and to the failed HSDP and HSWP). In fact, the formation of the government confirms the relevance of the left–right political scale, since it is based on a centre–right HDF–SHP–CDPP coalition.

The *economic dimension*, however, does not overlap with this distinction. Though the HSP and the HSDP had some contact with the trade unions, which coincides with their 'leftist' character, the two main parties, the HDF and the AFD, have a 'deviant' character in this dimension. The AFD (and the FYD) has a deregulation-oriented, more libertarian economic programme, while the HDF was less radical and slightly *etatist* in its economic policy. (For example, while the AFD is committed to fast privatization, the HDF is more cautious on that question and aims at creating a domestic bourgeoisie; it worries about the unlimited influx of Western capital into the Hungarian economy.)

The different attitudes to the concept of private property and to privatization are also worth mentioning. Private property is a 'natural right' for the parties on the right, especially for the historical parties (SHP, CDPP). Therefore, they do not consider the former socialist collectivization of agriculture legitimate. The SHP inclined towards interpreting the way of privatization as giving back the confiscated or nationalized private property to its original owners, even though the confiscation happened more than 40 years earlier.[12] (The line of the HDF is less strong on this issue than that of its allies.) By contrast, for the parties on the centre–left (AFD, FYD), privatization is a question of economic efficiency, and they regard the status quo in property rights as legitimate.[13] The socialist left (HSP, HSDP) also regard privatization as an economic necessity, but they have not entirely given up their alignment to some form of collective ownership.

In general, the economic and ideological left–right scales cross-cut each other. The libertarian economic line of the left–liberal AFD is on the right of the economic scale, while the recent economic programme of the centre–right HDF is to the left of the AFD position. Regarding the general *left–liberal* character and the libertarian economic philosophy of the Free Democrats and the Young Democrats, they can be classified as liberal centre parties.

In addition, there is one more factor on the issue level which underlines the *centre-party nature* of the AFD and FYD. Post-materialist issues,[14] like the green issue, the disarmament question, the anti-death penalty or the pro-abortion view, already appeared at the margin of Hungarian politics. The appearance of the 'new issue' politics connected more with the left–liberal parties (FYD, AFD) than with the right. The interweaving of the 'old' and 'new left' underlies the centre-party nature of the AFD and FYD.

The current social basis of the Free Democrats is also a factor of its centre-party character. It is dominated by urban intellectuals and professionals (by the 'new middle class') and it does not have any institutional link either to the blue collar trade unions or to the blue collar workers themselves.

This leads to a more general question: what is the social character of the new parties? The new political parties were initially organized by small groups of intellectuals or old politicians of the historical parties (who had not been active in politics since the last multiparty elections in

1945/1947). Could they acquire an appeal to specific social groups and forge institutional links to them?

The social character of the political parties

One of the main characteristics of Hungarian politics is the lack of organized interest groups behind the political parties. The electoral failure of the HSDP, which tried to establish links with eight trade union associations, showed the weakness and lack of credibility of the trade unions. But parties backed by other interest organizations (the Party of Entrepreneurs had the support of KIOSZ and KISOSZ, the interest organizations of artisans and small shopkeepers; the Agrarian Alliance was backed by the association of collective farms) also failed to pass the 4 per cent threshold and to gain effective representation in the unicameral Hungarian parliament.

The lack of either a Polish Solidarity-type working-class movement or Western-type trade unions partly explains the weakness of the left. On the whole, the party formation had a strong middle-class character in Hungary.

The social composition of the constituency of the different parties, however, was divergent. The electorate of the historical parties (SHP, CDPP, SDP) has the most specific character.

The *Smallholders' Party*'s strongholds were in rural Hungary. The SHP became a sectional party, backed by the poorly educated old-aged groups of the rural areas, by those who agree with the project to restore the 1947 private farming. The constituency of the *Christian Democratic People's Party* was very similar to that of the SHP, i.e., elderly, poorly educated citizens with relatively low social status. There were, however, three major differences: the sexual, professional and regional composition. Diverging from the Smallholders, there were more female than male voters among the electorate of the Christian Democrats, and its constituency was not limited to rural areas but concentrated in the highly Catholic regions.

There were two other historic parties (HSDP, HSWP) which were not able to become parliamentary parties but had a very specific social backing. Both the *Social Democrats* and the *Hungarian Socialist Workers' Party* had a working-class electorate, but each of them was from the old-aged groups.

The *Free Democrats* and the *Hungarian Socialist Party*, had a support more evenly spread among each social group than the historic parties, without extreme regional differences. However, both of them had a strong elite character: high income groups, professional groups with high social status, and the Budapest and urban population were strongly over-represented in their electorate. To put it more specifically the HSP was strongly supported by the old 'ruling-class' (the elite of the former regime, like managers, high-ranking officials), while the AFD was backed by the new elite groups (professionals, intellectuals). Both had support from each age-group, but while in the HSP electorate the elderly were over-represented, in the AFD electorate their proportion was small. The peculiarity of the AFD constituency was that in spite of its elite character it was slightly over-represented among the lower income groups. The *Federation of Young Democrats* also had support from all social strata, but it was highly over-represented among the younger age groups. In addition, the constituency of the FYD did not have an elite character: on the contrary, it was over-represented among the lower income groups.

The *Hungarian Democratic Forum* had a strong middle-class character. In spite of this, the HDF was the only Hungarian political party which had a backing that was evenly spread among all social (income, residential, educational and age) groups. The HDF was able to create a 'catch-all' character, which became the main source of its landslide electoral victory. In the single-member constituency contest, there was a two ballot system. Without an absolute majority victory a run-off was held (in 171 out of the 176 single-member constituencies) between the first three candidates. The HDF could increase its votes by 30 per cent,[15] in spite of the serious decline of turn-out (from 65 per cent to 45 per cent). The HDF could gain most of the voters of the unsuccessful parties, i.e. the HDF was the second preference of the originally non-HDF voters.

Electoral behaviour and party competition

How can we characterize the voting behaviour of the Hungarians at the first post-communist election? Though it is difficult to draw serious conclusions after one general election, an assessment of the main models of electoral behaviour might yield some results. In the following I will survey the main models[16] of voting behaviour in order to find out whether they are applicable to the recent Hungarian elections.

The *party identification model*, which assumes strong party alignments of the electorate, explains some votes, especially the votes of the SHP, the HSP, the HSDP and the HSWP. These four parties had long traditions, and have some electorates with strong party alignment. But most of them were able to regain only a fraction of their former electorates. The SHP was founded in 1930 (and it had a predecessor in the 1920s as well) and was on the political scene until 1948. The HSP and HSWP are the heirs of the more than five-decades-long Communist Party tradition. The CDPP does not have a strong *party* tradition: its direct predecessor, the Democratic People's Party, took part only in one election in 1947. Just like the CDPP, however, the Christian social parties of the inter-war period had good results in Western Hungary. The AFD, the FYD and HDF are new parties, without a long party tradition.

The *sociological model*, which assumes that people vote in accordance with the interests of their social location, explains only marginal votes. Since the links between the political parties and the social interest groups in society were rather weak and the electoral programmes of the parties were far from clear in terms of special group interests, the 'interest vote' did not characterize the 1990 Hungarian elections. There might have been some 'interest votes' in some areas.

The *issue voting* model assumes that the voters rationally analyse the programme of the parties on various issues of the political agenda and vote for the party which is the closest to their own viewpoints. Voters also evaluate the *policy* of the incumbents (and compare it with their previous promises). The defeat of the incumbent (ex-)communist HSP in the first round of the Hungarian elections demonstrated the general dissatisfaction with its previous record. In spite of the fact that the last government of the one-party rule was much more responsive to the people than its predecessors, the election became a verdict over the four-decades-long past of the one-party regime. The first ballot was much more a referendum on the transition towards a multiparty democracy than a vote on specific policy issues. The competition of the opposition parties, however, especially in the second round, might have made the issue voting model more relevant. The AFD, in particular, as a *programme* party, raised specific policy issues with a clear-cut view on them. But, in general, the electoral competition of the three major opposition parties was much more that of political parties with different political characters, styles and images, than competition of clear standpoints on specific policy issues. (The HDF, which appeared as a *people's party*, had a rather vague political programme.)

However, there were some issue cleavages among the political parties. The most important ones are: 1. the speed and methods of privatization; 2. control over the central mass media (state-owned TV channels and radio broadcasts); 3. the political responsibility of civil servants and economic managers for the previous policy; and 4. the question of landed property. In general, however, the issue dimension played a secondary role.

The party system: revival of the past or a new beginning?

The dominance of the new parties in Hungarian politics has been emphasized above, but their role was not overwhelming. The historic parties, i.e., the SHP, the CDPP and the HSDP, gained altogether 21.79 per cent of the (list) votes. In addition, the heirs of the communist ruling party, i.e., the HSP and the HSWP, which also had a long historical tradition, gained altogether 14.57 per cent. Though these votes meant support for the former incumbents, it also represented a loyalty to the inter- and post-war social democratic and communist tradition (the left-wing of the HSDP fused with the Communist Party in 1948). Though the new parties, the HDF, the AFD and the FYD, did not have any direct political predecessors, at the *ideological* and *issue* level they represented a strong continuity with the 1930s and 1940s. (The traditional ideological subcultural division of the Hungarian intelligentsia as the origin of the HDF and the AFD in this split has already been mentioned above.) The rural–urban, agrarian–industrial, denominational–secular and national–international dichotomies of the 1930–40s still dominate the division between the political right and the left. (On the 1947 political scale, the Smallholders' Party, the (Catholic) Democratic People's Party and the Hungarian Independence Party were on the right, while the Communist Party, the Social Democratic Party and the tiny Hungarian Radical and Civilian Democratic Party were on the left.)

These unexpected findings raise the question of historical continuity. S.M. Lipset and S. Rokkan set up a model which emphasizes strong continuity of the party systems (see Note 22). According to their 'freezing thesis', the party cleavages, which had appeared by the time of universal suffrage, tended to be 'frozen' and determined the further development of the party structure. But if Lipset and Rokkan's 'freezing-thesis' on the continuity of party structure fits the development of the Hungarian political scene at all, what period should be regarded as a 'starting point'? Before 1945 there were no free elections with secret ballot and the freedom of political parties to enter the contest was also limited.[17] The 1945 elections achieved a universal franchise and the secret ballot, but excluded all but one of the political parties on the right, therefore the Smallholders' Party took all the votes on the right. The 1947 elections gave more parties on the right the chance to enter the contest (viz. the Smallholders' Party fragmented into three major parties – the Catholic 'Democratic People's Party' ((C)DP), the 'Hungarian Independence Party' (HIP) and the SHP itself), but restricted the franchise and excluded about 10 per cent of the citizens, most of whom were voters of the right. In spite of these restrictions, the 1947 general elections gave an opportunity for the expression of a wide range of political preferences. Therefore the political scene and party structure of the 1947 elections can be regarded as a 'starting point' which could have determined the further development of the party structure if the multiparty system had not been abolished. Therefore, if the 'freezing thesis' of Lipset and Rokkan is relevant in our case – which is my hypothesis – the party structure produced by the 1990 elections should be a revival of the 1947 one.

The 1988–90 period showed signs of historical continuity on the *issue* and *ideological* levels, as has been described above. The 1990 general elections demonstrated to a certain extent even the *sub-cultural cleavages* of society survived, as the strong regional character of the historic parties shows. Namely, the votes for the historical parties were far above their national average in those regions which were their strongholds in 1947 at the time of the last multiparty elections (see Tables 9.3–9.6). This shows some continuity in electoral behaviour.

Hungary is divided into five politico-geographical regions. The first is the metropolitan area of Budapest, which is the most developed part of Hungary and represents one million voters by itself. The second is the heavy industrial North East (Nógrád, Heves and Borsod-Abaúj-Zemplén counties) with its high working-class population and communist tradition. In addition, this region has a high Catholic population. The third region is the rural south-eastern 'Tiszántúl' (Békés, Szolnok, Hajdu-Bihar and Szabolcs-Szatmár counties). This is the only region in Hungary which has a Protestant character. The fourth is rural Mid- and South Hungary (Pest,

Table 9.3 The regional character of Smallholders' constituency in 1947 and 1990. Difference from the national average (proportion of total votes, in %) by regions

	1947	1990
Metropolitan Budapest	− 8.0	− 5.0
Industrial north-east	− 0.6	− 3.1
Protestant–rural 'Tiszántúl'	+ 7.1	+ 5.9
Rural mid-south	+ 1.4	+ 2.7
Urbanized north-west	− 2.4	− 0.9

Source: calculated by the author.

Table 9.4 The regional character of the 1947 Democratic People's Party* and of the 1990 Christian Democratic People's Party. Difference from the national average (proportion of total votes, in %) by regions

	1947	1990
Metropolitan Budapest	− 11.3	− 0.7
Industrial north-east	+ 1.2	+ 5.0
Protestant–rural 'Tiszántúl'	− 8.7	− 3.9
Rural mid-south	+ 5.0	+ 0.2
Urbanized north-west	+ 17.4	0.7**

* Together with the result of the Christian Women's Camp.
** In one of the four counties (Fejér) the CDP did not have a party list, while in the other three counties of the north-west region the party got 9.7 per cent of the total votes, i.e. + 3.2 per cent over its national average.

Source: calculated by the author.

Bács-Kiskun, Csongrád, Baranya, Somogy, Zala, Veszprém and Tolna counties).[18] The fifth is the most developed and urbanized rural region, the North West (Vas, Györ-Sopron, Komárom and Fejér counties). Each region has its own particular political character.

The votes of the *Smallholders' Party* were concentrated in the southern and south-eastern regions where they surpassed their national average by 3–10 per cent. In these rural regions, the SHP had strong political traditions and gained over its average in the 1947 parliamentary elections as well. On the other hand, Budapest turned out to be their weakest region in 1990, as it was in the post-war elections (see Table 9.3).

Though the 1990 results of the *Christian Democratic People's Party* (CDPP) were much poorer than in 1947, their regional distribution follows the same pattern (see Table 9.4). In most of the Catholic counties (Györ-Sopron, Heves, Nógrád, Tolna, Vas and Zala counties) the CDPP got 10–15 per cent of the votes at the 1990 general elections, which is twice as high as its national average. They had the poorest result in the south-eastern Protestant 'Tiszántúl' region. In most of the 'Tiszántúl' constituencies the CDPP could not even put up candidates.[19]

Table 9.5 The regional character of the 1947 Hungarian Communist Party and the 1990 HS(W)P.* Difference from the national average (proportion of total votes, in %) by regions

	1947	1990
Metropolitan Budapest	+ 5.2	+ 2.5
Industrial north-east	+ 7.1	+ 3.9
Protestant–rural 'Tiszántúl'	− 0.9	+ 1.9**
Rural mid-south	− 3.7	− 2.5
Urbanized north-west	− 1.9	− 2.9

* HP(W)SP = HSP + HSWP votes.
** The reason for the good HS(W)P result is that the 'Tiszántúl' region was the stronghold of the radical agrarian National Peasant Party (NPP) at the 1947 elections. The NPP was the rural ally of the Communists and in 'Tiszántúl' it gained almost twice the number of votes as in general (+ 8.2 per cent over its national average). The NPP could not reorganize itself by the time of the 1990 elections, so the HSP and the HSWP got all the votes of the radical-left tradition.

Source: calculated by the author.

The (ex-)communist *HSP and HSWP* altogether gained between 9 and 14 per cent of the votes in Western Hungary while in Budapest and eastern Hungary they gained 16–20 per cent (see Table 9.5). This divergence can also be explained by historical traditions. In Budapest and in the north-eastern heavy industry region the industrial character and the strong social democratic and communist tradition explains their high votes. In the Protestant south-eastern 'Tiszántúl' region there is no direct correlation between the 1947 result of the Hungarian Communist Party (HCP) and the 1990 result of the HS(W)P. While the HCP got slightly

Table 9.6 The regional character of the 1947 Social Democratic Party and the 1990 Alliance of Free Democrats. Difference from the national average (proportion of total votes, in %) by regions

	SDP – 1947	AFD – 1990
Metropolitan Budapest	+ 9.8	+ 5.7
Industrial north-east	– 0.4	– 4.2
Protestant–rural 'Tiszántúl'	– 5.5	– 4.2
Rural mid-south	– 2.2	– 2.1
Urbanized north-west	+ 1.1	+ 4.8

Source: calculated by the author.

under its average in 1947, the HS(W)P exceeded it by 1.9 per cent. The explanation might lie in the historical role of agrarian radicalism in this region, which was expressed by high National Peasant Party (NPP) votes at the 1945 and 1947 elections. The NPP became the rural ally of the Communists (HCP) and got almost twice the number of votes (16.5 per cent) in the 'Tiszántúl' region as in general (their national average was 8.3 per cent).

Although the new parties, the two major parties, the HDF, the AFD and the minor FYD do not have direct political predecessors, the question of whether they follow any historical voting pattern should nonetheless be answered. The *Hungarian Democratic Forum*, as a 'catch-all' party on the right, had a relatively evenly spread constituency and does not have a strong regional character; neither does it follow any historical pattern. The same is true of the *Federation of Young Democrats*, which had the most evenly spread constituency in regional terms, though it slightly correlated with the Free Democratic votes. Diverging from the HDF and the FYD, the *Alliance of Free Democrats* has a remarkable regional character. The metropolitan Budapest region and the rather developed and urbanized North-West Hungary turned out to be the strongholds of the AFD, and it got weaker results in all the other rural regions. In addition, there is a positive correlation between the regional distribution of the 1990 AFD and the 1947 Social Democrat votes (see Table 9.6).

This correlation prevails not only in the five bigger regions, but in 17 out of 20 counties as well.[20] One of the three exceptions is the southern rural Békés county, a traditional stronghold of agrarian radicalism, where the HSDP has a long historical tradition. Another exception is the north-east industrial Borsod county, where the trade union-based HSDP was strong (but much weaker than the Communists) in the post-war period. The example of Borsod underlines the basic difference between the 1947 and the 1990 AFD constituencies. While the former received a high working-class vote, the AFD got much less. Besides its trade union bases, the post-war SDP was not a pure blue-collar party. It was the main moderate parliamentary political party on the left,[21] so it also collected the votes of the urban middle class, who were alienated from the national, clerical and/or agrarian-rural character of the right. The AFD (and the FYD) had the same democratic (but more liberal) appeal in 1990 and occupied the same position on the political scale.

The emerging Hungarian party structure is different from that of 1947 in three important aspects. First, while in 1945/47 the Social Democrats and Communists, backed by trade unions, dominated the left, the 1988–90 period was marked by fragmentation and the lack of a working-class base. Second, while in the post-war years the Hungarian political scene developed towards a bipolarization, in 1988–90 the emergence of a strong left–liberal centre (AFD, FYD) produced a tripolar structure. Thirdly, the emergence of a strong 'catch-all' party (the HDF) in 1990 is a new phenomenon. Therefore, strictly speaking, the 'freezing thesis' of Lipset and Rokkan lost its validity in the Hungarian case. In a wider sense, however, it is more relevant. The revival of the historical parties and of their constituencies, and the positive correlation between the 1947 HSDP and the 1990 AFD constituency, lead to the conclusion that there is a remarkable continuity between the pre- and post-communist Hungarian politics. It exists not only on issue and ideological levels but in the dimension of social cleavage as well. As the examples of the AFD and the HSDP show, it is a wider phenomenon than the revival of the historical parties. Though with the emergence of the new parties the party structure has changed significantly, traditions are still alive in the dimension of political culture and attitudes as well.

Regarding Lipset and Rokkan's thesis, we might put up another hypothesis and consider the period of 1989–90 as the 'starting period' of the model. The following elections will show whether the emerging party system will follow Lipset and Rokkan's 'freezing thesis'[22], the party system of the 1990 election period becoming stabilized, or whether it will change significantly. My assumption is that the party formation and constituency of the right (HDF, SHP, CDPP), which was able to revive its traditional constituency and party alignment and produce a modern 'catch-all' party as well, has a strong potential to preserve its current political character and party structure.

The stability of the status quo that has emerged is, however, less likely to be maintained from the left of the centre. The reason is that on the one hand, the traditional political loyalty of the working-class disappeared; the socialist left became fragmented and dispersed. On the other hand, two new left–liberal *programme* parties (ADF, FYD) emerged, and, becoming the main rivals of the winning right coalition, occupied the political position of the moderate left. In spite of this, since the AFD did not have a clear and stable electoral basis and because of the logic of political competition, the AFD might be compelled to seek a social democratic political character. Since most of the parties on the left of the centre (except the FYD) endeavour to recreate and occupy the political position and especially the constituency of a classical social democratic party, restructuring on the left of the political scene is very likely.

Hungarian democracy: social cleavages and party system

With the 1989 constitutional amendments and 1990 free multiparty elections, Hungary fulfils the two major criteria for democratic political systems.[23] The constitution and the political practice have tended towards a parliamentary form of democratic government.[24] The political traditions and the electoral law have produced a multiparty parliament. Since the political scene and the electorate were rather fragmented, no party gained the majority of the seats and a coalition government was formed. But what prospects does Hungary have for a stable democracy? What kind of democracy has emerged in terms of social-political cleavages and party system? The political scene of the pre-election period was rather polarized. Finally, six parties gained 97 per cent of the parliamentary seats (376 out of 386 seats), which is still a rather fragmented political scene.

In general, two major factors are taken into account as far as the nature and stability of democratic regimes are concerned: first, the nature of the social cleavages (homogeneous or plural society), and secondly, the character of the party system.

Homogeneous or plural society?

Hungary society was clearly a plural one in the inter-war and the immediate post-war period. The more than four-decades-long communist rule, however, destroyed the institutions of the subcultures and carried out the greatest social homogenization programme in human history. It was very successful, as far as the institutional level is concerned. The institutions of the different social, residential, religious and professional groups were banned and abolished. People were either atomized or forced into organizations strictly directed and controlled by the Communist Party. Though a great industrialization programme of the 1950–60s[25] radically changed the fabric of society (the occupational structure, etc.), producing 'rootless' generations, the homogenization programme was less successful on the level of attitudes, values and social habits. Non-institutionalized, informal (religious, residential, national, occupational, racial, etc.) group loyalties as well as the memories of pre-communist political alignments and loyalties survived, as the fast revival of political traditions in the years 1987–90 and the electoral successes of the historical parties testify. Since then, there have been no administrative obstacles to the institutionalization of the segmented social groups; therefore the plural character of Hungarian society might strengthen in the future.

Contemporary Hungarian society can be described as slightly *segmented* rather than plural; a segmented society with various 'objective' social (religious, cultural, ideological and 'class') cleavages, which are not institutionalized but exist in inherited attitudes, instincts and memories of the people. This social segmentation, however, has an effect on the electoral behaviour of the people, as the voting patterns of the 1990 elections showed.[26]

The party system: moderate or extreme pluralism?

In general, homogeneous societies tend to produce a two-party system (or a moderate pluralism) and a stable form of democratic government. Plural societies, however, have to face more difficulties in creating a stable democracy. Much depends on the way social cleavages are transformed into political cleavages by the party system.

G. Sartori distinguished between bipolar and multipolar party competition. A bipolar party competition, either in a two-party or in a multiparty system, tends toward a moderate pluralism with *centripetal* party competition. A multipolar competition in a multiparty system, however, leads toward a *polarized* (extreme) pluralism with a *centrifugal* party competition.[27] The short history of the Hungarian multiparty competition of the 1988–90 pre-election period was a multipolar one, where the HS(W)P, the HDF and the AFD formed the three main poles. After the marginalization of the HS(W)P, however, the competition tended to follow a bipolar pattern, where the political contest was dominated by the Hungarian Democratic Forum–Free Democrats competition.

The prospects for bipolar or multipolar party competition are still unclear. In spite of the bipolarity of contemporary Hungarian politics, the left–liberal centre-party character of the Free Democrats and Young Democrats leaves room for the tripolar development of Hungarian politics. If the Socialist Party (HSP) regains its political credibility and moves successfully towards the unoccupied position of a classical social democratic party, the AFD and FYD might be closed into a centre party position.

Other scholars emphasize that the polarity of the political scene depends very much on the depth of the social and political cleavages of a plural society, i.e. on the breadth and intensity of the polarity. If there is no consensus among the main political actors on basic constitutional or procedural questions, the form of government and of democracy itself might be fragile.

A. Lijphart emphasizes the role of political elites in stabilizing the democratic form of government in a plural society, where the social cleavages are deep and directly transformed into political cleavages. Hostile elite behaviour may deepen the political fragmentation and produce a *centrifugal* party competition and therefore a fragile democracy, as in the classical examples of the Weimar Republic and the Fourth French Republic. A consensus-oriented, coalescent elite behaviour, however, might moderate and counterbalance the hostile political cleavages of a plural society, and produce a 'consociational democracy' as the Dutch, Belgian and Swiss examples demonstrated. In consociational democracies, the forms of coalition government prevail.[28]

Where can we place Hungary in Lijphart's typology? Its *society* is between a 'plural' and a 'homogeneous' type. Its *elite behaviour* is much more 'adversarial' than the nature of the social cleavages (while at a social level the homogenization programme eclipsed the traditional cleavages, the emerging new parties – the HDF and the AFD – were rooted in the traditional subcultural hostility of rival elite groups of the 'intelligentsia').

If some cautious conclusion could be drawn it might be the following: on the rather fragmented and multiparty Hungarian political scene there are tendencies towards 'centrifugal party competition', but this is much more the consequence of adversarial elite behaviour than the cleavages of the segmented and slightly plural society. Hungary is an example of a 'reversed' adversarial policy.

Notes

1. G.A. Almond, 'Introduction: A Functionalist Approach to Comparative Politics', in G.A. Almond and J.S. Coleman, *The Politics of Developing Areas*, 1960, pp. 40–44.
2. Jonathan Eyel, 'Pledge of Peace Turns to Rule by the Sword', *The Guardian*, 15 June 1990, p. 10.
3. G. Almond and S. Verba, *Civic Culture*, 1960.
4. The more moderate and liberal character of the Bulgarian regime and the more violent and repressive character of the Romanian regime are due to their different origins. While in Bulgaria the (peaceful) internal power struggle within the ruling Communist Party and the victory of the 'progressives' led to the political reforms and to free elections, in Romania a popular revolt and a violent struggle led to the transition.
5. In Hungary it was the 'human right' or *'democratic opposition'*, formed by leftist dissident intellectuals in 1977, which came into existence as a *radical* anti-system opposition. They published the leading 'samizdat' journals, like the *Beszélö* and the *Hirmondó* during the 1980s. The human rights principle united the different Marxist, Maoist, liberal socialist and plebeian radical groups into a loose, political alliance. Leaving the extreme leftist approach behind, it became a group of intellectuals with left-liberal views (in an American sense) and radical democratic views (in a French sense) by the mid-1980s. They considered the liberalism and middle-class radicalism of Hungarian political thinkers like Jászi, Csécsy and Bibó as their intellectual forefathers. Their political model was, however, the Polish Solidarity movement. Besides the rights of the citizens, the democratic procedures of the political institution became the centre of their political thinking. Their political critique of the regime also emphasized the lack of individual political rights: the illegal procedures carried out by the police, by the judiciary and by the state administration. Their political ideal has been, since the mid-1980s, a Western-type parliamentary democracy with a strong welfare state. The sociological composition of the 'democratic opposition' was marked by

Budapest urban intellectuals, philosophers, historians, sociologists and economists, with a significant proportion being of Jewish origin.

6. The *moderate opposition* came into existence with the foundation of the *Hungarian Democratic Forum* (HDF) in September 1987. The HDF had its own ideology of the populism. The HDF was founded by populist writers and intellectuals. The HDF tried to keep an intermediate position between the regime and the opposition and enjoyed the support of the reform wing of the ruling Communist Party. The intermediate self-positioning of the HDF between the regime and the radical opposition was due to different factors. The crucial one was the traditional split of the Hungarian intelligentsia between the *populist* and the *urban* wing; therefore the reviving populist movement established its own organization and did not join the 'democratic opposition', which was the political expression of the radical urban intellectuals.

7. For example, F. Fejtö, P. Ignotus, B. Zsolt, I. Hatvany and A. József. The 'urbanists' rallied around journals like the *Századunk*, *Szép Szó*.

8. For example, Gy. Illyés, L. Németh, P. Veres and T. Kovács. The 'populists' wrote in journals like the *Válasz* and *Tanú*.

9. 'Urbanist' liberalism was accused by the populist view of being the intellectual expression of the Budapest Jewish middle class and bourgeoisie. For many 'populists', liberal parliamentarism and Manchesterian liberalism meant first, a danger for the traditional Hungarian values, and second, the reservation of the power monopoly of alien social groups. The populists were for some 'third road' between East and West, between capitalism and socialism. Their ideal was the formation of co-operatives based on private farming in agriculture, private ownership and a free market in small-scale industry and nationalization of the banking system and big business.

10. One of the watersheds was, for example, the interpretation of the 1848 Independence War against the Habsburg-rule and of the 'Pact' of 1867.

11. R.J. Dalton, 'The West German Party System Between Two Ages', in R.J. Dalton, S.C. Flanagan and P.A. Beck, *Electoral Change in Advanced Industrial Democracies: Realignment or Dealignment?*, 1984, pp. 104–33.

12. The view of the SHP is very clear in the case of landed property, where they would like to reinstate the 1947 situation. There were some endeavours within the CDPP to take back the historical role of the churches, involving the plan partly to give back former church property.

13. The Free Democrats considered the former nationalization of industry and the collectivization of the private farms as an historically given fact, which could not be reshaped to the 1947 situation in a fair way. They were more technocratic on the question of privatization and refused the orthodox version of property right.

14. R. Inglehart, 'The Changing Structure of Political Cleavages in Western Society', in R.J. Dalton, S.C. Flanagan and P.A. Beck, *op. cit.*, pp. 25–69.

15. In those 125 single-member constituencies, where both the HDF and the AFD took part in the run-off, the votes for the HDF candidates increased by 29.13 per cent while the votes for the AFD candidates grew by only 4.98 per cent.

16. M. Harrop, 'Voting and Electorate', in H.M. Drucker *et al.*, *Developments in British Politics*, 1986, pp. 34–59.

17. By the inter-war period universal suffrage was introduced, but the secret ballot (except in the 1939 general elections) was limited to the cities. However, the HSDP was excluded from the contest in the countryside and the Communist Party was banned during the whole period.

18. Mid- and South-'Dunántúl' (Danubia) and the 'Alföld' without the 'Tiszántúl' region.
19. Szabolcs-Szatmár county was the only exception from the four south-eastern 'Tiszántúl' regions where the CDPP had candidates (and votes). It is religiously more mixed, with a higher Roman and Greek Catholic population, and the CDPP here has political traditions as well.
20. The three exceptions Borsod, Békés and Vas counties. The correlation is less striking in the case of the 1945 results of the HSDP. Comparing the 1945 HSDP and the 1990 AFD votes, there are positive correlations in only 13 out of the 20 counties.
21. Beside the HSDP two tiny urban liberal parties existed – the Hungarian Radical Party and the Civilian Democratic Party.
22. S.M. Lipset and S. Rokkan, 'Cleavage Structures, Party Systems and Voter Alignments: An Introduction', in S.M. Lipset and S. Rokkan (eds), *Party Systems and Voters Alignments*, pp. 1–64.
23. There are several others, like the durability of the regime, which is especially important in the case of new democratic regimes. G. O'Donnell and P. Schmitter consider the first change of power within a permanent regime (i.e. whether the freely elected democratic government would pass on the power if it is defeated at the following elections). (P.C. Schmitter, G. O'Donnell and L. Whitehead, *Transition from Authoritarian Rule: Prospects for Democracy*, 1986.)
24. The political concept of a semi-presidential regime had already been defeated during the political fight of the winter of 1989–90. The President of the Republic, who has very limited constitutional power, had been elected indirectly, i.e. by the parliament, in summer 1990.
25. Which was carried out parallel with the collectivization of agriculture and the enforcement of the peasantry towards industrial jobs.
26. The votes for the CDPP in Catholic areas, the votes for the SHP in rural Hungary and the votes for the HSP and HSWP in heavy industrial districts demonstrated it.
27. G. Sartori, 'European Political Parties: The Case of Polarized Pluralism', in J. LaPaLambora and M. Wiener (eds), *Political Parties and Political Development*, 1969.
28. A. Lijphart, *Democracy in Plural Societies*, 1977.

10 The making of political fields in post-communist transition (dynamics of class and party in Hungarian politics, 1989–90)[1]

Tamás Kolosi, Iván Szelényi, Szonja Szelényi and

Bruce Western

The research puzzle

In February 1989, the Hungarian Socialist Workers' Party (MSZMP, as the Communist Party was called) formally accepted the principles of multiparty democracy. Within 13 months of this decision, free elections were held and a complex political system emerged in which six parties came to represent distinct 'political fields' in parliament. These 13 months offer a fascinating study of political institution building.

The objective of this paper is to describe the emergent 'political fields'. We will identify the principal issues around which these fields are organized, the political constituencies upon which they draw, the way in which actors competing for these fields emerge, and the process by which their struggle unfolds. Our empirical investigation is confined to Hungary, but many of our conclusions might well be extended to the whole region that is in post-communist transition.[2]

During the post-communist transition, three different political fields are in the making: Christian-nationalist (i.e. centre-right), liberal and social-democratic. The Hungarian elections in March–April 1990 produced an impressive victory of Christian-nationalist parties: the Hungarian Democratic Forum (MDF), the Smallholders' Party (FKgP) and the Christian Democratic Party (KDNP) won almost 60 per cent of the seats in the parliament. The liberals, the Alliance of Free Democrats (SZDSZ) and the Alliance of Young Democrats (FIDESZ) took a third of the votes, while the only party representing the 'left' in the parliament, the Hungarian

Socialist Party (MSZP), had to be content with less than 10 per cent of the seats.[3]

The outcome of the 1990 elections reflected a return to the political traditions. Similar trends can be observed in the whole region. The only exception is Czechoslovakia. Here the victorious Civic Forum – fundamentally a liberal party – opted voluntarily rather than was forced to enter a coalition with the Christian Democrats. Otherwise the shift to the Christian-nationalist centre-right seems to be the dominant trend in the whole non-Balkan region of Central Europe. Such parties won the election or such movements dominate the political discourse in East Germany, Poland, Croatia and Slovenia.[4]

In a way, this is no surprise. The region is returning to its political traditions. An American political commentator recently called the Central European transformations a 'conservative revolution': a return to traditional political, economic and social values.

Just a few facts to support these claims. In early November 1945 the Smallholders' Party, which then represented the centre-right, won 57 per cent of the votes. At the end of May 1938 the Party of Hungarian Life (Magyar Élet Pártja), which then represented the centre-right – its policies were between the social democrats and the pro-Nazi ultra-right – won 70 per cent of the votes. In April–May of 1906, the then moderately centre-right Independence Party (Függetlenségi Párt) gained 62 per cent of all seats.

As the sociologist-commentators have tried to predict events during 1989–90 they have felt themselves seated in a theatre with the curtain still down. They have wondered what may be in preparation behind the curtains after 40 years of Communism. Astonishingly, as the curtain went up the audience was confronted with a still-life: the 'act' which was interrupted by the transition to socialism continued as if nothing has happened.

This return to the past poses the central puzzle for this paper. For political sociologists who try to link political processes to social structure and class relations, this almost boring return to the status quo ante requires some explanation. After 40 years of communist voluntarism, one of course expected that the historical pendulum would now move in the 'right-wing' direction. However, the restoration of pre-war politics needs an explanation. During the previous 40 years, the social structure had undergone fundamental changes. The peasantry and the genteel middle class, the usual social base for the Christian-nationalist course, were virtually eliminated, proletarianized or cadrefied. A large class of industrial workers was created. In the light of these changes, one would have expected a general weakening of the traditional centre-right and a strengthening of social democratic parties. Liberals would be expected to do well as a response to the communist experience, but in the absence of a class of proprietors they would not be anticipated to play a major role. As we saw before, the outcome of the March–April 1990 elections was drastically different. How can one account for the exceptionally poor predictive power of structural factors and the apparent continuity of the political culture?

We shall proceed in four steps and our paper is organized accordingly into four sections: first we will present a hypothetical scheme of post-communist Hungarian social structure, or a 'class map', and we will locate the above-outlined three political fields in this structure.

Second, we shall confront this hypothesis with public opinion poll data. These data were collected after the Hungarian national elections and they provide us with information on the social composition of voters, enabling us to explore how well class structure explains who votes how. The differences in the constituency of Christian-nationalists and liberals at least correspond to what our hypothetical 'class-map' suggests. However, for our analysis the relatively high rate of 'non-vote' is particularly interesting. In the Hungarian two-round voting system, in the second and crucial round 55 per cent of voters stayed at home. We regard this as an astonishingly high rate of indifference at the first free elections ever held in Hungary.[5] In this second step we will not only explore how people with different socio-demographic characteristics vote, but we also analyse the differences in social composition between voters and non-voters.

Third we will analyse attitudes. The opinion poll also generated information on social and economic attitudes, thus we can assess how well constituencies and electoral behaviour, and constituencies and attitudes, 'match'. Like in the earlier section, we shall analyse the differences in political attitudes by party preference, but shall focus our attention on the differences in attitudes among voters and non-voters.

Finally, in the fourth step we will complement the statistical analysis, which mainly operates within the framework of social stratification with an institutionalist interpretation of Central European politics. We will look at the dynamics of political institution building and the problem of leadership, in order to explain why no party was interested, able or willing to speak to that third of the electorate which would normally vote centre-left.

1. Class structure and political fields: theory-driven hypotheses

The post-communist social structure is basically tripolar. In the classical model of state socialism, in which the redistributively integrated economy had the monopoly, there was a single-rank hierarchy (Bauman, 1974; Konrád and Szelényi, 1979; Szelényi, 1986–87; Szelényi, 1988) – the cadres being at the top and the working class at the bottom. With the gradual erosion of the system, this single hierarchy is being complemented by a second hierarchy based on market integration. Both Kolosi and Szelényi noted already during the mid 1980s the emergence of such a new dual social structure (Kolosi, 1988; Szelényi, 1986–87). In this second hierarchy ascent and descent are determined by wealth and entrepreneurship – owners and entrepreneurs being at the top, and their workers at the bottom. As of 1990, Central European societies have not yet become capitalistic; they are – probably temporarily – socialist mixed economies in which the statist sector has retained its dominance, and the market sector, though it is rapidly expanding, still plays only a subordinate, complementary role.

But the post-communist transition, despite the retained hegemonic role of the redistributive sector, has significantly changed the power relationship within the dominant elite. The old cadre elite, whose power and privilege were primarily based on access to political assets, and on loyalty to the party (Sz. Szelényi, 1987) and the boss, is either increasingly isolated and its influence reduced, or forced out of the elite position altogether, unless it succeeds in converting its political assets into cultural assets or economic capital. But within the old elite (those whose privilege was already based on access to cultural assets), the professionals in high ranking positions – especially those who were 'low' on political assets in the past, were even not members of the Communist Party or left it early enough – are now rising in power and privilege. Thus in post-communist transition the elite is highly fragmented. The 'old-line bureaucracy', in the Gouldnerian sense of the term, is shrinking in size and declining in influence, while Gouldner's 'New Class' of intellectuals is becoming hegemonic (Gouldner, 1979). This intellectual and cadre elite itself represents about 5–10 per cent of the total population, with two-thirds or four-fifths of them now belonging to the New Class of technical intelligentsia and humanistic intellectuals in positions of decision-making power.

The emergent new entrepreneurial/ownership class is also fragmented. It is composed of at least three fractions. Its first and largest section can be accurately called the 'new petty bourgeoisie' (this is of course not the poulantzian, but the more conventional use of the term). This is the class which grows out of what used to be the 'second economy'. The class is constituted of small proprietors in agriculture, service industries and in manufacturing. This is potentially a large class-fraction. During the mid 1980s, 10–30 per cent of the population of Hungary already earned half or more of their incomes in 'markets' in the 'second economy', and in family work organizations (Gábor, 1985; Szelényi, 1988). According to the recent opinion polls, the proportion of those who expressed a wish to start their own business was around 25 per cent in mid 1989.[6] This rose to about a third of the respondents by early 1990. This is the proportion of those who aspire to become petty bourgeoisie. The number of actual small entrepreneurs rose fast, it is still small and in autumn 1990 was around 10 per cent.

But there is also another type of entrepreneurial or propertied class in the making: this is that fraction of the former cadre elite who, through management buy-outs or joint ventures with Western firms, successfully converted their political assets into economic capital and became a political bourgeoisie. This is the term used by Jadwiga Staniszkis (1991), but the phenomenon was also noted by Elemér Hankiss and Erzsébet Szalai (Staniszkis, 1989, 1990; Hankiss, 1989a, 1989b; Szalai, 1989a, 1989b). This new propertied class is much smaller in size than the new petty bourgeoisie, but it has attracted a great deal of political interest and it could potentially be of great importance. Though at present its size is small, unlike the new petty bourgeoisie, its political influence may be significant.

Finally, by autumn 1990 foreign capital had begun to play its role in Central Europe. Through joint ventures and by direct investment, through the sale of private firms to foreigners, foreign owners and their 'comprador intelligentsia' (those professionals, who are hired by them to run their local affairs for salaries, which are several times those of domestic professionals) began to play a role. Their number is small – a few multinationals and a few dozen smaller/larger foreign capitalists and a few hundred professionals employed by them – but their influence is considerable. They are present in the media. One of the first areas where foreign capital began to be invested was newspapers – this may be an indication of political aspirations, since ownership of newspapers for the time being or in the foreseeable future hardly promises to be profitable. The extent of the sale of public property to domestic and foreign owners is unknown. However, from what we know it appears that foreigners own less than 10 per cent of all formerly publicly owned assets. Privatization was made legally possible in June 1989. From mid-1989 until autumn 1990, some 50–100 billion forint-worth of property was sold to private proprietors (the majority of this is believed to be to foreign capitalists) out of a total of around 2,000 billion forint-worth of national productive capital.

Finally, the 'third class position', that of the broadly defined working class is also highly fragmented. Here, besides the conventionally known fragmentation of the working class (friction between blue collar and white collar, skilled and unskilled, supervisors and supervised), in Central Europe and in particular in Hungary, the 'second economy' created another and vitally important division within the manual workers – namely between those involved and those left out of the second economy (Szelényi, 1986–87). By the mid-1980s about two-thirds of Hungarian income earners gained incomes from the second economy. Most of them lived mainly from their wages and salaries but a growing proportion had a genuinely dual existence between market and redistribution: they earned incomes both from the government and from private economic activities. The second economy introduced a division in the working class which cut across other sources of class fragmentation (Kolosi, 1989). Most significantly, the urban proletariat in heavy industry, the best paid fraction of the industrial working class during the classical epoch of redistributive economy, were the least likely to be able to earn incomes from the second economy. This traditional industrial proletariat had the least to gain and most to lose from marketization and privatization. The current shift from state socialism towards capitalism may seriously threaten many of them. Jobs in heavy industry and manufacturing are the most likely to disappear if Central European economies adapt their economic structure to the capitalist world system.

Hypothetically, we believe we can locate the three 'political fields' among these three fundamental class positions. The liberal field opens between the intellectual elite, especially among its technocratic fraction, and the new entrepreneurial class. SZDSZ and FIDESZ are the two parties which competed so far for this field. In an interview, Bálint Magyar, one of the main and most articulate theorists of SZDSZ, put it quite unambiguously: 'our social base is composed of three groups – the radical salaried workers, the small entrepreneurs and a significant proportion of the intelligentsia.' It is significant that he – in our judgement accurately – uses the term 'salaried workers' (*alkalmazottak*) and not 'wage earners' (*munkások*), thus recognizing the white collar instead of blue collar support his party seeks and gets.[7]

The Christian-nationalist field, on the other hand, is located between the entrepreneurial class and the working class. In particular, it links those fractions of the working class who work in the second economy (in terms of their social status they are semi-proletarian and semi-petty bourgeois) with the new petty bourgeoisie. The Christian-nationalist field reaches out towards the emergent large bourgeoisie as well. This field in Hungary is contested by MDF, FKgP and KDNP. The relative success of the 'centre-right' in Hungarian politics – beyond the reasons of political culture mentioned above – can be explained by the exceptionally large size of the semi-proletarian, semi-petty bourgeois masses.

Finally, the social democratic field opens up between the working class and the intellectual elite. During the mid-1980s we noted that the old-line bureaucracy may try to counteract the market-oriented reforms by trying to create a class alliance with those fractions of the proletariat who are left out of the benefits of the market, and are threatened by marketization and privatization. With the current dramatic shift towards a capitalist economy, that fraction of the working population which may suffer from the transition to capitalism (lose their jobs, fall into poverty) may be increasing rapidly. This fraction of the working class may find allies not just or primarily in the old-line Stalinist bureaucracy, but among those professionals who either have ideological reservations about full-scale privatization or on ethical grounds want to defend the institutions of the welfare state. Some of these professions may also be threatened existentially by the current transformations. Not only workers lose their jobs if profit criteria decide who can keep their jobs, so do many professionals in social science research, film, publishing, etc. There are thus professionals who for various reasons may find it difficult to cope with the demands of the emergent market economy, and they may be interested in defending the kind of role for the state that Western social-democrats typically stand for.

Schematically, we can describe the emergent new social structure and political fields as shown in Figure 10.1.

Figure 10.1 has some explanatory power. It foreshadows a centre-right victory and allows for a good showing of liberals (depending what proportion of the new petty bourgeois vote they can get). The shortcoming of the figure is that it could not predict the poor showing of parties competing for the social democratic field: they only won 8 per cent of the seats, though our figure would predict at least 20 if not 30 per cent for them. We assume workers involved in the second economy would

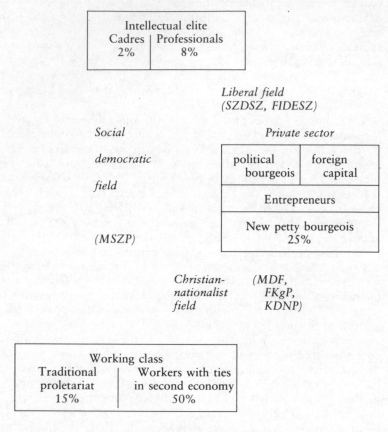

Statist sector

Intellectual elite
Cadres | Professionals
2% | 8%

Liberal field
(SZDSZ, FIDESZ)

Social

democratic

Private sector

political bourgeois | foreign capital

field

Entrepreneurs

New petty bourgeois
25%

(MSZP)

Christian-   *(MDF,*
nationalist   *FKgP,*
field   *KDNP)*

Working class
Traditional proletariat | Workers with ties in second economy
15% | 50%

Figure 10.1 Social structure and political fields in the transition to post-Communism (the case of Hungary, 1989–1990)

represent the 'swing-vote' for social democrats: if they vote as wage earners the social democratic vote can be above 30 per cent, if they vote as petty bourgeois the left vote can be as low as 20 per cent. The failure of social democracy requires an explanation.

First we shall analyse the quantitative data. With these data we shall try to substantiate two claims: 1. the social composition of voters of liberal and the Christian-nationalist parties are reasonably accurately predicted with our theory; and 2. what are the social characteristics of those who did not vote? Could they be the potential social democratic constituency? Is it possible that they decided not to show up at the elections because none of the parties articulated their interests? During the first round 35 per cent and in the second round 55 per cent of the electorate decided they did not have a stake in this election. The key to the future of

Hungary and possibly to that of the whole region, is which way this 'silent majority' will go? Who can mobilize them and with what kind of political programme? Even if one assumes that 20–25 per cent abstention is 'normal', some 30–35 per cent of the votes are up for grabs out there.

2. The effect of class on party preferences and the explanatory power of social structural variables in discriminating between voters and non-voters

First, we shall present the data, hypothesis and research strategy for our quantitative analysis both for this section and the third section; then we will present our findings on the social composition of constituencies of different parties and differences between voters and non-voters in terms of their socio-demographic characteristics.

Data and variables for quantitative analysis

In May 1990 TARKI conducted a public opinion poll with 981 respondents from a national random sample of the population. They asked their respondents if they voted or not at each round of the elections, how they voted and they also asked a series of political attitude questions both on 'economic' and 'social' issues. After sorting out the data we were left with 694 responses for the first round and 527 for the second round that we were able to analyse, the answers of other respondents being lost for various technical reasons.

This amount of missing data could result in a non-representative sample of completely observed cases and the resulting estimates would be biased. We have therefore weighted the data to correct for sample bias. The weights are calculated so that the joint distribution of the completely observed variables (age, sex and education) in the reduced sample with missing responses discarded, is the same as their joint distribution in the full sample.

Our independent variables are education; occupation (in which blue collars and white collars are split into upper and lower strata according to the level of their education, skilled workers being coded into the upper, semi- and unskilled workers into the lower strata of workers, professionals, those holding university degrees into the upper, high school graduates, clerical workers in the lower stratum of white collars; agricultural physical workers both in the collectives and private sector are coded as farmers); age; and sex.

We use two types of dependent variables. One of our key dependent variables is party preference: which party did people vote for. In the regression models voting behaviour is measured by four indicators: V1 refers to those who voted in the first round, V2 to voters in the second round, MDF1 to those who voted MDF during the first round and MDF2 to those who voted MDF in the second round.

We also use political attitudes as variables (both dependent and independent). We created three attitude variables both for the cross-tabs and for the regression models and analysis of variance; each of them are composed of several items. These are: CIVIL which is composed of measures of civil liberties and civil rights issues;[8] W1 contains those economic items which are linked to questions of 'safety-net',[9] thus those who expressed strong preferences on W1 basically share centre or right-wing social democratic values; W2 contains measures related to job security and social inequality.[10] Those who express moderate or strong support for such propositions are sympathetic to the left labour party policies.

In this analysis we estimate separate regression models for each dependent variable and we use component scales to estimate the attitude effects. Ordinary least squares are used to estimate the models of the attitudes. Logistic regression is used for the models of the turn-out and vote choice.

Data-driven hypotheses

We intend to test the following hypotheses:

1. We expect some difference in the social composition of those who vote Christian-nationalist and liberal. We expect the Christian-nationalist parties to win more votes from the lower classes and from the older people, while the liberals should get a higher proportion of their votes from the better educated and from the younger generation;
2. We expect that occupation and education will have a greater explanatory power when our task is to predict who votes and who does not.
3. We expect the lower classes to be over-represented among non-voters, especially among those who did not vote during the first round of the elections.
4. In the second round of elections we expect there to be a weaker link between structural variables and voting behaviour, since in the second round those whose candidates were eliminated in the first round mainly did not vote, thus here the effects which operated cross-cut each other;
5. We expect to find some difference in the political attitudes of the Christian-nationalist and liberal voters. We expect to find most of this difference in social issues, the Christian-nationalists being more conservative, and the liberals – by definition – being more liberal.
6. We expect major differences in political attitudes, especially economic attitudes, between voters and non-voters. We expect that non-voters will be much more committed to social democratic, and in particular to left-labourite, values – not articulated by any of the parties – than voters.

Strategy of analysis

We shall begin our analysis with descriptive statistics[11] and we will show the differences in the constituencies' voting for different parties in terms of their education, occupation, age and sex. We will look at differences in party preference, and also at differences between voters and non-voters. We will also compare the two rounds of the elections to find out if the impact of our independent, structural variables increased or decreased between the two rounds.

We shall also begin our analysis in section 3 with descriptive statistics on political attitudes and we will explore the power of our independent variables in explaining variance in attitudes. In addition, we shall analyse cross-tabulations between political attitudes and party choice and the differences in attitudes between voters and non-voters.

These descriptive statistics are not sufficient to test in a rigorous way our above-outlined hypotheses. For hypothesis testing we rely on multivariate analysis.

First, we build a series of logistic regression models. We begin the analysis with a baseline model (MODEL1 – columns (1) and (3) and Tables 10.1 and 10.2) in which our independent variables are occupation, age and sex. We construct MODEL1 with four different dependent variables – VOTE1, VOTE2, MDF1 and MDF2.

Next, we expand our baseline model and include our attitude variables (CIVIL, W1 and W2) as independent variables, thus we build MODEL2. We construct MODEL2 also with four different dependent variables, thus with VOTE1, VOTE2, MDF1 and MDF2.

Thus we analyse the following eight models:[12]

MODEL1VOTE1 = Table 10.1 column (1)
MODEL1VOTE2 = Table 10.2 column (1)

MODEL1MDF1 = Table 10.1 column (3)
MODEL1MDF2 = Table 10.2 column (3)

MODEL2VOTE1 = Table 10.1 column (2)
MODEL2VOTE2 = Table 10.2 column (2)

MODEL2MDF1 = Table 10.1 column (4)
MODEL2MDF2 = Table 10.2 column (4)

Hypothesis (1) will be supported if in MODEL1MDF1 the occupation will not have a particularly strong effect. It would be damaging to our hypotheses if lower class were to have a strong negative effect in this model.

Hypotheses (2) will be supported if MODEL1VOTE1 produces a better fit than MODEL1MDF1.

In order to find support for Hypothesis (3), we expect that in MODEL1VOTE1 higher occupations will have significantly higher positive parameters than lower occupations.

Hypothesis (4) will be supported if MODEL1VOTE1 and MODEL1MDF1 produces a significantly better fit, than MODEL1VOTE2 and MODEL1MDF2.

Hypothesis (5) assumes that in MODEL2MDF1 W2 will not be negative, and may even not be significant, but CIVIL will be negative and significant.

Finally, Hypothesis (6) is not falsified as long as in MODEL2VOTE1 W2 has a significant and negative parameter.

We also calculate the OLS regression scores W1, W2 and CIVIL as dependent, and age, sex and occupation as independent variables (Table 10.3, columns (1), (2) and (3) respectively). Hypotheses (5) and (6) will be supported if in the case of W2 a strong and positive lower class and strong and negative upper class parameters are found; in the case of CIVIL we expect the opposite, thus we expect to find robust and positive parameters from the upper classes, and we have no hypotheses as to what parameters the lower classes will have.

Findings: class determinants of party votes

After we presented our 'class map' we noted that the better electoral performance of the Christian-nationalist parties was according to our expectations, since they draw more on the lower classes. These lower classes – according to our theory – fall outside the reach of the liberal field. The TARKI data now enable us to assess if indeed there is any difference in the social composition of Christian-nationalist and liberal voters.

The cross-tabulations show a weak effect of class on party preference, but the effect goes in the direction predicted by our class map for a Christian-nationalist and liberal comparison.

Both the MDF and the SZDSZ received significantly less votes from lower blue collar workers and from those with only primary school education. However, it is still beyond doubt that the Christian-nationalist centre-right reached out more effectively towards the bottom of the social hierarchy. This can be shown by the MDF-SZDSZ comparison. While the MDF did not do badly among the lower blue collar workers it received many upper blue collar votes, while the SZDSZ did a little worse in this occupational category. The MDF received almost 3 per cent more votes from upper blue collar workers than its average vote, while the SZDSZ received 1.5 per cent fewer votes from this stratum. Furthermore, the SZDSZ received significantly fewer votes not only from those with primary school education, but also from those on the next educational level, those who had completed primary school and gone on to vocational training. In this educational category the vote cast for the MDF did not differ significantly from the average. The most striking difference between the MDF and the SZDSZ is in their support from farmers. While the farmers' vote was below average for both parties, in the case of the MDF this was only down by 3 per cent, while for the SZDSZ it was down by more than 11 per cent.

The better appeal of the Christian-nationalist field to the bottom third of the population is further supported by the electoral performance of the MDF's coalition partners – the FKgP and the KDNP. Both these parties received average or significantly above average votes from both categories of blue collar workers and farmers, and an above average amount of votes for the two bottom educational categories.

On the whole the MDF was the most balanced, the least class- or a stratum-based party. It reached out effectively to all social categories. Its weakness at the bottom of the social hierarchy is less pronounced than the weakness of the SZDSZ and it is compensated for by the constituencies of its coalition partners. The constituency of the SZDSZ's coalition partner, the FIDESZ, on the other hand, is less skewed towards the top than the SZDSZ is, but it is nonetheless skewed in the same direction and so does not compensate for the SZDSZ's lack of appeal to the lower classes.[13]

These data clearly prove Bálint Magyar right. While among those with tertiary education both the MDF and the SZDSZ receive votes far above their average, in this category the MDF does slightly – their difference is only marginally significant – better, than the SZDSZ does. However, the difference between the MDF and the SZDSZ among white collars is quite impressive: the SZDSZ was indeed doing extremely well among the routine white collar population. While the MDF received 2.3 per cent fewer votes from routine white collars than its average vote, the SZDSZ's electoral support in this stratum was 6.4 per cent above its average, which is a robustly significant difference.

From party choices it is impossible to substantiate our hypothesis concerning a social democratic constituency. The only party, the MSZP, which came the closest in its programme to a Western-style social democratic platform not only received few votes, but its constituency systematically came from the top of the social hierarchy; its vote from upper white collar workers was almost twice its average vote, while it received even less support from the workers than the SZDSZ. The MSZP was the least working class and the most intellectual party in the whole political landscape in Hungary during 1990.

Though the correlation is not overwhelming, and obviously class was not decisive in the struggle between the SZDSZ and the MDF, already the votes for the party list during the first round correspond to the predictions of the possible constituencies of the two political fields. As our theory predicted, the Christian-nationalist parties were doing better among the less educated and working class, while the liberals mainly appealed to white collars and the intelligentsia. Still, on the whole, class is a rather poor predictor of choice among parties, it explains only a fraction of the variance.

The demographic variables, age and sex, add little to our understanding of party choice. On the whole, men and older people are slightly more likely to cast their votes for the Christian-nationalists, while women and younger people are more likely to vote liberal.

The MDF received significantly less votes from those under 40 than its average vote, while the SZDSZ and of course the FIDESZ did the opposite: from this cohort they received significantly more votes than one could expect on average performance. The MDF got very strong support from the middle aged (those between 40 and 60), while the FKgP, and in particular the KDNP, had very strong support among those over 60.

The gender effect is less pronounced and is only marginally significant, though the tendency appears to be quite clear. The MDF and the FKgP together have a significant male majority (while the third party of the ruling coalition, the KDNP, seems to be more likely to receive women's votes). The SZDSZ and the FIDESZ together seem to be slightly more appealing to women voters. This is interesting and as we will see shortly somewhat inconsistent with our other results. When it comes to attitudes, women seem to be significantly less liberal than men. This is a particularly complex puzzle to solve, since liberalism on social issues (on the CIVIL variable) is a strong predictor of the liberal vote, which cross-cuts the gender effect. We will need a more detailed analysis, which can only be included in another study on the gender dynamics of post-communist politics.

Between the two rounds of elections the social base of the two major competing parties did not change drastically. Both parties became slightly more balanced, and the power of class as a predictor seemed to have declined. There is no dramatic shift in voting patterns either in terms of age or gender effect on party choice between the two rounds of the elections.

The baseline models (MODEL1) in our logistic regression analysis reconfirms the above interpretations of our descriptive statistics. First of all, in MODEL1MDF1 the parameters for upper blue collar workers and farmers are positive and for farmers the parameter is quite robust; the lower white collar parameter is negative and significantly so; while the upper white collar parameter is not significant. This indeed offers support to Hypothesis (1). The gender effect is not significant, thus what appeared to be a gender effect from the cross-tabulations disappears when one looks at the data in terms of age and occupation, but the age effect remains significant though weak.

MODEL1VOTE1 produces a slightly better fit than MODEL1MDF1,[14] though interestingly for MODEL1VOTE2 and MODEL1MDF2 this changes, and in Table 10.2 column (3) indicates a better fit than column (1). This later finding questions the validity of Hypothesis (3), as it suggests that the relative importance of class differences changes in the opposite direction to that predicted in the second round of voting; in comparison with the first one, they are becoming less important for predicting abstention from voting and *relatively* more important for predicting who will vote MDF or SZDSZ.

Findings: class as predictor of abstention from voting

One key hypothesis of this paper is that high degree of abstention from voting requires explanation, and that class will better explain abstention from voting than party choice.

In this chapter we can't explore in any systematic way how unique this level of abstention from voting is and how unique the weak predictive power of class is for party preference and the better performance of this variable, when the task is the prediction of non-voting. Like on the question of gender effect, we are planning to write another article comparing Hungarian voting behaviour with voting studies from other countries, such as the United States and Great Britain. Thus while this analysis will have to be done at a later point in time, our working hypothesis is that in both respects the 1990 Hungarian elections and possibly elections in other post-communist societies in the recent past or near future are unique. We would like to support this with two claims: 1. while 35–55 per cent abstention from elections is quite 'normal' in Western democracies (and in electoral systems, which operate with two rounds, voters interest frequently declines the second time around), such apathy at the *first* free elections ever held in a country is still surprising; 2. while it may not be that surprising that among non-voters the less educated are over-represented in European political systems, especially in countries where social democratic parties compete in elections, there is a stronger class effect on party preference elsewhere than in Hungary. Our minimum hypothesis is that while class may indeed always be a good predictor of abstention from voting, the difference in the power of class in explaining party preference or predicting abstention from voting was unusually high in the 1990 Hungarian elections.

The descriptive statistics indicate the robust class effect on abstention from voting. The population is split into two groups by education: those with high school diplomas or above are much more likely to vote than those who did not finish high school. It is particularly obvious that those who have only primary school education, or did not even finish primary school, are the least likely to vote. Abstention from voting is also highly correlated with occupation – lower blue collar workers and farmers are the least likely to vote, upper blue collar workers votes are around average, while the participation in voting rapidly increases from lower white collars to upper white collars. One of the largest statistical differences we could find in the data was in the abstention from voting of upper white collars in comparison with average abstention: 17 per cent fewer white collars abstained from voting than the average. The difference between farmers and upper white collar workers is 30 per cent.

Thus our cross-tabs indicate a massive class effect on abstention from voting. The demographic variables on the other hand play a lesser effect than in the explanation of party preference. There is no significant gender difference among voters and non-voters. Age has a significant effect and quite surprisingly the older are much more likely to vote than the younger. Abstention from voting gradually decreases, the difference between those older than 60 and those younger than 40 being already 10 per cent. The oldest age-group is significantly more likely to vote, and the youngest cohort is significantly less. This cuts across the class effect.

Younger people are on average more educated, thus the apathy of the youngest cohort is particularly notable. The explanation that older people have more experience of multiparty democracy does not hold much water: those who were 60 in 1990 were too young during the post-war years to take party in elections – only those who are aged 65–70 had voted once or more than once in freely contested elections.

The base-line logistic regression models with VOTE1 and VOTE2 as dependent variables give further and more rigorous support to our hypothesis that abstention from voting is class-determined. MODEL1-VOTE1 produces a good fit (all false positive and negative rates add up to only 66.6 per cent), and this is slightly better than the fit of MODEL1MDF1 (the difference is 12.8 per cent). This difference offers the strongest support so far that class is indeed a more powerful predictor of voting than vote choice. The detailed parameters of MODEL1VOTE1 further strengthen this claim. While the value of the AGE parameter does not vary much between MODEL1VOTE1 and MODEL1MDF1, in MODEL1VOTE1 the value of class parameters jump several-fold.

The greater likelihood of abstention from voting of the less educated blue collar workers can be interpreted in different ways. First, this may indicate their lack of interest in politics altogether, or it may be that none of the parties offered a political package to them that they felt may make a difference. Accordingly, one could offer two alternative theories, one about 'apathy' and the second about the 'social-democratic constituency'; thus one would conceptualize the non-vote as protest against the lack of a social democratic alternative.

Obviously both factors worked. A question was asked about political participation/interest. The non-voters of course reported less interest in politics, though about a third of them did express an interest. Two measures of political interest/apathy were used: 1. how often do you discuss political issues? and 2. how interested are you in politics? For the first measure, on a three-point scale ranging from 'not at all' to 'frequently' the distribution of non-voters was 34.9, 44.3 and 20.9 per cent. The distribution of those who voted was 25.5, 47.1 and 27.4 per cent. As far as the second measure is concerned, 34.9 per cent of non-voters said they were 'quite interested' or 'very interested; the same answer was given by 47.1 per cent of the 'voters'. These are significant and important differences, but they are actually smaller than the class effects of non-voting. Thus 'apathy' explains only part of the story.

The finding that class participation is more prevalent than class voting is a striking contrast to the post-war trend in Western European electoral politics. Comparative researchers have shown that in Scandinavian countries participation varies relatively little across class lines, but that vote choice continues to be shaped by class position (Korpi, 1983, pp. 60–64, 87–89; Esping Andersen, 1987). In Sweden, for example, workers are only 2 per cent less likely to vote than others, while they are 40 per cent more likely than others to vote for a left party (Korpi, 1983, pp. 61, 88). While this relationship is perhaps unsurprising for the archetypal class parties of Northern Europe, similar although less spectacular effects can be found in Britain where turn-out is about 15 per cent lower (Rose, 1989, pp. 154, 164, Table VI.4).

. Researchers have also distinguished the United States from Western Europe as in the U.S., as in Hungary, there is no major left party to attract workers to the polls. In the U.S., class has a strong effect on participation but is only weakly related to vote choice (Lipset, 1963, p. 194; ch. 7). Comparative political sociology therefore indicates both the unique and the ordinary in the Hungarian case. On the one hand, Hungary stands apart from its Western European counterparts where there is more class voting than class participation. On the other hand, this seems consistent with a more general pattern in which the presence of a labour or social democratic party tends to equalize class participation in elections.

We also found quite a strong correlation between political attitudes and voting behaviour. The non-voters seem to demonstrate a profile in terms of their political attitudes which is quite distinct from the political attitudes of the voters. We will try to show that the political attitude profile of non-voters offers some further evidence to support the fact that among non-voters those with social-democratic values were significantly over-represented.

3. Political attitudes and voting behaviour

The punchline of our analysis so far is this: while class explains relatively little regarding party choice (at least in the first round of the elections) – there is no striking difference in the social composition of the constituency of the two largest parties, they both are skewed towards the middle and upper middle of the social hierarchy – the silent majority, the non-voters, are strikingly different in their class composition from the voters. Those who abstained from voting, particularly during both rounds of the elections, come from social strata that, in countries with labour parties like Great Britain and Australia, would usually vote social democratic.

In this section of the chapter we want to offer evidence that non-voters are not only more like social democratic voters in terms of their social composition, but they are also more likely to share the values that left-wing labour parties advocate. We want to look therefore at the political attitudes, to explore who has what kind of attitudes and how these attitudes are related to party choice and to abstention from voting.

We expect that political attitudes will greatly influence voting behaviour, and in two ways: 1. As far as party preferences are concerned, in the absence of class determination attitudes about social issues will be particularly important in explaining who votes for which party. Thus, we anticipate that the inclusion of political attitudes into our logistic regression models will significantly improve the fit of the model when the dependent variable is MDF1 (this is MODEL2MDF1 in comparison with MODEL2MDF1).[15] In MODEL2MDF1 we expect CIVIL to perform well and to have a negative parameter and this is indeed the case;

2. Abstention from voting is well explained by class. As a result the inclusion of attitude variables in the models with VOTE1 as the dependent variable does not improve the fit significantly.[16] But the effect to some extent is still mediated by political attitudes. In particular, those who score 'left' of W2 will be the least likely to vote. Thus from our extended MODEL2VOTE1 we would expect to have a significant negative effect of W2, which is indeed the case.

In this section we will perform two tasks: 1. We will explore the correlation between socio-demographic variables and political attitudes. After a brief exploration of descriptive statistics, we will present results of regression analysis using W1, W2 and CIVIL as dependent variables (Table 10.3); 2. We will analyse the correlation between party preference and abstention from voting and political attitudes, thus here we will use political attitude as an independent variable. We shall conclude this exercise by expanding our logistic regression models, including the political attitude variables and testing the above-outlined detailed hypothesis that we gained by including political attitudes in our analysis.

The effect of socio-demographic variables on political attitudes

We created from several items three political attitude variables: CIVIL measures attitudes about civil liberties, W1 attitudes towards 'safety-net' issues, and W2 attitudes towards 'job-security and social equality'.

The generally surprising result is how strongly 'left' Hungarian public opinion was both in W1 and W2. While the dominant political rhetoric is already cast in the discourse of liberal capitalism on most economic items, Hungarian respondents expressed a desire for a social-democratic welfare state with a significant role for the government in assuring work and housing for everybody and in decreasing social inequalities. For example, about 90 per cent of the respondents believed the government ought to assure work for everybody, more than 80 per cent wanted the government to intervene and decrease social inequalities, and of course between 80 and 90 per cent of the respondents wanted the government to spend more on education, health care and other usual social welfare institutions. This huge discrepancy between the hegemonic political discourse and public opinion may be a sufficient explanation for voters' apathy.

If we separate these items into two factors, W1 and W2, we can observe that these two sets of attitudes are shared by different social strata. The two measures are also skewed in different directions: while W1 is skewed towards the 'left', W2 is skewed towards the centre. On a three-point scale, the overwhelming majority of the respondents scored on W1 as 'moderately' or 'strongly' supportive of a 'left-wing' position, while on W2 the swing goes in the other direction – here the overwhelming majority expressed only 'weak' or at best 'moderate' support for the 'left' values or policies.

There is quite a sharp class effect on both W1 and W2, both in terms of education and occupation, but the effect goes in the opposite direction. On W1, the better educated and members of higher classes are more likely to be on the 'left' (for instance, while blue collars and farmers are divided 60 to 40 among moderate and strong supporters of 'left' policies, the division of the two white collar groups is 50 to 50). The same holds for education; among those with tertiary education, 54 per cent are strongly in favour of creating and maintaining a safety net, while among those whose education is only primary school or less this is only 40 per cent. On W2 exactly the opposite is the case: among those with only primary education, about 60 per cent supports at least moderate 'job security and equality' policies, but among the university graduates this falls to only 10 per cent. About 60 per cent of farmers and low blue collar workers offers at least moderate support for W2, while among white collars this proportion is down to 10 per cent.

Both age and gender are closely correlated with W1 and W2. Younger people are more likely to be 'strong' on W1 and weak on W2, which is surprising since in abstention from voting younger people behave like the bottom third of the population (thus they are not very likely to vote), but obviously for different reasons. Women are more likely to be more 'moderate' or 'strong' on W2 than men. This is also surprising since we know that women vote more for the liberals, who otherwise get votes from the more highly educated, who would be the most strongly opposed to W2.

In terms of political attitudes about economic issues, the Hungarian electorate – unlike their professional politicians – seem to profess social-democratic values, but the upper half of the social hierarchy is supportive of a West German type of right-wing social democratic system, while the bottom half of the social hierarchy expresses more interest in a British-style Labour Party platform. This is somewhat contradicted by the fact that at the same time among the same respondents, about two-thirds of them also wanted less state intervention, about three-quarters of them were sympathetic towards privatization, and four-fifths of them had no objection to the foreign purchase of Hungarian national assets. People have attitudes that are fluid and somewhat inconsistent, which may be not that surprising in the current, rapidly changing socio-economic situation.

In the cross-tabs CIVIL works in the anticipated way. The class effect is slightly weaker than in the case of W2 but it is there, and as anticipated it means that the further you go up the social hierarchy, the more people score 'left' on social issues.

There is a greater age and gender effect on CIVIL than on W1 and W2. Women and older people score more 'right-wing' on the social issues items; they are more likely to oppose strikes and demonstrations, and are more sceptical about the right to free speech. This contradicts the voting behaviour of people belonging to these categories; women who vote liberal supposedly should be 'left' on these issues, and the young here again obviously abstained from voting for different reasons from the less educated or less qualified – the latter ones score conservative, while the young people score liberal on CIVIL.

The regression analysis in which W1, W2 and CIVIL are used as dependent variables does not contradict the findings of the descriptive statistics and they contain few surprises, though the anticipated effects are slight. While class is important in explaining CIVIL in this mode, the striking fact is the strong performance of gender, which in Table 10.3 column (3) performs almost as well as the class variables. The model with W1 produces in general a weaker fit than the models with W2 and CIVIL, but while in comparison with the model with CIVIL as dependent variable the effect of gender is greatly reduced, at least some of the class indicators retain most of their strength; and while farmers did not show a significantly different attitude towards CIVIL, now they come out in support of W2. The model with W1 produces a weak fit but the parameters go in the anticipated direction – W1 gets more support from the top of the social hierarchy than from the bottom.

The impact of political attitudes on voting behaviour

Differences in political attitudes may be responsible for the fact that class predicts voting better than vote choice. The MDF and the SZDSZ campaigned on 'social issues' or 'ethical issues', the SZDSZ being very outspoken on civil liberties and attacking the MDF for not being sufficiently committed to those liberties. The MDF, though it accepted civil liberties and human rights, ranked closer to a conservative position on these issues. The closing speeches by the two party leaders on TV just before the vital second round of the elections, describe this difference well. Mr. Antall promised that those who vote for the MDF will vote for 'the quiet force', while Mr. Kis, the leader of the SZDSZ, promised a 'radical change' and a 'smashing of the party state'.

But on economic issues the two parties differed little – both advocated privatization and free markets, and neither of them paid too much attention to questions such as unemployment, inequalities etc. Thus our main contention is that while the MDF and the SZDSZ offered a rather clear choice between conservative and liberal values on social issues, neither of them appealed to those who wanted to cast their vote for the welfare state, security of employment and egalitarian social policies.

The difference between the voters and non-voters is smaller on social issues and more pronounced on economic issues. While generally it is true that the non-voters are more conservative on social issues, CIVIL is more closely associated with party choice than with voting. Most astonishing is the opinion on strikes: 60 per cent of the non-voters opposed strikes, while only 48 per cent of the voters did so. Non-voters being more working class, one would expect them to be more pro-strike.[17]

Economic measures, especially W2 and to a lesser extent W1, are important to predict who does not vote. Those who vote are more likely to be 'left' on W1 and 'right' on W2.

As far as party choice is concerned, political attitudes have exactly the opposite type of effect: MDF and SZDSZ voters differ little from each other on economic issues W1 and W2. SZDSZ voters on W2 are slightly to the right of MDF voters, but the difference is far less significant than it was among voters and non-voters. However, while CIVIL was not important in determining who will vote and who will not, it offers the best possible explanation as to who voted MDF and SZDSZ – SZDSZ voters scoring much more on the liberal and MDF voters on the conservative end of the scale.

One also finds that education and gender have an extremely strong effect on these political attitudes. The less educated, blue collar workers and women seem to share the political profile of non-voters even if they voted. The dramatic gap is between those with tertiary education and the rest of the population. Thus, for instance, among those educated to the tertiary level the proportion of those who do not think the state should reduce inequalities jumps to 38.7 per cent (among those with primary education this is 10.1 per cent, and among those with secondary education it is 16.7 per cent), or the proportion of those who think it is a good idea for the government to regulate wages climbs from the modest 11.8 per cent among the tertiary educated, to the impressive 42.8 per cent among those with only primary education.

Our extended logistic regression models support our hypotheses in several ways. First of all, MODEL2VOTE1 produces a slightly better fit than MODEL2MDF1 (the difference between the false positive rates is a modest 6.2 per cent, favouring MODEL2VOTE1). In MODEL2VOTE1, W2 shows a strong effect while CIVIL is not significant, and exactly the opposite is the case in MODEL2MDF1, namely here CIVIL is a strong variable – it works as well or better than most class measures – and as anticipated, and since this model predicts who votes MDF is has a negative value. When we move from the first round to the second round of the elections, the fit of the model with MDF2 remains about the same as it was with MDF1, while the fit of the model with VOTE2 gets worse than it was with VOTE1. It is particularly interesting to note that in MODEL2MDF2 (Table 10.2, column (4)), the explanatory power of CIVIL becomes even stronger; only age produces an even more significant association with MDF votes than conservative attitudes towards civil rights issues. The MDF's victory in the second round is thus a victory for conservatism. In MODEL2MDF2 neither W1 nor W2 is significant and the class variables are also quite weak.

Our major conclusion is that there is indeed a large social-democratic constituency (both in terms of their class position and the nature of their political attitudes) in Hungary. This constituency, however, was unrepresented during the last elections. People with such views usually did not bother to vote, or if they voted they cast their ballots almost randomly. Hungarian political parties are skating on thin ice. What we see of Hungarian politics is only the tip of the iceberg and dramatic changes can easily occur. The strong correlation between the welfare statist values and conservative values makes the situation particularly explosive. This constituency can be mobilized either around welfare issues or around issues of law and order – i.e. around conservative values. The

MDF has probably won, since it scared away less of those concerned for welfare and drew towards it at the same time more of those with conservative values. But a 'Peronist' regime is as much within the range of possible futures for Central Europe as a West European-style welfare state.

4. Why was the social-democratic constituency unrepresented? The dynamics of institution building and the role of political leadership

The question our following analysis should try to find an answer to is this: if there is a potential social-democratic constituency, why could no party 'cash in' on this? So far our analysis has been framed a bit rigidly within a structuralist framework, but now we ought to shift slightly in the institutionalist direction. In these closing remarks we will try to show that the unique dynamics of political institution building and questions of political leadership are probably as important as social composition of potential constituencies in the process of making political fields.

First, we will briefly review the history of the SZDSZ–MDF struggle, and will try to explain what institutional dynamics led to the defeat of the SZDSZ.

During the summer of 1989 the SZDSZ perceived the MDF as a centre-left party with close links to the Communists, especially to its populist wing represented by Imre Pozsgay. As a result, the SZDSZ focused its fire on the left of the MDF. Bálint Magyar, in an interview during the summer of 1989, called the MDF a crypto-communist party – Pozsgay's invention to prepare himself for the collapse of Communism and preserve his power base. The MDF was viewed as the equivalent of the so-called Peasant Party after 1945, which indeed was the gathering of a number of left-wing populist writers, the party of the 'Third Way', which proved to be only communist 'fellow travellers'.

The MDF did not quite know how to handle this challenge. The SZDSZ made a major coup during the autumn by attacking the MDF–MSZP link around the issue of presidential elections. It appeared that the MDF, which during spring–summer 1989 was beyond any doubt the major opposition party (in polls, by late summer/early autumn it was receiving 25–30 per cent of the 'votes', while the SZDSZ and the FIDESZ trailed behind with 5–8 per cent each), had made a deal with the MSZP. According to this deal, the MDF will give a relatively strong presidency to the MSZP, and personally to Pozsgay, while the MDF will form the government, but possibly they will have the MSZP in the government as 'junior partners'. The way to get there was to hold early presidential elections (following the Polish patterns, which also allowed the election of Jaruzelski as president for the transition period). If elections could be held by the end of 1989 or very early in 1990, it appeared to be guaranteed that Pozsgay would win. He was far ahead of anybody else in public opinion polls. The opposition politicians had not had a chance yet to make their names known. In late September, an agreement was indeed reached in the opposition–Communist Party negotiations; it was to have the presidential election first sometime late in 1989, and then to have the parliamentary election early in 1990.

The SZDSZ, with good political instinct, did not sign this agreement but called for a referendum. According to Hungarian law the parliament has to call for a referendum if more than 100,000 signatures demand it. The SZDSZ easily collected 200,000 signatures and at the end of November this crucial referendum was held. The MDF was in total disarray as to how to respond. They sensed that their ties to Pozsgay were becoming a handicap to them and that they would have to demonstrate some distance from the MSZP. The MSZP advised its supporters to vote 'no' at the referendum (the referendum was about having the parliamentary elections before the presidential elections, thus those voting 'no', voted for an early presidential election and by implication for the presidency of Pozsgay). The MDF finally opted for the worst possible strategy. It did not dare to encourage its constituency to vote the way the MSZP wanted, but it called for a boycott of the referendum. According to Hungarian law, 50 per cent of the electorate has to vote in order to have a valid referendum. Thus the SZDSZ could have lost the elections if less than half the population voted. After a heated campaign the referendum produced a good turn-out (about 60 per cent voted) and by a tiny margin the 'yes' vote won.

This was a perfect strategy as far as the SZDSZ was concerned. It indeed split the MSZP and the MDF. The MDF was humiliated and it began to perform poorly in the polls. While during late September the MDF polled 26 per cent, the SZDSZ and the FIDESZ were under 10 per cent, and the Communists still did well with about 30 per cent; however, all this had radically changed by early December. The MSZP, after a messy party congress in October where it split into the MSZMP (the old-line Communist Party) and the MSZP (the reform Communist Party), began to lose votes rapidly, its support falling rapidly down to 10 per cent. But the MDF, instead of picking up the support that the MSZP and the MSZMP had lost, lost support itself and went down to 20 per cent, while the SZDSZ jumped to 20 per cent to form a 'draw' between the two new 'big parties'.

So far so good. The SZDSZ achieved this spectacular result by locating itself on the right of the MDF and attacking them for their communist connection and their dubious 'Third Way' fellow-traveller ideology. But now the dynamics of political institution building took a new turn. József Antall took charge of the MDF. A historian whose father was a leading government official under Admiral Horthy, he had little to do with the left-wing populist writers who were the founders of the MDF. He and the circle around him had some aristocratic connections and they were more centre-right Christian-democrats than left-wing populists. Antall cut off the left populist wing from the MDF and moved comfortably to the right. He realized that if the name of the current political game was anti-Communism, he could play this better than the SZDSZ. The SZDSZ leadership was mainly composed of people with a left-wing past: János Kis was a Lukács disciple and a prominent young Marxist during the early

1970s, Miklós Haraszti was a Maoist, and even Gáspár Miklós Tamás, the most articulate nineteenth-century liberalism ideologue of the party, started as a sort of anarcho-syndicalist. For quite some time what became the 'democratic opposition' was indeed an opposition to state socialism from the left, rather than from the right. Many of the SZDSZ leaders were also from cadre families, children of high-ranking former communist officials. From January onwards the MDF did beat the SZDSZ at its own game. Antall and his circle emerged as more authentically right-wing than the SZDSZ.

The SZDSZ hesitated for a while about which role to take. Kis himself is deeply left-wing in his values and he could live comfortably in a social-democratic party In a trip in December to Paris, he even called the SZDSZ a 'centre-left' party. But Antall went on the attack: of course they are left-wing, so far they have only pretended to be right-wingers. Somehow the SZDSZ chickened out at this point; they felt it was too risky in the general anti-communist atmosphere to take a left-wing stand, thus Kis' Paris statement was shelved and the party became dominated by free-marketeers and with nineteenth-century liberalism. Thus it was trying to keep itself right of the MDF.

In our judgement this was a strategic error. The SZDSZ, by sticking to its referendum-winning tactics as a strategy, lost. It could have done better by changing tactics in early December. After the split between the MSZP and the MDF was created, the SZDSZ should have moved into the political space between the MSZP and the MDF to become what Kis described the SZDSZ as in Paris: a centre-left movement which has an attractive programme for wage and salary earners.

After the elections the SZDSZ found itself in a very difficult situation, i.e. in a parliament in which the government was centre-right, Antall's confessed political model being Adenauer. There is no real room to the right from this position. The SZDSZ tries to demonstrate its liberalism on 'social issues', thus it fought the reintroduction of religious education in schools etc. This is a noble cause but hardly one which will win votes. Indeed by the end of June, according to a survey by the Public Opinion Research Institute, both parties were losing support, but the SZDSZ was the bigger loser. The SZDSZ is probably doomed to become something like the Free Democrats in Germany or the Liberal Party in England if it sticks to its current policies. From this position it is unlikely that it will ever be able to take the power away from the MDF. A move towards the centre-left and a programme centred around the issues of the welfare state and social justice seems more promising for the party which intends to unseat the current Christian-nationalist coalition.

Despite its strategic errors it is still the SZDSZ which is the best located to do this job. The other contenders for the social democratic constituency are in worse situations. First of all, the successor parties, the MSZMP and the MSZP, just do not appeal to the social democratic electorates. As we have demonstrated, the MSZP is the party which relies more on the upper-middle class than any other party; its support in the working class is the weakest among all the parties. This is not so surprising. The Communist Party betrayed the working class for 40 years, why should they trust them now?

The poor performance of the Social Democratic Party (MSZDP) is more of a surprise. Most political commentators anticipated that this party would do well. Four to five years ago, when the possibility of multiparty elections first appeared on the horizon, political scientists and sociologists took it as granted that some social democratic party would take the power away from the Communists. On top of this, the MSZDP received a great deal of support from Western social democratic parties and it was naturally located on the winning spot on the political field. However, the MSZDP did not even get 4 per cent of the votes and does not have a single MP. The reasons are complex. Most importantly, the MSZDP had a great deal of difficulty in institution building. First the 'old guard' tried to rebuild the party, but these were men in their seventies and eighties who also could not get along with each other. They fought and split. Then many young people, some of them with considerable talent, tried to join. This did not work either. They clashed with the old guard and many of them were former communist party members, and thus vulnerable as politicians. The party, after it tried to put its show together, also made a few major mistakes. In terms of image it went back to the traditions of the 1920s, using some of the old social democratic posters and trying to appeal to the old working class constituency, to the 'worker with the hammer in the hand'. This was unauthentic and cost them more votes than it won. Finally, they elected a chairwoman who proved to be of considerable charm but little charisma. She also had a communist past and stirred the party to the ultra-right of the Second International. Internal conflicts, lack of leadership, wrong policies (who wants a Thatcherite labour party?) and wrong images added up to nothing.

The final conclusion of our chapter is: a large social-democratic constituency around which a possible challenger of the current Christian-nationalist regime can emerge exists, but its interest for institutional reasons remained unarticulated. The future of Hungarian politics depends on whether these institutional problems can be corrected. If no centre-right force emerges, then the MDF's rule will last for a millennium, or if a major crisis evolves, due to the explosion of unemployment or unbearable increases of social inequalities, then a right-wing force, far right of Mr. Antall, will fill the gap that the potential centre-left parties failed to fill.

Appendix A: Models

Table 10.1 Logistic regression estimates of voting and vote choice for the first
round of the Hungarian elections, 1990

	Election participation		MDF vote	
Independent variables	(1)	(2)	(3)	(4)
Constant	− .707	− .726	− .979	− 1.138
Sex	.107	.084	.077	.176
	(.587)	(.673)	(.714)	(.422)
Age	.025	.025	.030	.026
	(.000)	(.000)	(.000)	(.000)
Upper blue collar	.795	.784	.369	.552
	(.003)	(.004)	(.227)	(.080)
Lower white collar	1.237	1.188	− .414	− .237
	(.000)	(.000)	(.132)	(.408)
Upper white collar	2.278	2.095	− .099	.228
	(.000)	(.000)	(.767)	(.530)
Farmer	− .042	.020	.750	.778
	(.885)	(.946)	(.083)	(.079)
Safety net issues	–	.056	–	.089
		(.360)		(.215)
Labour party issues	–	− .185	–	.052
		(.049)		(.618)
Civil rights issues	–	− .020		− .104
		(.543)		(.006)
− 2 Log likelihood	719.97	715.16	618.01	587.67
Model chi-square	48.52	53.20	34.65	44.01
Degrees of freedom	6	9	6	9
False positive rate	23.6	23.3	33.2	32.3
False negative rate	40.0	45.0	42.6	42.2
N	694	694	476	476

Table 10.2 Logistic regression estimates of voting and vote choice for the second round of the Hungarian elections, 1990

Independent variables	Election participation		MDF vote	
	(1)	(2)	(3)	(4)
Constant	.315	− .423	− .719	− .037
Sex	.151	.013	− .036	.071
	(.485)	(.954)	(.883)	(.778)
Age	.016	.020	.027	.023
	(.028)	(.007)	(.001)	(.009)
Upper blue collar	− .168	− .301	.292	.499
	(.597)	(.355)	(.414)	(.178)
Lower white collar	− .141	− .316	− .566	− .306
	(.289)	(.290)	(.072)	(.351)
Upper white collar	.372	− .049	− .007	.412
	(.324)	(.902)	(.986)	(.306)
Farmer	− .478	− .434	.768	.798
	(.203)	(.253)	(.140)	(.138)
Safety net issues	–	− .005	–	.039
		(.943)		(.634)
Labour party issues	–	− .254	–	.078
		(.015)		(.531)
Civil rights issues	–	.054	–	− .129
		(.137)		(.004)
− 2 Log likelihood	592.71	581.64	452.17	441.26
Model chi-square	9.88	20.99	24.22	36.01
Degrees of freedom	6	9	6	9
False positive rate	26.3	26.1	34.7	33.2
False negative rate	100.0	50.0	45.5	44.7
N	527	527	363	363

Table 10.3 OLS regression analysis of safety net (W1), labour party (W2) and civil rights (CIVIL) issues

	Safety net	Labour party issues	Civil rights
Independent variables	W1	W2	CIVIL
Constant	12.592	2.518	11.141
Sex	−.138	−.281	1.037
	(.244)	(.001)	(.000)
Age	.010	.006	−.043
	(.013)	(.028)	(.000)
Upper blue collar	−.108	−.283	1.293
	(.534)	(.017)	(.000)
Lower white collar	.316	−.389	1.497
	(.046)	(.000)	(.000)
Upper white collar	.477	−1.155	2.657
	(.020)	(.000)	(.000)
Farmer	−.064	−.326	−.188
	(.749)	(.018)	(.632)
R square	.033	.193	.193
Significance of F	.000	.000	.000
N	694	694	694

Notes

1. There are two accompanying articles that we have written on the same subject. The first is by Iván Szelényi and Szonja Szelényi: 'Classes and Parties in the Transition to Post-Communism: The Case of Hungary, 1989–1990' is forthcoming in G. Marks and Ch. Lemke (eds): *The Crisis of Socialism in Europe*, Duke University Press. This paper briefly sketches the theoretic arguments without offering data analysis. The second is by Szonja Szelényi, Bruce Western, Tamás Kolosi and Iván Szelényi: 'Making Democracy under Post Communism: Classes, Institutions and Pre-Communist Political Legacy' and is being reviewed for publication. This second article focuses on data analysis and uses different models from the ones presented here.
2. We use the term 'post-Communist' in a descriptive way. When we claim that Central Europe entered post-Communism, we only mean that it eliminated three key characteristics of those societies, which conventionally were referred to as 'communist' or 'Soviet-type' societies. These characteristics were: 1. in Soviet-type societies there was a virtual monopoly of the state as owner of strategically important capital goods; 2. these societies were one-party states in which the ruling party legitimated itself with Marxism/Leninism; 3. these societies had a social structure which could be described by a single pyramid, with cadres on top and workers at the bottom. In this hierarchy the main

criterion of ascent is political loyalty. Central Europe by mid-1990 was post-Communist, since it had adopted a 'sector neutral' property law, treated private property as equal to public property and in all countries multiparty elections were held. The social structure has also changed: the earlier single pyramid has been transformed into a tripolar system, in which a second avenue of social ascent – ascent by ownership of private property – is now being opened up. The cadre-professional and worker axis is now complemented by a third position around which a neo-bourgeoisie is being created.

3. The distribution of parliamentary seats among the above-described parties was as follows:

   The governing Christian-nationalist, centre-right coalition: 59.5%; MDF 42.7%; FKgP 11.4%; KDNP 5.4%; The liberal parties 29%; SZDSZ 23.6%; FIDESZ 5.4%.

   The 'socialist' party (MSZP) gained 8.5% and other parties and independent candidates of different persuasions won the remainder of the 386 seats.

   The Hungarian electoral system is quite complicated. People voted in two rounds. In the first round (25 March 1990) they cast one vote for the party list (which decided the fate of 210 seats) and one for the contestants of the 176 individual seats (this adds up to 386 seats). Individual seats, however, could only be won when a candidate received an absolute majority. The overwhelming majority of individual seats in the first round thus could not be filled, and were recontested among the front-runners in the second round (8 April).

   The gap between the centre-right and liberals was significantly smaller in terms of the popular vote than appears in the distribution of seats. During this second round most seats were contested in very close competition by MDF and SZDSZ candidates, thus the number of seats won by the MDF exaggerates the extent of its victory.

4. The 'Eastern region' of Central Europe, Romania, Bulgaria and Serbia, have so far followed a rather different trajectory of development. As of October 1990 they were still run by Communists or the successor organizations of the former Communist Parties. It may be coincidental, but this division corresponds to an old division of Central Europe into two sub-regions, one dominated by Western, the other by Eastern Christianity.

5. End of September 1990 local government elections were held. The election campaign was launched as a milestone in the change of the regime, as the event which would get rid of dual power, duality of democratic central power and local communist power. Sixty-three per cent of the eligible voters did not cast a vote, offering further proof of the seriousness of political indifference in the country. In March 1991 at two parliamentary by-elections, the turn-out rate dropped to 15–20 per cent.

6. These data were provided for us by György Lengyel who conducted a survey on attitudes towards private business.

7. In this outspoken interview Magyar repeats some of the themes other SZDSZ leaders articulated elsewhere, namely that social democracy is outdated: 'Both the social democratic and liberal parties in Western Europe are captives of a historical situation . . . they are unable to step out of their traditional role, though the difference between them is shrinking.' He also questions the value of the distinction between left and right, and suggests instead a distinction between liberals and conservatives. This is questionably true: social democracy in Western Europe is well and healthy, some 16 parties are in government, while the liberal parties typically never capture more than 10 per cent of the votes, and when the crunch comes they are more likely to form coalitions with

the conservatives than with the labourites. This is certainly true for the two major countries where there is a tripartite division of politics between social democrats, conservatives and liberals, namely Germany and England. (See *Magyar Nemzet*, 1 Aug 1990, p. 5)

8. The variable CIVIL was composed of the following items:
   1. Is a meeting against the government legal?
   2. Is a demonstration against the government legal?
   3. Is a strike against the government legal?
   4. Is a book inciting revolution legal?

9. W1 variable was composed of the following items:
   1. How much should the government spend on health care?
   2. How much should the government spend on education?
   3. How much should the government spend on pensions?

10. W2 variable was composed of the following items:
    1. Which is the better, to stop inflation or decrease unemployment?
    2. Should the state provide secure jobs for all?
    3. Should the state reduce the differences in income?

11. Due to space limitations we are not including the cross-tabulations in this chapter.

12. See the tables which contain these models in Appendix A.

13. Just a word of caution: this is, of course, the way that people remembered that they voted two months earlier. Their recollection failed them in more than one way: for instance, fewer people remembered not having voted, than the actual proportion of non-voters, and more people remembered voting for the victorious MDF than actually did. At the end of May only 24 per cent of our random sample remembered that they did not case a vote, though the actual proportion of non-voters was 35 per cent. This trend is known, of course, from other studies on voting behaviour: people are less likely to report not having voted than the actual proportion of non-voters, and people seem to readjust their memories and are likely to tell opinion polls that they voted for the victorious parties. But these errors in recollecting electoral behaviour should not systematically distort the distribution in the cross-tabs; errors – we hope – are randomly distributed in the population.

14. In order to compare fits among models with different dependent variables, we look at the proportion of cases that are misclassified under the model. This means predicting whether a person would vote or not (or vote MDF or SZDSZ) and comparing this prediction to how they actually vote. This gives the false positive rate, the proportion of cases mistakenly predicted as positive (i.e. predicted to vote, or to vote MDF) and the false negative rate, the proportion mistakenly predicted to be negative (i.e. not to vote, or to vote SZDSZ). Both these are reported in Tables 10.1 and 10.2.

15. We evaluate the differences in the fits of models with the same dependent but different series of independent variables by subtracting the model chi-squares and finding the significance level with the degrees of freedom for the difference. Comparing in Table 10.1 columns (3) and (4), thus for MODEL1MDF1 with MODEL2MDF1 the difference is 9.36 with 3 degrees of freedom, $p = .03$. In this case the inclusion of the attitudes improve the fit.

16. Following the procedure outlined in Note 14, we find a difference in chi-squares of 4.68 with 3 degrees of freedom, which is not significant.

17. It can, of course, be a source of error that these questions are put as opinion and not as attitude questions, thus the question posed was: 'Is it legal to strike?' rather than 'Is it appropriate to strike?'

References

Bauman, Zygmunt (1974) 'Officialdom and Class: Basis of Inequality in Socialist Society', pp. 129–48 in *The Social Analysis of Class Structure*, edited by Frank Parkin, London: Tavistock.

Benda, Gyula (1983) *Magyarország Történeti Kronológiája* (Chronological History of Hungary), Budapest: Akadémiai Kiadó.

Berelson, Bernard R., Paul F. Lazersfeld and William N. McPhee (1954) *Voting: A Study of Opinion Formation in a Presidential Campaign*, Chicago: The University of Chicago Press.

Bobo, Lawrence and Frederick C. Licari (1989) 'Education and Political Tolerance', *Public Opinion Quarterly*, 53 (Fall): 285–308.

Brown, Courtney (1987) 'Voter Mobilization and Party Competition in a Volatile Electorate', *American Sociological Review*, 52: 59–72.

Gábor, I (1985) 'The Major Domains of the Second Economy', pp. 133–79, in *Market and Second Economy in Hungary*, edited by Péter Galasi and György Sziráczki, Frankfurt: Campus Verlag.

Gouldner, Alvin (1979) *The Future of Intellectuals and the Rise of the New Class*, Oxford: Oxford University Press.

Hamilton, Richard (1972) *Class and Politics in the United States*, New York: John Wiley.

Hankiss, Elemér (1989/a) 'Reforms and the conversion of power', Paper read at a conference in the Konrad Adenauer Stiftung, Bonn, 29–31 May 1989, 'Ost-Mittel Europa, Die Herausforderung der Reformen.'

—— (1989/b) *Kelet-Európai Alternatívák* (East-European Alternatives), Budapest: Közgazdasági es Jogi Könyvkiadó.

Kolosi, Tamás (1988) 'Stratification and Social Structure in Hungary', *Annual Review of Sociology*, 14: 405–19.

—— (1989) *Tagolt Társadalom* (Stratified Society), Budapest: Gondolat Kiadó.

—— (1990) *International Social Survey Program: Role of Government, Hungary 1990*, [MRDF], Budapest: Social Research Informatics Society [producer and distributor].

Konrád, George and Iván Szelényi (1979) *The Intellectuals on the Road to Class Power*, New York: Harcourt, Brace and Jovanovich.

Lipset, Seymour Martin (1981) *Political Man: The Social Bases of Politics*, Baltimore, Maryland: The Johns Hopkins University Press.

—— and William Schneider (1987) *The Confidence Gap*, Baltimore: The Johns Hopkins University Press.

Little, Roderick J. A. and Donald B. Rubin (1987) *Statistical Analysis with Missing Data*, New York: Wiley.

Magyar, Bálint (1990) Interview for the daily newspaper, *Magyar Nemzet*, 1 August, p. 5.

Miller, Warren E., Arthur H. Miller and Edward J. Schneider (1980) *American National Election Studies Data Sourcebook, 1952–1978*, Cambridge, Massachusetts: Harvard University Press.

Staniszkis, Jadwiga (1989) 'The dynamics of breakthrough in Eastern Europe', *Soviet Studies*, October.

—— (1990) 'Patterns of change in Eastern Europe', *East European Politics and Society*, January.

—— (1991) *The Dynamics of the Breakthrough in Eastern Europe*, Berkeley: University of California Press.

Szalai, Erzsébet (1989a) 'Az új elit' (About new elite), *Beszélö*, No. 27.

—— (1989b) 'Ismét az uj elitről' (Once again about the new elite), *Élet és Irodalom*, 8 December.

Szelényi, Ivan (1986–7) 'Prospect and limits of the New Class project in Eastern Europe', *Politics and Society*.

—— (1988) *Socialist Entrepreneurs: Embourgoisement in Rural Hungary*, Madison: University of Wisconsin Press.

Szelényi, Szonja (1987) 'Social Inequality and Party Membership: Patterns of Recruitment into the Hungarian Socialist Workers' Party', *American Sociological Review*, 52: 559–73.

Korpi, W. (1983) *The Democratic Class Struggle*, London: Routledge and Kegan Paul.

11 The Hungarian transition in a comparative perspective

András Bozóki

Can social scientists studying the East Central European post-communist transition, learn anything from the historical experiences of other political transitions?

In order to be able to give an answer, first the nature of the discredited system, which was the communist (state socialist) one in our case, should be studied.[1] The proposition that *a close interrelationship can be identified between the nature of the old system and the type of political change* seems to be well founded. The transition began first in the less autocratic systems, where it took a more peaceful, slow and evolutionary shape. The more the earlier regime had limited human rights, the more drastic the break was. The angle of the analysis of the post-communist transition is partly decided by what is considered to be the essence of the original state, of the *ancien régime*.

The post-communist transition is a new, hitherto unknown political change of history, where not only the earlier dictatorial political system is replaced by a more liberal or democratic one, but also the collectivized and centrally planned economy is replaced by a market economy based on private ownership. Trends of *renewal* and *restoration* are simultaneously present in transition because of this dual nature of change. Successful transition means the establishment of a democratic system based on human rights (examples of which can only be found rarely and in certain historical moments), and 'remedying'[2] the blind alley of development, a return to capitalism in the countries of the region. In this respect the paradoxical term '*conservative revolution*'[3] seems to be appropriate; the political agents themselves can be differentiated by their desire to return to a pre-communist system, or by emphasizing the transformation of the post-communist system into a new democracy. In the Hungarian Parliament there are 'historical' parties looking back to the past and emphasizing the continuity of the pre-communist system (the Independent Smallholders' Party, the Christian Democratic People's Party), as well as modern parties stressing the importance of a new beginning as against the old traditions (the Alliance of Free Democrats, the Federation of Young

Democrats). Both approaches are present in the largest governing party, the Hungarian Democratic Forum, and either the representatives of the one or the other standpoint dominate in the policy decisions of the party. The Hungarian Socialist Party is in a special situation as it has been transformed into a modern parliamentary party out of the old state party, hence it has been able to get rid of the depressing heritage of its past with difficulty.

In Hungary, systemic change in the narrower sense of the term was completed with the local elections in the autumn of 1990, as far as the institutional transformation of the central and local authorities was concerned. In the meantime the transformation of the economic system is a slower and longer process, which is yet in its initial stages. Therefore the present chapter mainly deals with the issue of the *political transition*. Despite the different nature of the *ancien régime*, there are certain similarities between it and the earlier South European and Latin American transitions in a political sense, as in most of the East Central European countries (with the exception of Romania) the old systems could not be described fully by the concepts of totalitarianism. From the sixties onwards these countries were rather authoritarian dictatorships which tried to retain some elements of the earlier totalitarianism with varying degrees of success.

In Hungary, after the suppression of the 1956 revolution, the communist leadership gave up the total politicization of the society after the reprisals; it gave up the idea of permanently mobilizing the citizens in order to legitimize the system. It was satisfied by the fact that the people had resigned themselves to their inability to change their destiny by collective political action, therefore their aspirations were pushed back into the depoliticized world of individual advancement. The post-Stalinist-paternalistic system, hallmarked with Kádár's name, was based on the political neutralization of the citizens and gave up the ideological legitimation.[4] The leadership made the system temporarily function better by economic reforms, the consolidation and stability (the state of social peace) of which were considered more important than its legitimacy and acknowledgement by the people. Here was a society infantilized by the representatives of the different levels of counter-selected state bureaucracy, and escaped into private life and hoped for the 'good king' during the decades after 1956. *Survival* became the most important life strategy of people. For this purpose they themselves were forced to join the informal networks of the clientele of interest lobbying, which made the system more tolerable and life easier to endure, as contrasted to the hopelessness of passive resistance. Hence a significant part of the society had something to lose when the system began to disintegrate: the protective net of informality had to be abandoned.

The communist political leadership of the eighties reacted upon the erosion of the system with ill-assorted measures of liberalization so that a collective political protest of social dimensions could be prevented by the division of the social groups. Thus the tiny groups of political opposition evolving from the late seventies onwards, could be isolated from the society, but the growing influence of economic autonomies could not be counterbalanced. As the reform of the centralized command economy proved to be illusory, the leadership needed the economic autonomies in the interest of maintaining social peace and its own rule in the short run, but even these economic autonomies, free of politics, got into conflict with the limitations of the system in the longer run. The economy of 'neither plan, nor market', the subtle system of intricate mechanisms of bargaining, only extended the deepening of the crisis of the system. In Hungary systemic change could be peaceful because the circle of people, squeezed out of the possibility of a political career by political discrimination, was relatively narrow; on the other hand, the circle of those who could have safeguarded their own future exclusively by the maintenance of the nomenklatura was getting continuously narrower within the political leadership. The second generation of the Communist Party elite did not consist primarily of worker cadres picked out of their environment, but of technocratic intellectuals with a convertible expertise, who were not existentially exposed to the party. The growing petty bourgeoisie, appearing from the seventies onwards as a positive heritage of Kádárism, gradually disrupted and disintegrated the monolithic structure of the system, independently of the original intentions of the political leadership. Thus the changing situation of foreign policy – Gorbachev's ascent to power in the Soviet Union – did not launch, but encouraged and justified from the outside, the process of structural transformation slowly unfolding in the daily routine of Hungarian society.

On the concept of transition

The concept of transition can be interpreted broadly as well as narrowly. In a *broad sense* transition – according to O'Donnell and Schmitter's definition – is nothing other than an *interval between two different political systems.*[5] It includes the dissolution of the old authoritarian system as well as the laying of the institutional foundations of the new one. The definition concentrates only upon the fact of change between systems, irrespective of *how* this change takes place. In this approach, transition is the *collective concept* of the process of systemic change which can include a revolution or a coup just as much as slow evolution. It is the advantage of this approach that the often inextricable linkages of the forms of change can be interpreted historically with greater flexibility, and there is no need to make strict distinctions among the forms as to whether change had started from above or from below, whether it had been violent or peaceful, whether it had been accompanied by the mobilization of the masses, or not, etc. But it is a disadvantage that the concept of transition may thus become a relative one, it can be interpreted too broadly and can lose just the meaning by which it had been originally distinguished from the long-term trends of social changes. To some extent it is left to the voluntary decision of the social scientist as to which interval he or she considers a transition among the social processes of multiple components, and when he or she would regard a transition as completed, hence interpretations of an excessively normative approach may also fit into the definition.

In a *narrower interpretation*, transition is essentially an *alternative of revolution*. In this approach such a systemic change is involved the basic characteristic of which is to accomplish the objectives of revolution while avoiding the sacrifices as corollaries of revolutionary change. Thus transition bears upon itself the features of reform as well as revolution to some extent, yet it is fundamentally different from both. According to this approach, democratic transition is *controlled transformation from a more illiberal state to a more liberal one*.[6] Transition begins when the old authoritarian system is unable to observe its own rules and makes allowances for the extension of the rights of individuals and groups outside itself. Hence its legitimacy is challenged, and the regime may get into the condition of *anomy* in the Durkheimian sense by the relativization of the set of rules, resulting in the development of a power vacuum. Transition can be regarded successful if the life-chances of the people prospectively improve within the evolving institutional system compared to the previous one. From this angle the 'Glorious Revolution' of 1688–89 in England was the first successful *transition*, according to Ralph Dahrendorf, whereas the French Revolution of 1789–93 can be regarded as the basic pattern of *revolutionary* change.[7]

Social scientists analysing the post-communist change of 1989 see that it went beyond the framework of reform everywhere, but – with the exception of Romania – it was nowhere accomplished in the shape of the classical revolutions. One can find such expressions in the descriptions of change like 'negotiated revolution', 'velvet revolution', 'peaceful revolution', etc. Timothy Garton Ash, when studying the East Central European changes, reached the conclusion that the usual categories could not be employed, therefore he has created a third term out of the words reform and revolution: that is *refolution*.[8]

It is the advantage of the narrower interpretation of transition that it lays emphasis on the manner of change, thus offering a more differentiated typology, and it is suitable to grasp shorter historical periods on the basis of certain formal criteria (such as free elections, etc.). Its disadvantage, however, is that every transition can be compared too easily, too 'comfortably', by the priority of formal elements, hence typology, as a theoretical construct may lose its content of reality. In addition, the closely related categories may be separated and result in unhistoricalness.

In this chapter a relatively short historical period is under survey and as I do not consider the description of these changes precisely as 'revolutions', I shall attempt to interpret the post-communist changes and summarize their general features by employing the narrower interpretation of political transition.

In this approach political transition can be isolated from the other forms of political change as shown in Table 11.1.

Of the East Central European changes of the past decades, the policy of the Hungarian 'new phase' (1953–54) and the 'new economic

Table 11.1

	Reform	Coup	Revolution	Transition
start:	from top	from top	from below	from top and below
process:	peaceful	peaceful or violent	violent	peaceful
opposing agents:	conservatives vs. reformers	rival power groups	old elite vs. social opposition	*leadership:* conservatives vs. reformers vs. *opposition:* moderates vs. radicals
relationship to society:	demobilization	demobilization	mobilization	mobilization and demobilization
result:	usually the system does not change	usually the system does not change	systemic change	systemic change

mechanism' (1966–72), the 'Prague Spring' (1968) starting as a reform but launching social movements in Czechoslovakia, and the Soviet 'perestroika' (from 1987 onwards) can be mentioned in the series of *reform efforts*. There were two *revolutions* in the classical sense of the term: in Hungary in 1956 and in Romania in 1989 (accompanied by a coup-like replacement of the leadership). The Polish 'self-limiting' revolution of 1980–81 occupies a special place in the history of the region. It could not become a successful political transition, and though it could destroy the remains of the legitimacy of the communist system, yet the Polish party leadership, enjoying Soviet support, considered its compromises with Solidarnost only temporary and tactical ones and responded with the introduction of a military dictatorship the moment it was feasible.

As history shows, no democratic transition is possible from the totalitarian regimes. In such regimes the ruling group is not responsible to any elected body, and it is impossible to remove it from power by any institutionalized, peaceful method.[9] Usually a democratic change can only be accomplished by revolution in totalitarian regimes, but the creation of a somewhat more tolerable authoritarian system by reforms following, or substituting, revolution or by a coup is a more typical process. In 1956 the revolution was suppressed in Hungary, but its memory was so strong that after the reprisals the new leadership introduced reforms and created a milder form of dictatorship. In 1968 the 'Prague Spring' began as the reform initiative of the leadership and was actively supported by the society. Though the possibility of a democratic transition was included in the reform movement – beyond the intentions of its initiators – the Soviet invasion thwarted it. In 1989 the outbreak of the revolution was accompanied by a well-organized coup in Romania and the new leadership applied the strategy of demobilization as well as the channelling of emotions into nationalism. After the consolidation of power, the new leadership created a political order that was anti-communist in its rhetoric but semi-democratic in its practice.

Revolution, as an alternative to democratic transition, is usually a risky solution accompanied by extraordinary sacrifices, which, in most cases, does not bring the expected results: it may develop into a dictatorship of the revolutionary extremists, as was the case with the Jacobin terror following the French Revolution, or the Bolshevik dictatorship after the democratic change of 1918 in Hungary, and all this may lead to attempts by the conservative regimes at restoration in the long run. The Hungarian revolution of 1956 and the Czechoslovakian reform movement of 1968 were suppressed by the superior force of the Soviet army, and learning from the lesson, the Polish, Czech and Hungarian opposition groups of the late seventies elaborated a new strategy: *new evolutionism* based on critical publicity, constitutional legality and human rights instead of open confrontation.[10]

In 1989 and 1990 a democratic political transition took place in most of the countries of the region, which was characterized by negotiations between the authority and the opposition in Poland and Hungary, and by mass protests in the GDR, Czechoslovakia and Bulgaria. In the following I am going to study those features of the process which can be generalized.

The process and the chief actors of the democratic transition

Three phases of the process can be theoretically distinguished, they are: 1. *the erosion of the old system*, which was accompanied by the appearance of the new, autonomous movements; 2. *the moment of collapse*, when the basic features of the regime changed; and 3. *the consolidation of the new regime*, the phase of institution-building. *Liberalization*, characterizing the first phase of transition, can also be distinguished from the following *democratization*, as suggested by O'Donnell and Schmitter. The former one expands the framework of the system based on autocracy and creates a liberalized autocracy (*dictablanda*), while the latter one surpasses it and at first creates a limited democracy (*democradúra*), and next a fully fledged political democracy.[11]

The chief actors of transition are partly the '*makers of politics*' (representatives of the old and the merging new political elites), and partly the pressure groups, or masses of *civil society*, which manifest their political will in a less articulated form, not only or not primarily through parties.

Conservatives and *reformers* can be distinguished among the representatives of the old political system within the sphere of the 'makers of politics', whereas one may differentiate between *moderates* and *radicals* within the new opposition groups. All four groups have a significant role in the process of systemic change: during the first phase of transition it is usually the struggle of conservatives and reformers within the state party which is in the forefront, and it is followed by confrontation between the power elite and the opposition, subsequently the struggle of the moderate and radical opposition forces become dominant with the retreat of the old power elite. As political transition is nearing its completion, the significance of the conceptual coupling of 'moderate and radical' – which indicated the relationship of the opposition forces to the communist system – is gradually pushed into the background, and different competing ideologies and party programmes comes into the fore. In such cases it may become obvious that the extent of moderateness and radicalism cannot always be identified with the proximity to, or the distance from, the ideology of the *ancien régime*. For instance, the Hungarian Christian Democratic People's Party was always very moderate and sometimes even loyal to the representatives of the earlier system during the negotiations of the Opposition Roundtable, whereas it had been the farthest away not only from the socialist-communist, but even from the leftist liberal values in its ideology.

Table 11.2

| | POLITICAL ACTORS | | | |
| | Authoritarian bloc | | Opposition bloc | |
	Conservatives	Reformers	Moderates	Radicals
POLAND	Bureaucratic faction	Globalists	Social democrats	Liberals
		Populists	Neo-conservatives	Populists
HUNGARY	Leninist party of order	Pragmatic technocrats	Christian democrats	Liberals
		Reform Communists	Populists	Social liberals

The location of the political actors of transition is represented by Table 11.2, which gives a comparison of the Polish and Hungarian cases on the basis of the 1989 situation.[12] It is a significant difference that while the individual actors were political forces that for the most part had been organized into parties in Hungary, these groups had not yet crystallized into party formations in Poland.

In the first phase of transition the opposition forces are still weak and unorganized, and their voice does not reach the broad layers of the society. They project a possible critical behaviour against the existing system, and spread the culture of a critical language, different from party jargon, in the secondary public sphere created by themselves. Initially most writers and artists appear besides the marginal autonomous intelligentsia, who know the metaphoric language of the critique of the regime which represents certain protection for them as well as a possible international solidarity. The influence of thinking differently gradually reaches the students and young intellectuals, who organize clubs, circles and networks, who participate in the development of new subcultures, or in the not directly political peace and environmental movements. At this stage they locate themselves *between* the authorities and the opposition, thus contributing to the slow blurring of the borderline between bipolar publicity (directed press versus samizdat), to the broadening of the limitations of expression and description.

What are the causes of transition? Why does a political leadership feel that government cannot continue along the old lines and its politics have to be altered? Why does a society feel that the 'time has come' when it can turn against the regime with good chances and without the communist leadership responding to its movements with a bloody showdown?

Several causes are enumerated by social scientists involved in the comparative analysis of political transitions.[13] One possible cause is *defeat in a war*. The most important cause of the democratic transformation of West Germany after 1945 was the overthrow of the Nazi system from the outside. But the possibility of an armed conflict had a role in the 1973–74 changes in Greece as well, when the Greek army realized that they could not emerge victorious from the Cyprus crisis against Turkey and hence turned against their own authoritarian leadership. The democratic transformation of Portugal and the fall of the Salazar-regime in 1974 was greatly accelerated by the fact that the army had been unable to retain the colonies. A democratic regime was needed which would give up goals that it was impossible to realize. The lost war waged for the Falkland Islands was a significant component in the Argentinian change and in Raúl Alfonsín coming into power. This is how the East Central European changes began in 1945, but their unfolding was hampered by the Soviet Union interpreting the Yalta agreement according to its own power intentions.

Though no war had a role in the 1989 changes, there was still the important realization that the Soviet bloc had *lost the cold war* in the eighties. The post-industrial-technological revolution, based on the decentralization of the media of information and unfolding in the early eighties, fundamentally challenged the functioning of the centrally commanded economies; it became obvious that these systems had been unable to halt the falling living standards of the population and, moreover, that the military-industrial complex of traditional structure, holding together the empire, had become obsolete. The Soviet world system, as an alternative, had crumbled.

The process of transformation can also be launched by *conflicts within the leadership*, within the power elite. It can become particularly sharp when the person symbolizing the system dies or has to give up his leading position for some other reason. Succession and the replacement of generations inevitably emphasizes the internal divisions and may become the catalyst of the beginning of transformation. This is what happened in Spain after the death of Franco, but it was the same in Hungary when Kádár and his inner circle were removed from the leadership almost by a coup at the 1988 May party conference.[14] The intra-party struggle of conservatives and reformers characterized the years after the death of Brezhnev in the Soviet Union as well.

A further cause of liberalization can be the success or decay of the *social and economic efficiency* of the system. It was the success of the economic productivity of the autocratic system which encouraged the reformers to launch changes and to establish contacts with social groups in Chile and in South Korea, and a similar process had started in China too, but there it confronted the opposition of the conservatives and was terminated by the merciless reprisal at Tienanmen Square. The economic *decay* of the system had a role in the East Central European changes. In Hungary the leadership sensed that there was no return to the policy of repression, and as it wanted to maintain social peace, it attempted to extend its rule by loans from the West. However, this policy soon led to indebtedness and an economic dependency upon the West, which further constrained the mobility of the conservative leadership. In fact, further loans would only have been forthcoming if stability had been guaranteed, and this could not be maintained by forcing people to overwork and to exploit themselves beyond a certain point. Thus a political 'opening up' ensued, at first by the introduction of free travel, then by the broadening of the freedom of the press and also by the acknowledgement of the demand of the right to association.

The *changing international environment* may also play an important role in the commencement of transition. In the final analysis the Communist Parties of East Central Europe were able to rise to power and to retain it for such a long time because their countries – with the exception of Yugoslavia and Albania – were occupied by the Red Army. The national sovereignty of these states was limited precisely in the most important issues. But when Gorbachev initiated a vigorous policy of reform in 1985, and particularly after 1987, it was an encouragement to the reformers of the communist parties and the opposition movements. And when in 1989 he overtly abandoned the Brezhnev-doctrine, the protective umbrella helping the ruling parties disappeared, and the crisis of legitimation of these systems suddenly became obvious.

If the conservative communist leadership retains its unity, the beginning of the transition may be delayed and may start from *below*, bursting forth. In such cases usually demonstrations and strikes break out, emigration from the country becomes a movement, subsequently autonomous initiatives develop, at first the movements express diffuse dissatisfaction and later on they are politically articulate. Adam Przeworski differentiates between two different models of the East Central European transitions: the '*top-down*' model, starting from above (Poland, Hungary), and the '*bottom-up*' model, starting from below (GDR, Czechoslovakia, Romania).[15] However, it is important to stress the role of the society even in the so-called 'top-down' model, partly because its desire for freedom had already been manifest in the earlier suppressed revolutions, and fearing any revolution contributes to the reform intentions of the leadership; and because the leadership by itself would not go beyond the reforms, leaving the basic structure of the system untouched. Incidentally, the case of Romania differs at significant points from the East-German and Czechoslovakian changes because of the initially different situation and the differences in the character of the change.

Thus transition may begin if the changes in the external or internal situation of the country force the leadership to seek new solutions. During the course of transition the various groups of the leadership may follow different strategies, subject to their desire to promote or to hinder the process.

During the first phase the objective is not systemic change as yet but *reform*, and public opinion is primarily preoccupied with the struggle of conservatives against reformers. The conservatives consider the survival of the old system in its unchanged form possible and desirable, sensing that the slightest change may endanger their power. In March 1988, just two months before his fall, János Kádár stated that Hungarian society was not in a crisis. And party Secretary-General, Károly Grósz, used the typical argument of the party of order when he warned that chaos and white terror were possible alternatives to the system represented by him, as late as November 1988.

As contrasted with the conservatives, the reformers realize that it is impossible to govern in the old way, and a controllable extension of liberties is necessary to make the system more efficient. The reformers seriously believe in the reformability of the system for a long time, they trust in the possibility of extending its base of legitimacy, hence their own social support can be enhanced to the detriment of the conservatives. As the reformers regard the legitimacy of their authority as important – yet another issue where they differ from the conservatives – no other choice is left to them but *opening up*, abandoning camarilla politics and moving towards the society, or at least towards the intelligentsia shaping political public opinion. Sensing social dissatisfaction, they want to take the lead and hope to safeguard the maintenance of 'social peace' and 'national consensus'.

Liberalization starts with the policy of 'opening up', when certain liberties are redefined and extended. However, this is always allowed within the sphere defined by the leadership. (For instance police and criminal procedures are relaxed, censorship is limited or abolished in a certain sphere, the opportunities of enterprise are extended, etc.) Liberalization is the result of the mutual influence of the power groups within the leadership, and the leadership and the autonomous groups of the society upon one another. The policy of opening up is expressed by such concepts as the 'new course' (1953), the 'new mechanism' (1968), and 'unfolding' (1987) in Hungary; 'apertura' (opening) in Spain; 'odnowa' (renewal) in Poland; 'distensão' (reduction of tension) in Brazil; or 'ottepel' (thaw, 1953), 'glasnost' (openness, 1987), and 'perestroika' (transformation, 1987) in the Soviet Union.[16]

If the conservatives become dominant within the leadership, *repression*, the more or less violent stoppage of liberalization, ensues. If it is successful – as it was in the post-Khruschevian Soviet Union – dictatorship may survive, but on a narrower basis of power; if it fails then a revolutionary situation may develop and an uprising may take place, the outcome of which is always uncertain (see China, 1989; Romania, 1990). Therefore the conservatives do not always turn against liberalization right from the outset as they may be confident in their ability to control the process and to compromise the reformers with it at a suitable moment.

If the reformers do not succeed in squeezing out the conservatives from the leadership – which first took place in Hungary at the party conference of 1988, its second wave coming between February and June 1989 – the question is not the issue of reform anymore, but whether there should be *reform* or *democracy*. At this stage the hitherto offensive reformers are suddenly forced on to the defensive in the face of the opposition which has gained force and become united. Here the question is no longer the extension of certain rights as if they were privileges, but the general *acknowledgement* of these rights and their consequences to be asserted within the political system. While liberalization means the redefinition of certain legal statuses, democratization means the acknowledgement of formal rights on the level of the individual as well as public institutions and governmental procedures.

During this period the role of expert intellectuals (lawyers, economists) becomes increasingly important within the opposition, who may criticize the operation of the system for violating human rights and the malfunctioning of its economy on a professional basis but with a political edge. The tactics of the opposition are based on the type of ideology such as 'civil society against the state',[17] and are to try to draw the borderline between the opposing parties as sharply as possible. This was the objective of the Opposition Roundtable in Hungary, whereas in Poland the opposition, which was far better organized and united due to Solidarity, did not require such self-legitimation, and could enter into the 'national roundtable' type of negotiations, bringing together all the significant political forces without qualms. As this is not a revolution but its peaceful alternative, the role of the moderates grows within the opposition during this period, as they may facilitate the beginning of negotiations due to their outlook being nearer to that of the reformers. In Hungary, for instance, the reform communist leadership agreed to negotiate because for a long time they could hope to reach such a compromise with the more moderate forces of the opposition which could be advantageous to them too.

However, the democratic transition is rarely a linear process. The reformist leadership may not wish to proceed towards political democracy but wants to maintain a reform policy managed from above for a longer period of time. There may be an attempt to avoid democratization by *cooptation*, in other words, the leadership may try to lift the moderate opposition groups considered constructive into power, thus canalizing social dissatisfaction. By the creation of a new power centre, the leadership may effectively turn against the radical groups labelled as extremists, and may push them to the margin of politics. A typical example of cooptation is the setting up of pseudo-movements of a popular front character in order to strengthen the support of the reformist leadership by the 'socialization' of leadership. These solutions are usually of the type of popular fronts, encouraging 'unity', the 'joining of forces', 'appeasement' and projecting the pluralization of society to be a dangerous and harmful phenomenon. When analysing the Hungarian political transition, it is worth studying the meeting at Lakitelek in September 1987, which was a demonstrative act by the reformers within the Communist Party and the moderate opposition representing the national idea. It is not quite clear whether the reformers met the moderates, excluding the radical opposition, already with the intention of coopting them into power, or whether it was only an opening towards the society, the beginning of liberalization. The intentions of the participants, representing the different groups, may have included the broadening of the social basis of the forces of reform, the elaboration of a new, popular socialist alternative, the re-arrangement and possible extension of the power centre, and the creation of the germs of political pluralism in Hungary. The creation of the so-called *Movement for a Democratic Hungary*, set up for the support of Imre Pozsgay's presidential candidacy in the summer of 1989 without effective social support, can be regarded as an attempt at cooptation. The movement soon faded away after the failure of its set goal.

The longest period of liberalization was achieved by the Polish General Jaruzelski, who introduced a number of democratizing institutions (a constitutional court, an administrative court, an ombudsman, a 'consultative council' of intellectuals aiding the government, etc.) in the eighties, but while the system absorbed neo-corporative elements (state party, the Church, trade unions),[18] its basic structure remained unchanged. Jaruzelski's 1986 decree on amnesty was also issued in the spirit of liberalization, but his calculations miscarried at this point and the amnesty became the starting point of the demand for the democratization of the political system.[19]

Once the process of democratization starts, the reformers, who have hitherto attempted to control the process, have to decide whether they want to return to the restoration of autocracy, or to allow the democratic emancipation of the society and the opposition. The trap of the reformer's position is that there *is no correct decision whatsoever* as the reformers may be squeezed out of power in either case: by the conservatives in the case of restoration, and by the opposition in the case of democracy. It is a self-extinguishing enterprise to be the reformer of the earlier authority, as the collapse of the system politically buries under itself even the reformers for some time. In the period of the broadening freedom of speech and of the press, the society is no longer satisfied with reform and wants real democracy. The concept of reform is rapidly discredited, the reformers' merits are swiftly forgotten, and soon they are regarded as a drag on transition.

As the legal and political outlines of systemic change appear, the situation of the opposition also becomes more difficult. They know that the anti-dictatorial forces have to act jointly for the success of transition, but they also know that they have to compete with one another if they want to rule in the evolving democratic system. Hence they have no alternative but to engage in a 'two-front struggle'. Moderates and radicals join forces against the representatives of the authoritarian system, but at some point they have to turn against each other too.[20] This was the case in Hungary at the end of the negotiations between the party state and the Opposition Roundtable, after the agreement of 18 September 1989, which was signed by some and rejected by others.

A too early separation of the opposition forces, or their staying together too long are both equally dangerous for the success of the democratic transition. If moderates and radicals break up too early, they make the job of their common political adversary too easy. This was the case in South Korea, where the representative of the earlier regime won the elections against the two opposition candidates. But if the different wings of the opposition do not separate from each other, there is the danger of the new regime becoming only a reflection of the old one: no competition evolves, no proportional representation, safeguarding the weights and counterweights of power, can develop. A similar situation has evolved in Romania after the landslide victory of the National Salvation Front, led by Iliescu, at the elections.

The changing dynamics of transition require moving closer at some points and distancing at others between the participants. An understanding between the reformers and the moderates is important in the interest of the success of transition, so that the peaceful nature of change can be preserved; whereas the radicals have a significant role in avoiding halts in transition, as they may hinder the development of a new power centre consisting of reformers and moderates, which can lead to elections where the results are influenced in advance.

From the viewpoint of 'policy makers' transition is no more than the successive process of agreements and the annulment of agreements. Temporary pacts, as the corollaries of elite politics, constitute a part of peaceful transition almost everywhere.

Another, often anonymous, chief actor of democratic transformation is *civil society*. The chances of the success of systemic change are better where there was a functioning civil society before the authoritarian regime and a democratic political culture (even if it was limited), than in places where there was nothing of the sort. In one of his writings, Giuseppe Di Palma argues that the chances of democracy in East Central Europe are better than in the other developing countries because the 'new structure of normative thinking'[21] could evolve in the region out of the heritage of dissidence and the success of 'cognitive mobilisation' launched by it, as contrasted to the prophecies of the ideologists of backwardness. Apparently the strengthening of civil society is a pre-condition as well as a result of democratic transition; where embourgeoisement had been more rudimentary, and the space for the development of the informal society was narrower, even the process of the democratic transition would be more difficult, or would turn towards a new authoritarianism.

Civil society may grow strong economically or politically, but the success of transition becomes doubtful in the long run if the two types of development are not linked.[22] In Hungary a depoliticized 'withdrawing' behavioural pattern and a social strategy of an 'entrepreneurial type' – seeking individual ways of success and a defence against state expropriation by extra work – were characteristic during Kádárism; whereas in Poland there was a politicized, mobilizing workers' resistance of a 'trade unionist type', asserting interests collectively, which was encouraged by the Church.

The process of transition is usually accompanied by *demonstrations*, by the celebration of political anniversaries of the opposition, and related *symbolic* acts. This has an important social psychological role in building up identity: it is in these events that the atomized society meets itself for the first time as a *great mass*. This is when fear is relaxed, the psychological inhibitions, hitherto hindering the possibility of social pressure coming from below, are dissolved. The great mass – no matter how disorganized it is – offers a sense of security to the participants. In this respect the demonstrations of hundreds of thousands in Leipzig, Berlin, Prague and Sofia, the demonstration on the occasion of the reburial of the martyrs of the 1956 Hungarian revolution, and the self-sacrificing Timisoara protest, launching the Romanian changes, had a significant role in the collapse of the Soviet bloc and in the post-communist transition. The initially unarticulated mass movements may contribute to the acceleration of the political institutionalization of the opposition and may exercise pressure on the representatives of power, so that liberalization should not be followed by reprisals, but by democratization. In June 1989, Li Peng ordered firing at the protesting Chinese students in Peking, but neither Honecker nor Jakeš dared to do the same in October and November 1989. Differing from the pioneering Polish and Hungarian transitions, the system collapsed almost at the stroke of a magic wand in the GDR and in Czechoslovakia. Even if certain social groups had a prominent role in the preparation of change and the building up of the new institutional system, in all these countries it was the vast majority of the society that got rid of the old system when the right moment came.

The democratic transition is the process of the broadening of civil society. This is usually accompanied by the growing strength of the political society and by the politicization of daily life. Yet transitions are often void of the moment of *euphoria* and *catharsis*. When transition is achieved by negotiations, the broad and liberating experience of system change that was forced by the masses is missing. There was such a cathartic moment in Portugal (1974), in Chile (1989), in the GDR (1989) and in Czechoslovakia (1989), but in Hungary many people spoke about a 'morose revolution', and the same thing happened in Poland too. With the passage of time, however, political 'hangover' and disappointment appeared even in countries where the changes had been accompanied by the enthusiasm of the masses.

Table 11.3 Summary of political systemic change in East Central European countries

Country	Former system	Process of change	New regime
Poland	authoritarian regime with limited neo-corporatist type pluralism	roundtable negotiations, limited free elections, presidential elections	opposition gained power although it still had to share it with the Communists ('diarchy'), parliamentary democracy with strong presidency
Hungary	liberalized authoritarian paternalistic regime	roundtable talks, referendum, free and fair elections	parliamentary democracy with competitive parties after the elections
GDR	authoritarian regime (no change from above)	emigration waves, mass demonstrations, limited power-sharing, free and fair elections	parliamentary democracy with competitive parties after the elections
Czechoslovakia	authoritarian regime (no change from above)	mass demonstrations, limited power-sharing, free and fair elections	parliamentary democracy after the elections
Bulgaria	authoritarian regime (no change from above)	mass demonstrations, provisional government, free elections	unstable democratic institutions
Romania	totalitarian or 'sultanistic'[23] regime	popular uprising, *coup d'état*, provisional government, free elections	unstable democratic institutions, anti-democratic pro-government movements

Social mobilization *cannot be identified* with civil society; as extensive mobilization does not necessarily mean the strengthening of civil society, so a decreasing mobilization, or even its disappearance, does not mean that the civil society is on the retreat, rather it means a return to daily life after a period of politicization. The success of democratic transition can be measured, among other ways, by the ability of civil society to carry out political self-organization in new conflict situations in the wake of the first free elections.

The process of the political systemic change of the East Central European countries is summarized in Table 11.3.

The Polish and Hungarian transitions were dominated by negotiations; the East German, Czechoslovakian and Bulgarian transitions were characterized by non-violent mass mobilization; whereas the Romanian transition was launched by an uprising that manifested itself in violent clashes and street fighting.

Systemic change took place in two phases in Poland as it set out on the road of political transformation. The rountable negotiations and the subsequent free elections constituted the first phase, where the Communists acquired parliamentary representation that was decided in advance, irrespective of the election results, and General Jaruzelski became the first President of the republic. During the second phase, a year after the elections, Jaruzelski was pressed to resign and Lech Walesa, the leader of Solidarity was elected President.

The Hungarian transition was a continuous one, where the opposition did not enter into a self-limiting pact with the authoritarian leadership, and the presidential aspirations of the HSWP, wishing to follow the Polish example, were impeded by a referendum.

The East German, Czechoslovakian and Bulgarian transitions are similar in so far as the earlier communist leadership, hallmarked by the names of Honecker, Jakeš and Zhivkov respectively, had not shown any inclination itself towards political reforms before the commencement of the social movements. Transition had begun from below and the reformer representatives of the party (Krenz, Modrow, Urbanek, Adamec, Mladenov) appeared in public only afterwards, but could not become the leaders of systemic change and were sooner or later squeezed out of politics. New governments were formed before the free elections in all the three countries, in the GDR and Czechoslovakia by the representatives of the opposition, and in Bulgaria by the reform communists.

In the GDR and in Czechoslovakia the opposition (the CDU, and the Civic Forum respectively) won the elections, whereas in Bulgaria the reform Communists (Bulgarian Socialist Party) retained power, a fact that soon became a source of new conflicts. In Romania too an essentially reform Communist group took over government after the December changes, and has tried to govern in a different style and under a different name because of the violent anti-Communism prevalent in the society. This group projected itself as the heir of the national revolution and thus it easily won the elections.

The opposition movements of the earlier regimes were only able to gain power in Czechoslovakia and Poland. In the GDR, following the West German party system, the New Forum who were launching the changes could not even enter parliament, and the heir of the Hungarian 'democratic opposition', the AFD, though it has become the second largest party of the country as a liberal force, has become a parliamentary opposition only. However, since then the process of pluralization has begun within the victorious political forces in Poland as well as in Czechoslovakia.

The political actors of the East Central European countries have learned a great deal from one another during the period of transition. The Hungarian opposition gained a lot from the experiences of the Polish roundtable talks, whereas the East German opposition learned a lot from both. In Hungary the erstwhile communist state party (HSWP) entered the political arena of the transformed political system under a new name (HSP), with new faces and with a socialist-social democratic policy. Its example was followed by the Polish, East German and Bulgarian Communist Parties, hence a certain degree of their social acknowledgement.

During the course of transition some leaders of the Communist Parties realized that they had to give up their rigid, exclusionary policies in their own interest and that they had to anticipate change. Gorbachev's visit to Berlin in October 1989 was accompanied by demonstrations against the regime resembling those of Peking, but Krenz and his comrades prevented Honecker from applying violence and a month later they opened the Berlin Wall. Miklós Németh's government strove to have consultations with the opposition, and, sensing social pressure, dissolved the Workers' Militia (the paramilitary armed force of the Communist Party before the plebiscite of November 1989), and banned the organization of parties in workplaces. In the meantime the leaders of the ruling parties realized that they could become victorious over the opposition forces, that were less organized and that had little access to the mass media, if the free elections were held as soon as possible. This strategy was applied by the National Salvation Front in Romania, by the Socialist Party in Bulgaria, and by the Labour Party in Albania.

In Hungary the basic phase of political transition was completed by the local elections in the autumn of 1990. In the towns the liberal opposition parties and in the villages the independent candidates had a landslide victory. In settlements with a population above ten thousand the candidates of the AFD and the FYD got 39.9 per cent of the votes in the individual constituencies, whereas the candidates of the three-party governing coalition (HDF–ISHP–CDPP) could obtain only 21.2 per cent; the AFD–FYD got 38.5 per cent, and the parties of the governing coalition attained 34.8 per cent on the list.[24]

However, the most conspicuous lesson of the elections has not been the surging ahead of the opposition parties due to the loss of society's confidence primarily in the governing coalition, but also in the parliamentary parties in general. During the first round 60 per cent and during the second round 70 per cent of the electorate absented themselves from the polls. In 1989–90 there were six national elections in Hungary, of which participation was above 50 per cent only on two occasions: at the referendum of 26 November 1989 it was 58 per cent, and at the first round of the parliamentary elections on 26 March 1990 it was 65 per cent. On both occasions the issue was the rejection of the *ancien régime*. Thus the society knew what it had *not* wanted, but it was far more uncertain about how to approach the future it did want. Thirty-five per cent of Hungarian society could not be moved from its distancing behaviour by either of the elections.

The advancement of the opposition can be explained by the fact that the government missed the favourable psychological moment after the parliamentary elections for launching economic changes. Parliament 'freely floating' above the society was working at full capacity on legislation, but in the meantime the parliamentary parties often entered into unnecessary ideological disputes. Economic transition, a resolute launching of privatization and the programme, were delayed behind the clarification of the issues of public authority, and internal conflicts put pressure on the governing coalition, and even the coalition parties. Inflation and unemployment were growing and the society had become uncertain as to whether the Hungarian Democratic Forum, posing with the slogan of being the 'calm force', was really safeguarding its security. The governing coalition's conservative–gentry–national rhetoric evoking the twenties and thirties was irritating for a significant part of the intelligentsia as far as the shaping of public opinion was concerned. Parallel to it the opposition parties, earlier called 'Thatcherite', have become more open to social issues, such as poverty, lack of housing, and the situation of the young and the retired. Hungarian society voted for the possibility of a *power balance* at the local elections.

Local elections have established a three-tiered power system approaching bipolarity in Hungary. It is a *bipolar* one in so far as it has become clear that the socialist–social democrat forces continue to play a marginal role in political life, thus the opposed political forces can be separated on the basis of conservative–national (HDF–ISHP–CDPP) and liberal–social liberal (AFD–FYD) values. The Hungarian political set-up had the potential of evolving a two-party system (or a two-bloc system) by the end of 1990, but with the growth of social tension the revival of the left, who are under-represented in parliament, cannot be excluded. The power structure has become *three-tiered* in so far as parliament and national politics are dominated by the conservative right-of-the-centre forces; the capital and the settlements of more than ten thousand inhabitants by the liberal parties; while in the villages the politically hardly predictable independents, the majority of whom had been members of the HSWP, have acquired a decisive influence.

After the election year of 1990 the setting up of the *institutions* of the system has come into the foreground and the related disputes have often contained conflicting world views. The disputes frequently reveal that the Hungarian parliamentary parties and those outside the legislation assess the transition in a way that is in keeping with their own ideas about the post-communist society. The political assessment of the democratic transition fluctuates between extremes: some stress the continuity between the old and the new systems, and hold that no systemic change has been accomplished, whereas others draw a sharp caesura between the two periods and consider systemic change to be a fact.

In the present political sociology two marked views can be distinguished regarding the issue *when a transition can be considered accomplished*. According to the *minimalist* concept, the chief criteria of democratic consolidation are the following: 1. each major political force acknowledges that democracy has no alternative; and 2. nobody challenges the legitimacy and right to action of the democratically elected decision-makers. On the other hand, the *maximalist* concept regards democracy to be consolidated only if: 1. all the elements of a democratic institutional system have evolved; 2. the party system is consolidated; and 3. power has shifted from the governing parties to the opposition parties on at least one occasion.[25]

The Hungarian political transition is very near to meeting the minimum conditions of a self-supporting democracy, though stands or demands indicating political discrimination occasionally still occur in the ruling coalition parties. Nevertheless, it sounds exaggerated to link democratic consolidation to the stabilization of the party system and to the first shift of power, as the changes of the party system – provided some other conditions exist – do not mean the fragility of democracies in themselves; there are some democratic countries where the shift of power from the government to the opposition has not taken place for decades after the political transformation.

Apparently it is indispensable to the success of a democratic political transition that:

– the majority of social conflicts should be channelled into the set of democratic institutions (the parliamentary multiparty system, local self-governments, democratically elected organs of interest representation);
– the outcomes of democratic decision-making should not be predetermined, or subsequently modified by extra-democratic means;
– the possibility of a democratic change of power should be available, together with the opportunity for carrying out a policy contrary to the earlier one, after the replacement of the old government by the new one;
– efficient civilian control should be exercised over the armed forces.[26]

The new East Central European democracies have not yet reached this level of self-supporting democracy. However, the shortcomings of democracy that are present in certain cases almost everywhere, cannot in themselves be identified with a lack of democratic consolidation.

The Spanish and Hungarian cases: similarities and differences

In Spain democracy was consolidated between 1975 and 1982, and an accepted and still functioning set of political institutions has evolved. When compared to Spain, Hungary is still at the initial phase of the process, but striking similarities can be found between the two countries regarding the nature of political transition. Therefore it is worth discussing in brief how relevant the Spanish example can be to Hungary to see whether the differences between the two countries make the similar traits too relative.[27]

Both countries have inherited a gerontocratic authoritarian system as a basic situation from which they had to build democracy. Franco's dictatorship lasted from the end of the Spanish Civil War until November 1975, and János Kádár's leftist paternalistic system continued from the suppression of the 1956 revolution until May 1988. The names of both dictators have been associated with a generation and have symbolized a period. In the twentieth century, no politician other than Franco and Kádár had such a long reign either in Spain or in Hungary. Initially Franco started to build a fascist and Kádár a neo-Stalinist system, but soon both dictatorships were 'softened'; neither became totalitarian as both were based on the political neutralization of the citizens. Both systems were able to have some internal liberalization and limited economic reforms. After the exhaustion of the inner reserves of the stricter dictatorships, the reforms of the sixties brought about relative successes in both countries, which, however, weakened rather than strengthened the political cohesion of the regimes. The leaderships reacted with a new series of limiting measures upon this 'softening': Spain again experienced growing internal pressure during Carrero Blanco's prime ministership (1969–73), whereas the Kádár leadership shifted to an anti-reform course between 1972 and 1978. However, the policy of repression only further deepened the gap between the regimes and the societies governed by them. Carrero Blanco was assassinated, and by the time Franco died the system was fundamentally shaken. After 1978, the Hungarian leadership was able to extend its agony by ten years through ill-assorted reforms and foreign loans, while its social support decreased year by year in line with the falling living standards.

As far as transition itself is concerned, here also the similarities are striking. In the initial stage the Spanish Prime Minister, Arias Navarro (1975–76) – like the Hungarian Károly Grósz (1987–88) – did not accept the transformation of the system towards a pluralistic democracy. Both of them spoke about a controlled liberalization guided from the top, while they wished to retain the decisive elements of the old system. The Spanish as well as the Hungarian transition was characterized by a gradual transformation through compromises, accompanied by the readiness of the leadership for reform and by the pressure of the opposition coming from below. In Spain and in Hungary the road of political change led through a series of *negotiations and political pacts*. The change of the political system was not accompanied by the broad and enthusiastic support of the masses in either country. This is indicated by the low level of participation in the first elections and by scepticism, pessimism and cynicism appearing in the societies. In both countries a national referendum preceded the free elections; in Spain it was on the democratic political transition in December 1976 (78 per cent participation), and in Hungary on the elimination of the privileges of the state party and on the constitutional set-up of the republic (58 per cent participation). Political scepticism was indicated by a low degree of party loyalties in both countries. If the memberships of the present Hungarian parties are added up (approximately 200,000 people), the total lags far behind the membership of the erstwhile state party, the HSWP (800,000), and even behind the proportions of party membership during the 1945–47 period of limited democracy. According to a Spanish public opinion poll in 1977, 25 per cent of the people stated that they had not trusted either party[28] and this proportion reaches 35 per cent in Hungary. The lack of interest has been explained by the depoliticizing, atomizing social strategy of the earlier autocratic systems in both countries, as a result of which people had identified politics with immoral activity and hotbeds of corruption.[29] But such a distancing can also be explained by the economic decline that accompanied transition in both countries. In Spain, during the year of the first free elections (1977) there was 30 per cent inflation and unemployment reached 7.5 per cent. In Hungary, initially unemployment was negligible beside the same inflation rate, but it has been dramatically increasing each month ever since.

The first free elections have made the hitherto blurred political fields clear and have considerably reduced the number of competing parties. In both countries a competitive parliamentary system has evolved with a stable governing majority and a strong opposition. A right-of-centre government has come into power under the leadership of Adolfo Suárez and József Antall respectively in both Spain and Hungary. The strongest parties have not had a clear political image in either country; rather they constitute the coalition of different trends. The Spanish Union of Democratic Centre (UCD) headed by Suárez is the union of a number of smaller parties and includes the liberal, Christian democrat, populist, and even the social democrat trends. The Hungarian Democratic Forum (MDF) headed by Antall includes three trends – the national liberal, the populist and the Christian democrat. In Spain the deep ideological differences between the right of centre and the left of centre have not allowed for a grand coalition, and this has been the case in Hungary too.

In both countries the parties who had formed the government for the first time were inclined to consider the inherited state as their own territory and to influence the most important television news programmes. The analysts of the Spanish case regarded the weakness of the democratic right as a sign of the fragility of the new democracy, because they were afraid of the possibility of an anti-democratic rightist change if the former one should prove incapable of absorbing the rightist basis. Though this danger has not occurred in any serious form either on the left or the right in Hungary, the uncertain outcome of the struggle between the democrats and the populists inside the largest governing party continues to be a cause of concern.

It is a further similarity that both countries have found a broadly acknowledged and legitimate head of state in the person of King Juan Carlos, and President Árpád Göncz respectively. Their activities have expressed their commitment to the democratic transformation of their societies. The first local elections after the parliamentary elections have brought the victory of the opposition parties in both countries (though in a higher proportion in Hungary), which has created a kind of power balance in these systems.

In Spain long years of economic crisis ensued; the country was shaken by strikes and terrorist attempts, by 1982 unemployment had risen to 12.6 per cent, and there was even an abortive coup in February 1981. However, the political leadership resolutely continued the *policy of compromises* with the opposition parties and the organs of interest representation even after the elections. It could reach an agreement with the Basque and Catalonian representatives on the handling of regional issues, and the new constitution of the country was confirmed by a plebiscite. The *Moncloa Pact* of the autumn of 1977, reached with the opposition parties and the trade unions, was the most important one in the series of compromises. This pact authorized the government to freeze wages, to reduce public expenditure and credit, and to increase financial discipline. In return the government promised the reform of the taxation system, a more efficient system of social insurance, the reorganization of the fiscal system and the implementation of the pressing political reforms. From a party political angle this was undoubtedly an unpopular programme, but the initially fragile democracy was almost definitely saved by it in the long run. Suárez's government was still able to win the 1979 elections, but lost those of 1982. In 1982 quite unexpectedly many people went to vote (87 per cent), and the Socialist Party, hitherto in opposition, had a landslide victory under the leadership of Felipe González. As Prime Minister, González (with the effective help of Finance Minister Boyer) could continue the liberal economic policy founded on the Moncloa Pact with large social support, so the economy started to develop and democracy was strengthened.

However, despite the striking similarities in the political transitions, there are also significant social and economic differences between the two countries. First of all, the most important difference is that the Franco regime was a *rightist authoritarian* dictatorship which, despite some limitations, had not destroyed the market economy, whereas the *communist* dictatorship of Hungary had not only liquidated political freedom, but also the market economy based on private ownership. It is undoubtedly easier to throw the doors wide open to already existing economic activities than to create the entire set of required conditions anew.

In Spain the labour movement has created traditionally strong trade unions which could not be disregarded by any government, whereas in Hungary strong trade unions are not only missing but it is in fact the trade unions which occupy the last place on the 'confidence scale' of social institutions.[30] However, on the basis of the successful Chilean and South Korean transitions one may argue that it is the *lack* of strong trade unions which makes the economic success of post-communist transitions hopeful, because the changes in the economic structure inevitably lead to the re-arrangement of the position of certain social groups. This is possible according to a purely economic logic, however, in Europe it seems to be more possible that the 'operation' would be successful but that the 'patient' would die. Apparently the irresponsible wage demands of the strong trade unions represent a lesser danger than the lack of the institutional conditions for the most elementary communication between the most important interest groups of the society. The former one – at least in the case of some South European countries – does not prevent the success of the economic and political transition, whereas the latter one may lead not only to a simply inevitable pact, but to an open social explosion. On the Iberian peninsula the important economic pact was also reached besides the political one, which, despite the initiative of some parties[31] has not yet been achieved in Hungary because of the weakness of the organs of interest representation and because of their doubtful legitimacy.

In Spain the Catholic Church had withdrawn its support from the authoritarian regime before Franco's death, and committed itself to democratic transformation, whereas in Hungary the most important churches have been passive onlookers rather than promoters of political transition.

In Spain a neat politico-ideological formula evolved because of the divisions within the right as well as the left wing, where the right has been represented by the more centrist (UCD) and more radical (AP) parties, and the left by the socialists (PSOE) and the Euro-communists (PCE). In Hungary the image is far less clear in respect to the left and the right, as while the governing parties are regarded as rightist because of their more conservative set of values, their announced economic policy of 'considered progress' ('social market economy') curiously mixes the elements of a leftist social sensitivity and rightist state corporatism, particularly if compared to the liberal interpretation of the economy by the AFD and the FYD. Nevertheless the success of Spanish transition has always been endangered by radical regional separatism and political violence that have been manifested in terrorism (the latter one caused the death of more than a hundred people during the years of transformation). Hungary does not have to face this threat, though a series of wildcat strikes and mass demonstrations cannot be excluded if the democratic interest representations are not strengthened in the society. The danger of a coup hung over the Spanish transition like the sword of Damocles, because the supreme military command continued to be controlled by the Francoist generals; in Hungary, however, the earlier Kádárist leadership of the army expressed its loyalty towards the new regime.

As far as the external conditions of transition are concerned, Spain had been in a more favourable situation all along as its political objectives were supported by all the neighbouring and Western countries. In Hungary political transformation could have started in the early eighties in theory, but it was made impossible by the outlawing of Solidarity and by the big power interests of the Soviet Union. The East Central European countries had to wait for the deepening of the Soviet crisis, for the emergence of Gorbachev, but they could not be quite sure whether the new Soviet leadership had really given up the Brezhnev-doctrine right until 1989. Thus the process of transition was delayed by a decade and started off from a far worse economic situation.

The fragility of the new democracy

The post-communist transitions have again sharply exposed the question: is democracy possible in poverty? Can a democratic system be maintained during a crisis threatening collapse? Can a freely elected parliament, and a government responsible to it, retain its legitimacy when the country becomes ungovernable? Can the strikes, collective disobedience movements and civil war situations destabilizing the new regime be avoided? Can it be avoided that the losers of transformation should drift towards political extremes and promote the strengthening of a nationalist-populist party endangering democracy?

The greatest obstacle to the consolidation of a democratic system is economic crisis, beyond the shortcomings of the political culture. It is not accidental that there are stable democracies in those parts of the world where there are advanced market economies, elsewhere – like in Latin America – the unfolding new democracies have to face the fragility of the system, the possibility of the loss of social confidence and a military takeover. Until the forties Argentina was among the richest countries of the world but its development halted during President Perón's populist regime, whereas in South Korea it was in fact economic boom which produced the possibility of a systemic change – the interests of a middle class with growing wealth were hurt by political autocracy, thus they could effectively turn against it with broad social support. The only lasting exception has been India, where dissatisfaction resulting from barely tolerable poverty has not shaken the institutional system of democracy, though it has repeatedly given birth to bloody violence. In the eighties a series of countries have set out on the path of democratization outside East Central Europe too, and there are such under-developed countries among them as Bangladesh, Pakistan, Namibia, Bolivia and Peru. Thus the issue of the relationship between democracy and relative wealth is again an open one.

The destiny of the erstwhile communist countries of East Central Europe has been different from those where the earlier political dictatorship had not limited economic growth. In Hungary the history of several decades of exercises in economic reform – ending up in failure despite partial successes – has shown that no change in the economy can be expected without breaking up the post-totalitarian political framework. Though the political leadership may have given up some of the functions through which it controls economic activities in the interest of social peace, its basic structure had remained unchanged. The essence of this structure had been the leading role of the Communist Party which could not be challenged, loyalty towards the Soviet Union and the economic and military alliance headed by it, and the taboo of the central management of the collectivized economy.

Therefore the task of the East Central European opposition movements was simply to attack the system at its strongest rather than its weakest points during the period of systemic change, because they had recognized that this was the only way of change. Therefore in Poland and in

Hungary, in the societies first setting out on the way of democracy in the region, the opposition had the task of turning against the representatives of the ruling authoritarian system in a self-restricting manner, but never missing their radical objectives. As the pillars of the system had been *political* ones, it was quite obvious that only the dismantling of an outdated political set-up could create the possibility of economic prosperity. However, many people have inferred from this correct assessment of the situation that a systemic change in politics as well as in economics can only be realized simultaneously, since the two are inseparable.

By now it can be seen that this is not so. The political and economic changes have been torn apart, and the political changes have not brought along automatically the restructuring of the economy. Transition has reached a delicate, imbalanced phase, where the emotions of the increasingly impoverished strata and the masses concerned about their jobs and existence are unleashed against the newly established democratic institutions. In Hungary in October 1990 there was a collective act of disobedience that exploded in the wake of an unexpected and drastic rise in petrol prices, where the taxi drivers and carriers blocked the most important road junctions of the country for three days and the country became ungovernable during that period. The event did not remain the affair of an occupational group only, as the majority of the population sympathized with their movement. In such cases the situation is particularly aggravated if the government have no uniform concept for the speed and extent of economic transformation, and the necessary social compensations, if they are unable to face the society with a programme which can be represented.

On such occasions, just as revolutionary situations produce their own revolutionaries, so the spokesmen of the dissatisfied society may come forth from anonymity, and in the better cases take the lead of autonomous interest representations, or in the worse, organize political movements appealing to mass emotions against the existing system. The new political forces can be incorporated into the flexible system by the democratic mechanism with the help of new elections, but a not yet consolidated democracy may be easily destabilized and pressed in extreme directions by too frequently held elections, because the logic of political campaigns inevitably pushes long-term ideas into the background in the face of advantages hoped for in the short term.

The fragility and uncertainty of the democratic systemic change was brought out in bold relief by the Polish presidential elections of the autumn of 1990. During the campaign Walesa, utilizing social dissatisfaction, concentrated his attack upon his earlier adviser, Mazowiecki, whom he regarded to be his chief rival, and he called Mazowiecki's government a new elite detached from the people, a group of intellectuals hindering faster progress. The danger of a populist turn was highlighted by the appearance of Stanislaw Tyminski, an unknown Polish millionaire returning from Canada who unexpectedly defeated Mazowiecki in the first round of the presidential elections, and was thus able to fight against

Walesa in the second round. Tyminski promised richness and a welfare democracy to Poland, he said what the people had been dreaming about and what they wanted to hear. This was the populist alternative to democratic change, where rationality and tolerance were substituted by emotions and the expectation of miracles, where democracy was set against charismatic leadership.

The electorate of Poland was split into three in the first round: the urban middle classes voted for Mazowiecki, the workers and peasants who were committed to Solidarity cast their vote for Walesa, and the less consolidated, less educated rural masses who were disillusioned by Solidarity voted for Tyminski. During the second round the political camp of Solidarity, which was pulling in different directions, was again united for a moment with the active support of the politically influential Catholic Church, and thus Walesa could occupy the presidential chair.[32]

Hungary, Czechoslovakia and Poland have been able successfully to avoid the dangers of turning the new democracies into nationalist-populist systems despite their grave economic situations. In Poland and Czechoslovakia the heads of state are the living symbols of the democratic opposition movements (Lech Walesa and Václav Havel), and in Hungary a conservative right-of-centre government has come into power whose rhetoric may take the wind from the sails of the more extremist right-wing groups that may gain strength as a result of the crisis.

The development of the organizations of interest representation and the strengthening of the local democratic self-governments may create links between the 'political class' and civil society, in which case there is a chance of democracy retaining its order despite the economic crisis, and for enduring the grave ordeal of the years of economic transition.[33] The experience of the successful democratic transitions after the Second World War shows that there is no direct causal relationship between the economic situation and the nature of the political system. In some cases the commitment of the society to democracy may be a more important factor and this can become manifest most unambiguously just when democracy is endangered.

Translated by Vera Gáthy

Notes

1. There are several conceptions of Communism as a system. *Totalitarianism* had the greatest impact among them, of which classic explanations were the works of Hannah Arendt and Friedrich-Brzezinski in the fifties. Other important approaches were the idea of *new elite* or *new class* (Trotsky, Djilas, Konrád-Szelényi), which examined the rule of party-bureaucracy (*nomenklatura*) and of technocratic intellectuals; the theory of *group conflicts* (Skilling); the conception of *clientelism* (Oi-Walder), which emphasized the role of patron-client relationships, and of informal networks; the theory of *synchretic society* (Campeanu), which pointed out the co-existence of different historical structures in communist systems; the conceptions of redistribution, bureaucratic coordination, *state socialism* (Kornai, Szelényi); the approaches which understand Communism as *cultural phenomenon*, political religion (Bell); and that

paradigm which finds strong correlation between the forced and centralized industrialization attempts of the economic *periphery*, and its power concentration (Wallerstein, Gerschenkron, Nove) etc.

On these concepts see further: András Bozóki-Miklós Sükösd 'Honnan, hová, miért? - a magyar átmenet megértése felé' (From where to where and why? Toward the understanding of the Hungarian transition) *Mozgó Világ*, No. 8, 1990, pp. 3–9.

2. Jürgen Habermas: *Nachholende Revolution*, Frankfurt am Main, Suhrkamp, 1990, pp. 179–204.
3. Jürgen Kuczynski is quoted by Habermas, op. cit., p. 180.
4. See for further details: Miklós Szabó: 'A legitimáció történeti alakváltozásai' (Historical changes of legitimacy) In: Miklós Szabó: *Politikai kultúra Magyarországon, 1896–1986* (Political Culture in Hungary 1896–1986), Budapest, Medvetánc, 1989, pp. 275–306.
5. Guillermo O'Donnell–Philippe C. Schmitter: *Transitions from Authoritarian Rule* Vol. 4. *Tentative Conclusions about Uncertain Democracies*, Baltimore, Johns Hopkins University Press, 1986, p. 6.
6. Ralf Dahrendorf: 'Politik, Wirtschaft und Freiheit' *Transit*, Heft 1, Herbst 1990, p. 38.
7. Dahrendorf, op. cit., p. 37.
8. Timothy Garton Ash: *The Magic Lantern. The Revolution of '89 Witnessed in Warsaw, Budapest, Berlin and Prague*, New York, Random House, 1990, p. 14.
9. Juan J. Linz: 'Transitions to democracy' *Washington Quarterly*, Vol. 13, No. 3, Summer 1990, p. 144.
10. Adam Michnik: 'A new evolutionism'. In: Adam Michnik: *Letters from Prison and Other Essays*, Berkeley–Los Angeles–London, University of California Press, 1987, pp. 135–48.
11. O'Donnell–Schmitter, op. cit., Vol. 4.
12. On the pluralization in Poland see: Jadwiga Staniszkis: 'Patterns of change in Eastern Europe', *East European Politics and Societies*, Vol. 4, No. 1, Winter 1990, pp. 77–97. On the Hungarian case see, András Bozóki: 'Post-communist transition: political tendencies in Hungary' *East European Politics and Societies*, Vol. 4, No. 2, Spring 1990, pp. 211–30.
13. Alfred Stepan mentions ten different versions: 1. internal restoration after external reconquest; 2. internal reformulation after external liberation; 3. externally monitored installation; 4. redemocratization led from within the authoritarian regime; 5. transition initiated by the military as government; 6. extrication led by military as institution; 7. society-led regime termination; 8. transition through a pact of political parties; 9. violent revolt; 10. Marxist-led revolutionary war. Alfred Stepan: 'Paths toward redemocratization: theoretical and comparative considerations.' In: O'Donnell–Schmitter–Whitehead (eds.) *Transitions from Authoritarian Rule*, Vol. 3, *Comparative Prospectives*, Baltimore, The Johns Hopkins University Press, 1986, pp. 64–84.
14. See for further details: George Schöpflin–Rudolf Tökés–Iván Völgyes: 'Leadership change and crisis in Hungary' *Problems of Communism*, September 1988, pp. 23–46.
15. Adam Przeworski, 'The Games of Transition', manuscript, January 1990.
16. Ibid.
17. On this idea see: Andrew Arato: 'Civil society vs the state' *Telos*, No 47, Spring 1981; Andrew Arato: 'Empire vs civil society. Poland 1980.' *Telos*,

No. 50, Winter 1981/82; Andrew Arato: 'Civil társadalom, társadalomelmélet és államszocializmus' (Civil society, social theory and state socialism) *Századvég*, No. 3, 1987, pp. 46–52.

18. David Ost: 'Towards a corporatist solution in Eastern Europe: the case of Poland' *East European Politics and Societies*, Vol. 3, No. 1, Winter 1989, pp. 152–74.
19. Adam Przeworski, op. cit.
20. Ibid.
21. Guiseppe Di Palma: 'Why democracy can work in Eastern Europe' *Journal of Democracy*, Vol. 2, No. 1, Winter 1991, pp. 21–31.
22. According to Iván Szelényi, the two social 'heroes' of the Hungarian transition were the enterprising petty bourgeoisie and the critical intelligentsia. Iván Szelényi: 'Polgárosodás Magyarországon' (Embourgeoisement in Hungary). An interview with András Bozóki, *Valóság*, Vol. 33, No. 1, 1990, pp. 29–41.
23. The term 'sultanistic' was derived from the use by Max Weber and it was reformulated by Juan J. Linz. Its explanation can be found in: Juan J. Linz: 'Transitions to democracy' *Washington Quarterly*, Vol. 13, No. 3, Summer 1990, pp. 145–6.
24. Source: *Magyar Hírlap*, 16 October 1990.
25. See for further details: Juan J. Linz, op. cit., pp. 157–60. The author argued for the minimalist conception of a democratic consolidation.
26. Juan. J. Linz, op. cit., p. 159.
27. On the Spanish transition see: José Maravall: *The Transition to Democracy in Spain*, London & Canberra, Croom Helm, 1982; Paul Preston: *The Triumph of Democracy in Spain*, London, Methuen, 1984; J. Maravall–J. Santamaria: 'Political change in Spain and the prospects for democracy', In: O'Donnell–Schmitter–Whitehead (eds) *Transition from Authoritarian Rule*, Vol. 1, *Southern Europe*, Baltimore, The Johns Hopkins University Press, 1986, pp. 71–108, etc.
28. José Maravall, op. cit., p. 39.
29. Juan J. Linz emphasizes that authoritarian regimes – unlike totalitarian ones – intentionally demobilize the people and apparently try to avoid ideological politics. See, Juan J. Linz: 'An authoritarian regime: Spain' In: E. Allardt–S. Rokkan (eds) *Mass Politics*, New York, Free Press, 1970.
30. Public opinion poll account, January–February 1991, Szonda-Ipsos Ltd, Budapest.
31. In April 1991 FIDESZ suggested six-party negotiations for the Hungarian parliamentary parties, realizing the necessity of a Moncloa-type agreement during the economic change.
32. Tomasz Zukowski: 'Three Polands' *Warsaw Voice*, 23–30 December 1990, p. 3; On the question of presidential or parliamentary system in new democracies see: Juan J. Linz: 'The perils of presidentialism' *Journal of Democracy*, Vol. 1, No. 1, Winter 1990, pp. 51–69.
33. As Dahrendorf sceptically put it: 'This is not exactly an encouraging story. Political transition leads to economic frustration which results in instability and unrest; economic transition leads to political frustration which also results in instability and unrest. Either way liberty is victim.' Ralf Dahrendorf, op. cit., p. 42.

Acknowledgement

The author expresses his thanks to the fellows of the Institute für die Wissenschaften vom Menschen in Vienna for allowing him to do research work there.

Index